T0213034

WRITING SCIENTIFIC SOFTWARE: A GUIDE TO GOOD STYLE

The core of scientific computing is designing, writing, testing, debugging and modifying numerical software for application to a vast range of areas: from graphics, weather forecasting, and chemistry to engineering, biology, and finance. Scientists, engineers, and computer scientists need to write good, clear code, for speed, clarity, flexibility, and ease of re-use.

OLIVEIRA and STEWART provide here a guide to writing numerical software, pointing out good practices to follow, and pitfalls to avoid. By following their advice, the reader will learn how to write efficient software, and how to test it for bugs, accuracy, and performance. Techniques are explained with a variety of programming languages, and illustrated with two extensive design examples, one in Fortran 90 and one in C++, along with other examples in C, C++, Fortran 90 and Java scattered throughout the book.

Common issues in numerical computing are dealt with: for example, whether to allocate or pass "scratch" memory for temporary use, how to pass parameters to a function that is itself passed to a routine, how to allocate multidimensional arrays in C/C++/Java, and how to create suitable interfaces for routines and libraries. Advanced topics, such as recursive data structures, template programming and type binders for numerical computing, blocking and unrolling loops for efficiency, how to design software for deep memory hierarchies, and amortized doubling for efficient memory use, are also included.

This manual of scientific computing style will prove to be an essential addition to the bookshelf and lab of everyone who writes numerical software.

WRITING SCIENTIFIC SOFTWARE:
A GUIDE FOR GOOD STYLE

SUELY OLIVEIRA AND DAVID E. STEWART

University of Iowa

CAMBRIDGE
UNIVERSITY PRESS

CAMBRIDGE
UNIVERSITY PRESS

University Printing House, Cambridge CB2 8BS, United Kingdom

One Liberty Plaza, 20th Floor, New York, NY 10006, USA

477 Williamstown Road, Port Melbourne, VIC 3207, Australia

4843/24, 2nd Floor, Ansari Road, Daryaganj, Delhi - 110002, India

79 Anson Road, #06-04/06, Singapore 079906

Cambridge University Press is part of the University of Cambridge.

It furthers the University's mission by disseminating knowledge in the pursuit of education, learning and research at the highest international levels of excellence.

www.cambridge.org
Information on this title: www.cambridge.org/9780521675956

© Cambridge University Press 2006

First published 2006

A catalogue record for this publication is available from the British Library

ISBN 978-0-521-85896-0 Hardback
ISBN 978-0-521-67595-6 Paperback

Contents

Preface

Mathematical algorithms, though usually invisible, are all around us. The micro-computer in your car controlling the fuel ignition uses a control algorithm embodying mathematical theories of dynamical systems; a Web search engine might use large-scale matrix computations; a "smart map" using a Global Positioning System to tell where you are and the best way to get home embodies numerous numerical and non-numerical algorithms; the design of modern aircraft involves simulating the aerodynamic and structural characteristics on powerful computers including supercomputers.

Behind these applications is software that does numerical computations. Often it is called scientific software, or engineering software; this software uses finite-precision floating-point (and occasionally fixed-point) numbers to represent continuous quantities.

If you are involved in writing software that does numerical computations, this book is for you. In it we try to provide tools for writing effective and efficient numerical software. If you are a numerical analyst, this book may open your eyes to software issues and techniques that are new to you. If you are a programmer, this book will explain pitfalls to avoid with floating-point arithmetic and how to get good performance without losing modern design techniques (or programming in Fortran 66). People in other areas with computing projects that involve significant numerical computation can find a bounty of useful information and techniques in this book.

But this is not a book of numerical recipes, or even a textbook for numerical analysis (numerical analysis being the study of mathematical algorithms and their behavior with finite precision floating-point arithmetic or other sources of computational errors). Nor is it a handbook on software development. It is about the development of a particular kind of software: numerical software. Several things make this kind of software a little different from other kinds of software:

- *It involves computations with floating-point numbers.* All computations with floating point arithmetic are necessarily approximate. How good are the approximations? That is the subject matter of numerical analysis. Proofs of correctness of algorithms can be irrelevant because either: (a) they completely ignore the effects of roundoff error, and so cannot identify numerical difficulties; or (b) they assume only exact properties of floating point arithmetic (floating point arithmetic is commutative $x + y = y + x$, but not associative $(x + y) + z \neq x + (y + z)$). In the latter case, they cannot prove anything useful about algorithms which are numerically accurate, but not exact (which is almost all of them).
- *It involves large-scale computations.* Large-scale computations can involve computing millions of quantities. Here efficiency is of critical importance, both in time and memory. While correctness is vital, efficiency has a special place in scientific computing. Programmers who wish to get the most out of their machine had better understand just how the hardware (and software) behind their compilers and operating systems work.
- *Requirements change rapidly.* Frequent changes in requirements and methods are a fact of life for scientific software, whether in a commercial or research environment. This means that the code had better be flexible or it will be scrapped and we will be programming from scratch again.

In every decade since the 1950s, the complexity of scientific software has increased a great deal. Object-oriented software has come to the fore in scientific and engineering software with the development of a plethora of object-oriented matrix libraries and finite element packages. Fortran used to be the clear language of choice for scientific software. That has changed. Much scientific software is now written in C, C++, Java, Matlab, Ada, and languages other than Fortran. Fortran has also changed. The Fortran 90 standard and the standards that have followed have pushed Fortran forward with many modern programming structures. But, many people who were educated on Fortran 77 or earlier versions of Fortran are unaware of these powerful new features, and of how they can be used to facilitate large-scale scientific software development. In this book when we refer to "Fortran" we will mean Fortran 90 unless another version is explicitly mentioned.

We have focused on C, C++ and Fortran 90 as the languages we know best, and are in greatest use for scientific and engineering computing. But we will also have things to say about using other languages for scientific computing, especially Java. This is not to say that other languages are not appropriate. One of the points we want to make is that many of the lessons learnt in one language can carry over to other languages, and help us to better understand the trade-offs involved in the choice of programming language and software design.

Occasionally we make historical notes about how certain systems and programming languages developed. Often important insights into the character of operating systems and programming languages, and how they are used, can be gleaned from the history of their development. It is also a useful reminder that the world of software (including scientific software) is not static – it is changing and changing rapidly. And often our best guide to the future is a look at the past – it is certainly a good antidote to the impression often given that programming languages are eternal.

This book has been divided into five parts. The first is about what scientific and engineering software is all about, and what makes it different from conventional software design: the approximations inherent in floating-point arithmetic and other aspects of scientific software make some approaches to software development of limited applicability or irrelevant. Instead, we need to understand numerical issues much better than with other kinds of software. Also, scientific software often has much more of an emphasis on performance – there is a real need for speed. But this must be tempered by the need to keep the structure of the code from becoming "fossilized", trying to maximize performance for some particular system. Instead we advocate a balance between flexibility and performance.

The second part is about software design. After a look at how things happen (how CPUs work, stacks and registers, variable allocation, compilers, linkers and interpreters), we emphasize practical software design and development techniques. These include incremental testing alongside some of the more practical of the "proof of correctness" ideas.

The third part is on efficiency – in both time and memory. To do this well requires a good understanding of both algorithms and computer architecture. The importance of locality is particularly emphasized. There is also a considerable amount on how to use dynamic memory allocation. This may be particularly useful for Fortran programmers who have so far avoided dynamic memory allocation.

Part IV is on tools for software development including online sources of scientific software, debuggers, and tools that have originated from the Unix operating system and have spread to many other environments.

Part V emphasizes the practicalities involved in programming scientific software. We have developed two medium-sized examples of numerical software development. One is a cubic spline library for constructing and evaluating various kinds of splines. The other is a multigrid system for the efficient iterative solution of large, sparse linear systems of equations. In these examples, the reader will see the issues discussed earlier in the context of some real examples.

As Isaac Newton said, "If I have seen far, it is because I have stood on the shoulders of giants." We do not claim to see as far as Isaac Newton, but we have stood on the shoulders of giants. We would like to thank Barry Smith, Michael Overton, Nicholas Higham, Kendall Atkinson, and the copy-editor for their comments on our manuscript. We would especially like to thank Cambridge University Press' technical reviewer, who was most assiduous in going through the manuscript, and whose many comments have resulted in a greatly improved manuscript. We would also like to thank the many sources of the software that we have used in the production of this book: Microsoft (MS) Windows XP, Red-Hat Linux, the GNU compiler collection (gcc, g++, and most recently g95), Delorie's port of gcc/g++ to MS Windows (djgpp), Minimal GNU for Windows (MinGW) and their port of gcc/g++ to MS Windows, Intel's Fortran 90/95 compiler, the GNU tools gmake, grep, sed, gdb, etc. (many thanks to the Free Software Foundation for making these tools widely available), the LyX word processing software, the MikTeX and TeTeX implementations of LaTeX and the DVI viewers xdvi and yap, Component Software's implementation of RCS for MS Windows, Xfig, zip and unzip, WinZip, Valgrind, Octave and MATLAB.

Part I

Numerical Software

1

Why *numerical* software?

Numerical software is the software used to do computations with real numbers; that is, with numbers with decimal points in them like $\pi = 3.141\,5926\ldots$. These kinds computations are commonly of great scientific and engineering importance. Real numbers can be used to represent physical quantities (position, height, force, stress, viscosity, voltage, density, etc.). Computation with real numbers can be for simulating the nuclear processes in the centers of stars, finding the stresses in a large concrete and steel structure, or for determining how many spheres of unit radius can touch each other without penetrating. This kind of software is about *quantitative problems*. That is, the answers to our questions are not simple yes/no or red/green/blue answers. They involve continuously varying quantities. But computers can only store a finite number of values. So we have to use an approximation to real numbers called floating point numbers (described in Chapter 2).

Numerical software is often used for *large-scale problems*. That is, the number of quantities that need to be computed is often very large. This happens because we want to understand what is happening with a continuously varying quantity, such as stress in a structural column, or flow in a river. These are quantities that vary continuously with position, and perhaps with time as well. Since we cannot find or store the values at all infinitely many points in a column or a river, we must use some sort of **discretization**. Discretizations are approximations to the true system, which are usually more accurate when more refined. Refining a discretization means that we create more quantities to compute. This does not have to go very far (especially for problems in three dimensions) before we are at the limit of current computers, including supercomputers.

How large are modern computational tasks? Here is an example. Consider water flowing through a pipe. If the flow is smooth, then we can use relatively coarse discretizations, and the scale of the simulation can be kept modest. But if we have turbulence, then the scale of the turbulent features of the flow are typically a fraction of a millimeter. To simulate turbulent flow in a pipe that is 5 cm in diameter and 2.5 cm long with a discretization spacing of a tenth of a millimeter would involve at least $3 \times \pi (25\,\text{mm}/0.1\,\text{mm})^3 \approx 147$ million unknowns to store the flow's velocity. Just to store this would require over a gigabyte of memory (in double-precision). Unless you can store this in the main memory of a computer (the memory banks of your computer, but excluding disk drives), your algorithm is going to be slow. This amount of memory is simply the memory needed to store the results of the computations. The amount of memory needed for the other data used in the computation can be equally large or even much larger.

These large-scale problems are computational challenges that require not only effective and efficient algorithms but also implementations that maximize use of the underlying hardware.

1.1 Efficient kernels

Since we are trying to compute a large number of quantities, we need our software to be efficient. This means that the core operations have to be written to execute quickly on a computer. These core operations are often referred to as *kernels*.

Since these kernels are executed many, many times in large-scale computations, it is especially important for them to run efficiently. Not only should the algorithms chosen be good, but they should also be implemented carefully to make the best use of the computer hardware.

Current Central Processing Units (CPUs) such as the Intel Pentium 4 chips have clock speeds of well over a GigaHertz (GHz). In one clock cycle of one nanosecond, light in a vacuum travels about 30 cm. This is Einstein's speed limit. For electrical signals traveling through wires, the speed is somewhat slower. So for a machine with a 3 GHz Pentium CPU, in one clock cycle, electrical signals can only travel about 10 cm. To do something as simple as getting a number from memory, we have to take into account the time it takes for the signal to go from the CPU to the memory chips, the time for the memory chips to find the right bit of memory (typically a pair of transistors), read the information, and then send it back to the CPU. The total time needed takes many clock cycles. If just getting a number from memory takes many clock cycles, why are we still increasing clock speeds?

To handle this situation, hardware designers include "cache" memory on the CPU. This cache is small, fast but expensive memory. If the item the CPU wants is already in the cache, then it only takes one or two clock cycles to fetch it and to start processing it. If it is not in the cache, then the cache will read in a short block of memory from the main memory, which holds the required data. This will take longer, but shouldn't happen so often. In fact, the cache idea is so good, that they don't just have one cache, they have two. If it isn't in the first (fastest) cache, then it looks in the second (not-as-fast-but-still-very-fast) cache, and if it isn't there it will look for it in main memory. Newer designs add even more levels of cache. If you want to get the best performance out of your CPU, then you should design your code to make best use of this kind of hardware.

There is a general trend in the performance of these kinds of electronic components that is encapsulated in "Moore's Law", which was first put forward in 1965 [81], by Gordon Moore one of the founders of Intel:

the number of transistors on a CPU roughly doubles every eighteen months.

Gordon Moore actually said that the doubling happened every twelve months. But, averaging over progress from the 1950s to now, the number of transistors on a "chip" doubles about every eighteen months to two years. This usually means that the number of operations that can be done on a single CPU also roughly doubles every eighteen months to two years. But memory speed has not kept up, and data has to be transfered between the main memory and the CPU. To maintain the speed, we need to get memory and CPU closer; this is why we have multiple level caches on CPUs. It also means that if we want to get close to peak performance, we need to take this structure into account. There will be more on this in Part III.

1.2 Rapid change

As scientists, we are interested in research. That means that we want to go where no-one has gone before. It means that we want to investigate problems and approaches no-one else has thought of. We are unlikely to get something profoundly important on our first try. We will try something, see what happens, and then ask some new questions, and try to answer those. This means that our software is going to have to change as we have different problems to solve, and want to answer different questions. Our software will have to change quickly.

Rapidly changing software is a challenge. Each change to a piece of software has the chance to introduce bugs. Every time we change an assumption about what we are computing, we have an even bigger challenge to modify our software, since it is easy to build in bad or restrictive assumptions into our software.

The challenge of rapidly changing software is not unique to research, but it is particularly important here. In numerical analysis, a great deal of thought has gone into designing algorithms and the principles behind them. The algorithms themselves, though, have often been fairly straightforward. However, that has been changing. Consider Gaussian elimination or LU factorization for solving a linear system of equations. The standard dense LU factorization routine is fairly easy to write out in pseudo-code or in your favorite programming language. A great deal of analysis has gone into this algorithm regarding the size and character of the errors in the solution. But the algorithm itself is quite straightforward. Even when we add pivoting techniques, there is much more to the analysis than the algorithm. But with the increasing importance of sparse matrices with general sparsity patterns, the algorithms become much more complicated. Current algorithms for solving sparse linear systems are supernodal multifrontal algorithms that use combinatorial data structures (elimination trees) that must be constructed using moderately sophisticated techniques from Computer Science. You can write a standard LU factorization routine with partial pivoting in an afternoon in almost any programming language. But current supernodal multifrontal algorithms require much more care to implement. This trend to increasing sophistication and complexity can also be seen in the development of finite element software, ordinary differential equation solvers, and other numerical software. When we start bringing together different pieces of software to solve larger problems, we should realize that we have a large software system, and it should be treated as such. Writing your own (from scratch) is no longer an option.

1.3 Large-scale problems

Problems in scientific computing usually involve large amounts of computation. These are called *large-scale problems* or *large-scale computations*. This can be because the problem requires a large amount of data (such as signal processing), produces a large amount of data (such as solving a partial differential equation), or is simply very complex (some global optimization problems are like this). Some tasks, such as weather forecasting, may both require and produce large amounts of data.

1.3.1 Problems with a lot of data

Signal processing is an area where vast amounts of data must be processed, often in real time – such as digital filtering of telephone signals, transforming digital video signals, or processing X-ray data in computerized tomography to get pictures of the inside of human bodies. Real-time constraints mean that the processing must be very rapid. Often specialized hardware is used to carry this out, and perhaps fixed-point rather than floating-point arithmetic must be used.

Other situations which do not have real-time constraints are seismic imaging, where pictures of the rock layers under the ground are obtained from recordings of sounds picked up by buried sensors. The amount of data involved is very large. It needs to be, in order to obtain detailed pictures of the structure of the rock layers.

In addition to the usual numerical and programming issues, there may be questions about how to store and retrieve such large data sets. Part of the answers to such questions may involve database systems. Database systems are outside the scope of this book, but if you need to know more, you might look at [26].

Many problems, such as finding the air flow around a Boeing 747, produce a great deal of data. After the relevant partial differential equations have been discretized, there are large systems of nonlinear equations that need to be solved. And the answer involves a great deal of data. Part of the problem here is making sense of the answer. Often the best way to describe the answer is to use computer visualization techniques to paint a picture of the airflow. Moving pictures can be rotated, shifted and moved enable aeronautical engineer to study different aspects of the problem. Computer visualization is outside the scope of this book, but if you need something like that, some good references are [37, 51, 68].

1.3.2 Hard problems

Sometimes, the data for the problem, and the data produced, are not very large, but solving the problem can involve an enormous amount of time. This can easily be the case in global optimization, where there can be very large numbers of local minima, but only one global minimum. Finding all the local minima and comparing them to find the best – the global minimum – can be like looking for a needle in a haystack. These problems are often closely related to combinatorial problems (problems which can be described in terms of integers rather than real numbers). Sometimes combinatorial methods can solve these problems efficiently, but often, continuous optimization methods are an essential part of the solution strategy.

Another area where there are hard problems which do not necessarily involve a lot of data are highly nonlinear problems. Highly nonlinear problems can have, or appear to have, many possible solutions. Perhaps only one or a few of the solutions is really useful. Again we have a problem of finding a "needle in a haystack".

2

Scientific computation and numerical analysis

2.1 The trouble with real numbers

Real numbers like $\pi = 3.141\,592\,65\ldots$ are a problem for computers because (in general) they have an infinite number of digits. Unless your computer has infinite memory (and ours don't), there is no way it can store π *exactly*. So we do the next best thing, and store a reasonable approximation. Of course, how accurately you need to know something depends on what you want to do with the information. And that is exactly how it is with computers.

2.1.1 Floating point numbers

Real numbers are stored as *floating point numbers*. Floating point numbers are numbers like $\pi \approx 3.141\,592\,6$, or Avogadro's number $\approx 6.03 \times 10^{23}$, or the charge on an electron $\approx 1.602\,1773\,3 \times 10^{-19}$ coulombs. These have the form $\pm x \times b^e$ where x, the *significand* or *mantissa*, is a number from 1 to b (or from $1/b$ to 1), e is the *exponent*, and b is the *base* of the floating point system. If the mantissa is in the range 1 to b, then it has the form $x = x_0.x_1x_2x_3 \ldots x_{m-1}$ in base b where each x_i is a base-b digit $(0, 1, 2, \ldots, b-1)$ and m is the length of the mantissa.

The length of the mantissa describes how accurately numbers can be approximated. Since

$$x \times b^e = (x_0.x_1x_2x_3 \ldots x_m \quad \text{base } b) \times b^e$$
$$= (x_0 + x_1\, b^{-1} + x_2\, b^{-2} + x_3\, b^{-3} + \cdots + x_{m-1}\, b^{-m+1}) \times b^e,$$

we can't approximate a number from 1 to b with a guaranteed error less than $\frac{1}{2}b^{-m+1}$. This tells us how many digits or bits we have to represent a number. If $b = 2$ (as it is in most computers), then we can assume that the leading digit is $x_0 = 1$; then it doesn't even need to be stored! Actually this assumption cannot hold for zero, which can be represented by a special value of e. There are also limits on the values of e as it must be represented using a finite number of bits or digits. This controls the range of the floating point system.

The best known and most used floating point system is the ***IEEE floating point system***, which is sometimes referred to as the IEEE 754 standard [59]. This specifies a set of three different floating point formats: *single-precision*, *double-precision*, and *extended precision*. These give increasingly precise and broad floating point systems. Most programming languages support single and double-precision floating point systems. Usually, `real` or `float` types represent single-precision numbers, while `double`, `double-precision` or `long real/longreal` types represent double-precision numbers. An excellent overview of floating point arithmetic with particular emphasis on the IEEE standard is Overton's book [84]. A shorter starting point is Goldberg's classic article [45]. Some history of the development of the IEEE standards can be found in [64]. A very useful reference that describes floating point arithmetic, but is mostly focused on the consequences of using floating point in numerical algorithms is Higham's book [52]. Most of the algorithms analyzed in [52] are for matrix computations, but the basics of error analysis are the same in every part of numerical analysis and scientific computing. An older book (pre-IEEE arithmetic) that deals with floating point and other aspects of numerical computing that is still well worth reading is Webb Miller's *The Engineering of Numerical Software* [79].

A fundamental quantity for any floating point system is the ***unit roundoff***. This is denoted by $\mathbf{u}$ and is the smallest positive number where the *computed value of* $1 + \mathbf{u}$ is different from 1. The ***machine epsilon*** is the smallest $a - 1$ where a is the smallest representable number greater than 1. We denote the machine epsilon by ϵ_{MACH}; in binary arithmetic with rounding we usually have $\epsilon_{MACH} = 2\,\mathbf{u}$.

Suppose we used four-digit decimal arithmetic, so we might store π approximately as $3.141 \times 10^0 = 0.3141 \times 10^1$. If we added $1.000 + 0.0001$ exactly we would get 1.0001. But if we can only store four decimal digits, we would have to drop the last digit: 1.000. To get a value different from 1.000 in the result we would have to add at least 0.0005 and then round 1.0005 up to 1.001 before storing. So for four-digit decimal arithmetic with rounding we would get $\mathbf{u} = 0.0005 = 5 \times 10^{-4}$. The smallest representable number > 1 is $1.001 = 1 + 2\,\mathbf{u}$.

Another fundamental quantity in floating point arithmetic is the range of the floating point numbers: what are the largest and smallest floating point numbers? This depends on the range of the exponent. If $-e_{max} \le e \le +e_{max}$ and $1/b \le x < 1$, then the largest representable number is close to $b^{e_{max}}$ and the smallest representable number is $b^{-e_{max}-1}$. Usually $b^{e_{max}}$ is given to indicate the range of the floating point numbers.

Table 2.1. *IEEE floating point quantities*

floating point data			bits			
precision	**u**	max number	sign	mantissa	exponent	total
single	6×10^{-8}	$\approx 10^{38}$	1	23	8	32
double	2×10^{-16}	$\approx 10^{308}$	1	52	11	64
extended	5×10^{-20}	$\approx 10^{9863}$	1	64	15	80

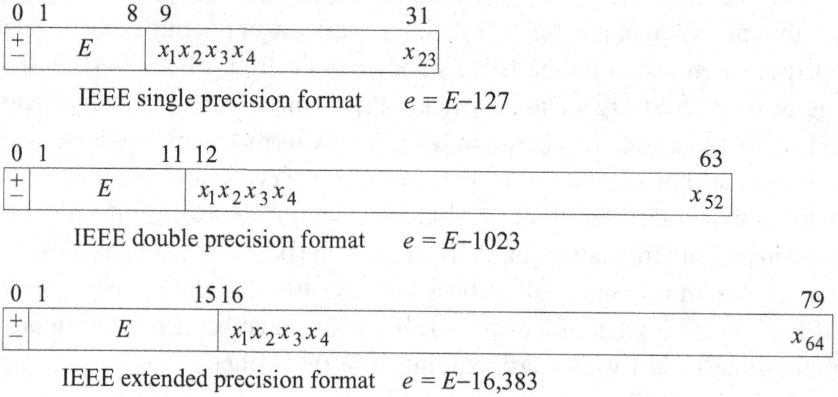

IEEE single precision format $e = E-127$

IEEE double precision format $e = E-1023$

IEEE extended precision format $e = E-16{,}383$

Figure 2.1. IEEE 754 floating point formats.

In Figure 2.1 we show how the components of the floating point numbers are stored. In Table 2.1 we give a list of the most important values of the above quantities for the IEEE floating point standards.

The floating point units on most CPUs now have registers which store floating point numbers in extended precision. In the past, when floating point operations were performed in software, it was considerably cheaper to use single-precision floating point numbers; adding double-precision numbers took about twice as long, while multiplying them took about four times as long. Now, however, to add single-precision numbers, they are loaded into extended precision registers and then the hardware adds the extended precision values. This limits the speed advantage of using single-precision arithmetic. The main penalty for using double-precision is the amount of memory it takes up, although in some situations where the memory bandwidth is limited, single-precision can be twice as fast as double-precision. As a practical matter, we recommend that floating point variables be declared double-precision (or better), and you should let the hardware do the actual operations in extended precision (or better) where this is under the programmer's control.

One of the important features of this is that

intermediate calculations should be done in higher precision than needed for the results.

This point-of-view is strongly promoted by William Kahan, one of the driving forces behind the IEEE floating point standards. For some scathing criticism of language "features" that prevent this, see [62].

2.1.2 Floating point arithmetic

Real numbers can be added and subtracted, multiplied and divided (at least provided the denominator is not zero); if a real number is not negative it has a square root; the basic trigonometric functions sin and cos are defined for all real numbers. So we would like to do all these things with floating point numbers. However, unless we are very lucky, most of these operations applied to floating point numbers will give us something that is not a floating point number, or at least requires more bits or digits to represent it.

As an example, suppose we had a computer that used five decimals digits for the mantissa. Then 1.0000 and 3.0000 are exactly represented, but $1.0000/3.0000 = 0.333\,333\,33\ldots$ cannot be. Even addition has this problem. Suppose we add 0.123 45 to 3.141 5:

$$
\begin{array}{r}
0.12345 \\
+ \quad 3.1415 \\
\hline
3.26495 \\
\hline
\end{array}
$$

and the sum has more than five digits in the mantissa. We can either **chop** the answer back to 3.2649 or **round** it up to 3.2650. Similar problems occur when we subtract or multiply floating point numbers, or if we consider computing square roots, powers, trigonometric or other functions.

Since we want to use fast hardware to do our floating point operations, and we don't want our mantissas to grow in size, we keep chopping or rounding the results of adding, subtracting, multiplying or dividing floating point numbers. This means that most operations with floating point numbers are approximate. What we can do is quantify how large those errors should be. For notation, suppose that x and y are floating point numbers, and "$*$" represents a standard arithmetic operation $(+, -, \times, /)$ and $fl(expression)$ is the *computed* value of the given *expression* using floating point arithmetic. The error in the result of a floating point computation is generally given by

$$fl(x * y) = (x * y)(1 + \varepsilon),$$

where $|\varepsilon| \leq \mathbf{u}$ and $\mathbf{u}$ is unit roundoff. This holds true for IEEE floating point arithmetic, provided there is no *overflow* or *underflow* (see next paragraph). For functions f like sin, cos, and square roots, the best we can expect is that

$$fl(f(x)) = (1 + \varepsilon_1)f((1 + \varepsilon_2)x),$$

where $|\varepsilon_1|$, $|\varepsilon_2| \leq \mathbf{u}$. If they are well implemented, we can expect an accuracy close to this for function evaluations that are provided in standard libraries.

2.1.3 Forward and backward error

Let's have a closer look at the formula for what is actually computed by a function call:

$$fl(f(x)) = (1 + \varepsilon_1) f((1 + \varepsilon_2)x).$$

The numbers ε_1 and ε_2 are small, but either positive or negative or possibly zero. Let us look at the effects of the two errors separately: first suppose $\varepsilon_2 = 0$. Then

$$fl(f(x)) = (1 + \varepsilon_1)f(x).$$

This says that the relative error (the actual error, or absolute error, $fl(f(x)) - f(x)$ divided by what we are trying to compute, $f(x)$) is ε_1. This is called the *forward error*. If we know what the input is, this gives us an estimate of what the error in the output is. We want this quantity to be small. The best we can expect is that $|\varepsilon_1| \leq \mathbf{u}$. Usually the forward error is small, but not always, particularly if $f(x) \approx 0$.

Here is a small example. The following computation was done in double-precision:[1] $y = \sqrt{2}, z = y^2$. The exact result is exactly 2, but subtracting two from z gave $\approx 4.44 \times 10^{-16}$. Dividing by the exact answer $(= 2)$ we obtained the relative error $\approx 2.22 \times 10^{-16}$ which is $\mathbf{u}$ for double-precision. This is about as good as we can reasonably expect for the accuracy of these computations.

Now trying $\sin(2\pi)$, the computed value in double-precision is $\approx -2.44 \times 10^{-16}$. This is good for the *absolute* error, but the exact value is zero! This gives infinite *relative* error. One reason for this problem is that the computed value of π is not exact, and even if it were, any computation that is carried out with it in floating point arithmetic will result in errors of about the size of $\mathbf{u}$. Since the trigonometric functions repeat themselves after every 2π, usually the first step in computing $\sin x$ for any x is to subtract off a multiple of 2π from x so that $0 \leq x < 2\pi$. This is called *argument reduction*. Carrying out this step before doing the main computations will result in absolute errors of size approximately $\mathbf{u} |x|$ for $|x| \geq 2\pi$. Then

[1] We used GNU Octave on a Pentium 4 computer to do this.

we are not evaluating sin x exactly, but rather $\sin((1 + \varepsilon_2)x)$. This is an example of **backward error**. Of course, when $\sin((1 + \varepsilon_2)x)$ is computed, there will be some forward error as well: $(1 + \varepsilon_1)\sin((1 + \varepsilon_2)x)$.

Often the computed value can be represented using *only* the backward error:

$$fl(f(x)) = f((1 + \varepsilon_2)x) \text{ for small } \varepsilon_2.$$

This says that the computed value *is the exact value for some nearby input(s)*.

2.1.4 Overflow and underflow

Since floating point formats use a fixed number of bits, there are only finitely many floating point numbers in a particular format. This means that there must be a biggest floating point number in a specific format – a biggest single-precision number, and a biggest double-precision number. When we have numbers bigger than this, we have **overflow**. What do computers do when there is overflow? The most common response is to terminate the program. With IEEE arithmetic it is possible to return "infinity" as a result (denoted by Inf). This often leads to other problems which will be discussed later in this section.

Overflow obviously should be avoided. Fortunately, the maximum number in well-designed floating point systems like IEEE arithmetic are really very large ($\approx 10^{38}$ for single-precision, $\approx 10^{307}$ in double-precision). It is difficult to give precise limits for when overflow will occur in most realistic computations, but some things can obviously cause problems: for example taking exponentials of large positive numbers are very large numbers; multiplying large numbers gives even larger numbers. An example is the tanh function which can be expressed by the quotient

$$\tanh x = \frac{e^{+x} - e^{-x}}{e^{+x} + e^{-x}}.$$

Here is an obvious implementation.

```
double tanh1(double x)
{
    return (exp(x)-exp(-x))/(exp(x)+exp(-x));
}
```

Here the obvious implementation can fail when x is moderately large, even though the result is never larger than one. For single-precision, overflow in tanh1 occurs for $x = 90$, while for double-precision overflow occurs for $x = 750$.

A more subtle issue is **underflow**, which occurs when the result of a floating point operation is too small to be represented as a floating point number (of the same format). This can happen when multiplying two very small numbers, or dividing a small number by a very large number. The limit of how small floating point numbers have to be for this to happen is usually close to one divided by the largest floating point number. So the smallest single-precision IEEE floating point number is about 10^{-38}, and the smallest double-precision IEEE floating point number is about 10^{-307}.

When underflow occurs, the FP unit usually returns zero, although on some old systems the program would crash! When underflow occurs, the formula

$$fl(x * y) = (x * y)(1 + \varepsilon), \qquad |\varepsilon| \leq \mathbf{u}, \qquad \text{where "*" is } +, -, \times, /,$$

no longer holds. Since the size of underflowing numbers are very small, this is usually not a problem. However, underflow does represent a loss of all significant digits, and this should be kept in mind.

IEEE arithmetic reduces the dangers of unexpected results from underflow by implementing *gradual underflow*. Once the exponent field reaches its minimum value, the system uses a form of fixed point arithmetic so that the loss of significant digits is made more gradual as the size of the floating point numbers is reduced. See Overton [84] for more details.

2.1.5 Things to avoid with floating point numbers

There are a number of things that you should avoid doing with floating point numbers because they are not exact representations of real numbers.

- *Don't test for equality between floating point numbers.* Don't do this even if you have assigned one to the other: `y = x;... if ( x == y )...` One of the authors got a nasty shock when this failed. Why didn't it work? The reason was that one was stored in a register in extended precision, while the other was stored in main memory in double-precision. When they were compared, the variable in main memory was loaded into a register, converted to extended precision, and the comparison was done in extended precision. As a result the two quantities compared were not exactly equal.

  There are many other situations where things that ought to be the same are actually not exactly the same in floating point arithmetic, so you should forget about testing exact equality between floating point numbers.

- *Don't subtract nearly equal quantities and then divide by something small.* This often results in **catastrophic cancellation** and all digits of accuracy are lost. An easy exercise: compute $(1 - \cos x)/x^2$ for $x = 10^{-k}$ with $k = 1, 2, 3, \ldots$ The limit should be $1/2$. But usually you end up getting zero for x small. Why? Because $\cos x$ becomes so close to one that it is rounded up to one; then the numerator becomes zero and the end result is zero. In general, if you subtract numbers where the first k digits are equal, you lose k digits of accuracy. For more information see Section 2.4.1.

- *Don't use floating point numbers as loop counters.* Since there is very little that can be trusted to be exact in floating point, we should not trust loops like

```
for ( x = 0.0; x <= 1.0; x = x + 1.0/9.0 )
  printf("%g  ", x);
```

For a start, 1/9 will not be stored exactly in a binary floating point representation. With roundoff error, after ten times through the loop we will have x close to $8/9 = 0.8888\ldots$. But then adding 1/9 to x will give something close to 1. If it is smaller, then we go through the loop one more time. If it is larger, we exit the loop straight away. Do we really want these decisions to be at the mercy of roundoff error? Not if we want reliable and accurate code. In summary: use integers (standard, short, or long) to control loops. Not floating point numbers.

2.1.6 Inf, NaN, and other traps

IEEE arithmetic has a number of bit-patterns reserved for things that are not truly numbers. The ones you will hear most about are *Inf* and *NaN*. These are represented by certain extreme values of the exponent. Inf stands for infinity, and there are both +Inf and −Inf. These can arise if you get overflow occurring. It is also possible to get −0 as $1/(-\text{Inf})$, for example. So there are both +0 and −0. However, these are equal to each other if you test them for equality.

Then there are things that are undefined – and are not infinity: 0/0 for example. This is simply a nonsense thing to work with as anyone who has proved that zero and one are the same will know:

$$0 = 0 \times 1 = 0 \times (0/0) = (0 \times 0)/0 = 0/0 = 1 \qquad \text{(oops)}.$$

Similar things happen with Inf − Inf, Inf/Inf and related expressions. Certain other undefined quantities like $\sqrt{-1}$ and $\log(-1)$ are represented by NaNs. IEEE handles such things by creating NaNs; NaN stands for "Not a Number". This is nice in the sense that it is clearly connected with the theoretical idea of an undefined quantity. In computations, if creating an NaN does not immediately cause program termination, they tend to spread widely (adding, subtracting, multiplying or dividing anything with a NaN will give a NaN) and you can easily have extensive output of nothing but NaNs from your code. MATLAB is an example of a system where NaNs do not stop the program, and one NaN can infect everything else.

As a practical rule, it is almost always best to immediately stop the program if you find a NaN. Generating a NaN is usually a sign of a bug in your program or algorithm. Since locating this bug is usually the first step to fixing it, having your program crash on finding a NaN, or at least alert you to it, is a good common-sense strategy.

Table 2.2. *IEEE floating point exceptions and the standard responses*

Note that N_{min} and N_{max} are respectively the smallest and largest *normalized* floating point numbers

Exception	Standard response
Invalid operation	return NaN
Division by zero	return $\pm\infty$
Overflow	return $\pm\infty$ of N_{max}
Underflow	return ± 0, $\pm N_{min}$, or subnormal
Inexact	return correctly rounded result

A simple way to test if a number is a NaN is to compare it to itself; NaNs are the only floating point numbers not equal to themselves. Here is how to test for NaNs in Fortran 90.

```
if ( x == x ) then
    print *, 'x is not a NaN'
else
    print *, 'x is a NaN'
endif
```

Don't test every variable to see if it is a NaN. Instead occasionally test a "summary" variable, like the norm, or magnitude, of a vector.

2.1.7 *Rounding modes and exceptions in IEEE floating point arithmetic*

The IEEE floating point arithmetic standard contains some features which there are, until recently, no standard ways of accessing. These include control of the rounding modes, and access to the different types of exceptions that can be generated.

The exceptions that can be generated by IEEE floating-point operations and the standard responses are shown in Table 2.2. The possible rounding modes in IEEE floating-point arithmetic are listed in Table 2.3. Note that the default rounding mode is *round to nearest*. In the case of a tie, the rule used is *round toward zero*.

Under the newer standards C99 and Fortran 2003 there are defined mechanisms for controlling the behavior when an IEEE floating-point exception occurs, and to enforce a particular rounding mode.[2] Included in the standard for C99 are macros

---

[2] Note that, at the time of writing, the C99 standard is partially supported by the well-known GNU C compiler gcc provided a suitable compiler option is used. However, the GNU C support for the IEEE arithmetic features is limited.

Table 2.3. *IEEE floating-point*
rounding modes

Rounding modes
Round down (towards $-\infty$)
Round up (towards $+\infty$)
Round towards zero
Round to nearest

for testing if a number is a NaN or a normalized floating point number, for example. For more details consult the relevant standards and/or your compiler manuals and documentation.

2.1.8 Rounding modes and debugging

The rounding modes of IEEE arithmetic provide a wonderful opportunity to expose rounding errors in most software. Re-running software with different rounding modes (especially the "toward $+\infty$", "toward $-\infty$" modes in addition to the usual "to nearest" mode) will give different results; the size of the difference will usually give a good estimate of the effects of roundoff errors. While it is not a foolproof method, there are currently no foolproof methods for detecting problems due to roundoff error. For a discussion of the problems with different schemes for identifying roundoff error, see Kahan [63]. The best is a detailed rounding analysis, but this is costly to carry out, and is done only by a few people, even amongst numerical analysts. According to Kahan, the next best approach is to re-run the code with different rounding modes to "smoke out" problems with roundoff.

With the C99 and Fortran 2003 standards, there is (at last) a standardized way of setting rounding modes. Here is an example in C99 that shows how to do this inside a program.

```
#include        <stdio.h>
#include        <fenv.h>

#pragma STDC FENV_ACCESS ON

double my_op(double x, double y);

int main(int argc, char *argv[])
{
    double a, b, x, y;
```

```
int old_fp_mode, status1, status2, status3;

x = 7.1;   y = 1.0/5.0;

old_fp_mode = fegetround();
status1 = fesetround(FE_DOWNWARD);
a = my_op(x, y);
status2 = fesetround(FE_UPWARD);
b = my_op(x, y);
status3 = fesetround(old_fp_mode);

/* All status values should be zero */
printf("Status values are: %d, %d, %d\n",
       status1, status2, status3);
printf("Difference is %g\n", b-a);
}
```

This was compiled and run using gcc 3.4.2 for MinGW. The pragma FENV_ACCESS is meant to turn off certain optimizations that subvert the control of rounding modes. However, gcc (at the time of writing) ignores this pragma; compiling the my_op function in the same file as main results in zero difference between the two rounding modes with optimization on (-O1 or -O2), but gives properly rounded results without optimization. The effects of optimization and the use of pragmas will undoubtedly change with the compiler and the version of the compiler; we just want to point out that care must be exercised in using IEEE rounding modes.

2.2 Fixed-point arithmetic

While almost all conventional scientific and engineering computations are done using floating-point arithmetic, in some real-time systems, fixed-point arithmetic is used because of its speed and simplicity compared to floating-point arithmetic. This is done, for example, in digital signal processing. Few programming languages support fixed-point arithmetic; Ada is one of them. Usually, fixed-point arithmetic is implemented using standard integer arithmetic.

We can think of fixed-point numbers as having the form

$$x = c \times z, \qquad z \text{ an integer,}$$

where c is a positive constant that defines the range of the fixed-point numbers. (If we were doing financial calculations, then we might set $c = \$0.01$ – that is, c might be one cent.) Since the error in performing a fixed-point arithmetic operation is at best c, we try to make c as small as possible. Our choice of c is constrained by the fact that integers are represented using a fixed number of bits (usually 32, but it could be 16 or 64, or some other number). Because of this, there is a maximum integer value; let's call it M. If we want to represent real numbers in the range $[-r, +r]$, we want $r \leq c\,M$. Since M is fixed by the integer arithmetic used, and we want c as small as we can, we usually want $r = c\,M$.

But there is a danger here. If most of any of our fixed-point numbers exceed r in magnitude, we get integer overflow. Often this will happen silently, and we will find that adding two large, positive fixed-point numbers might result in a negative fixed-point number! In other implementations (e.g., Ada), fixed-point overflow results in an error or exception being raised.

These problems mean that if we are using fixed-point arithmetic, we have to choose $c\,(> 0)$ large enough so that $r \ll c\,M$ to avoid fixed-point overflow (with a larger error for most computations). The two conflicting goals of reducing the error by reducing c, and increasing the range r to avoid overflow, must be carefully balanced. Whether the numbers to be represented lie in the permissible range must be carefully monitored to prevent overflow. Floating-point arithmetic is much more adaptable, and floating-point overflow *much* less likely.

The use of fixed point arithmetic has been common in digital signal processing and other applications requiring high speed with minimal hardware. However, it was a contributing factor in the Ariane 5 disaster discussed in Chapter 4. The initial event that triggered the Ariane 5 crash was a fixed point event.

2.3 Algorithm stability vs. problem stability

Even if we can't compute the exact answer to a problem with real numbers in it, we would like to get something close, preferably very close. The trouble with a criterion like this is that often we can ask questions without even realizing they're bad questions. Suppose we have a routine for solving linear equations $Ax = b$ for x, where A is a given square matrix and b a vector with consistent dimensions. If we ask our solver to solve

$$\begin{bmatrix} +1 & -1 \\ -1 & +1 \end{bmatrix} \begin{bmatrix} x_1 \\ x_2 \end{bmatrix} = \begin{bmatrix} 2 \\ 3 \end{bmatrix},$$

then we are asking a stupid question because there is no solution. (There is if we replace 3 with -2, but for almost all other changes there is no solution.) This is because the matrix

$$\begin{bmatrix} +1 & -1 \\ -1 & +1 \end{bmatrix}$$

is a singular matrix; that is, it has no inverse matrix. But if we change one of the entries by even a very small amount, the result is not singular:

$$\begin{bmatrix} 1+\epsilon & -1 \\ -1 & +1 \end{bmatrix}^{-1} = \frac{1}{\epsilon}\begin{bmatrix} 1 & 1 \\ 1 & 1+\epsilon \end{bmatrix}.$$

So changing the entries of our matrix will give us an answer. Unfortunately it won't be a very useful answer. But that is not the fault of our algorithm. It is the fault of the problem. Ideally, the numerical software will identify when the matrix is singular or nearly singular.

Linear equation solvers do not claim to give us an answer that is always close to the exact solution. But they usually claim to give *an exact answer to a nearby problem*. This is called **backward stability**. This property means that the algorithm has a small **backward error**. Provided the problem we ask is **well-posed** (small changes in the inputs give small changes in the exact solution), then backward stability of our algorithm will ensure that we will get answers close to the exact solution.

On the other hand, if a particular class of problems is always well-posed (multiplying a pair of numbers, for example), then we can have algorithms that always give answers that are close to the exact answers – provided the numbers are not so big as to overflow or so small as to cause underflow.

For solving a linear system, the data for the problem are the matrix A and the vector b; the output is x. Note that vectors can be added and can be scaled (multiplied by a number), but it usually does not make sense to multiply or divide vectors. Matrices can be added and multiplied, and can multiply vectors.

When we want to tell whether a vector or matrix is big or small, we need a way of measuring the "size" of a vector or matrix. To measure the size of a vector we use a *norm* $\|z\|$. All norms have three basic properties:

1. $\|z\| \geq 0$ for all vectors z, and $\|z\| = 0$ can only happen if z is the zero vector.
2. If α is a number the scaled vector αz has norm $\|\alpha z\| = |\alpha|\,\|z\|$. So doubling a vector doubles its size.
3. If x and y are two vectors then $\|x + y\| \leq \|x\| + \|y\|$. This is known as the *triangle inequality*. (See Figure 2.2.)

Although we can choose different norms, most often people use the Euclidean norm $\|z\|_2 = \sqrt{\sum_i z_i^2}$, the max-norm $\|z\|_\infty = \max_i |z_i|$, or the 1-norm $\|z\|_1 = \sum_i |z_i|$. There are many others, but these seem to be the most useful. For example, if

$$z = \begin{bmatrix} 3 \\ -2 \\ 5 \end{bmatrix},$$

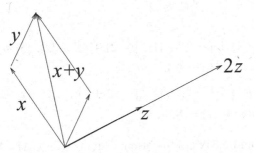

Figure 2.2. Vectors and vector operations.

it is easy to compute $\|z\|_2 = \sqrt{3^2 + (-2)^2 + 5^2} = \sqrt{38} \approx 6.1644$, $\|z\|_\infty = \max(|3|, |-2|, |5|) = 5$ and $\|z\|_1 = |3| + |-2| + |5| = 10$.

For each vector norm, we have a corresponding matrix norm $\|A\|$. The usual way of creating a matrix norm from a vector norm is through the formula

$$\|A\| := \max_{x \neq 0} \frac{\|Ax\|}{\|x\|}.$$

Note that in the fraction all the norms are *vector* norms. Vector norms and their associated matrix norms have two extra properties:

1. $\|Ax\| \leq \|A\| \|x\|$ for matrix–vector products, and
2. $\|AB\| \leq \|A\| \|B\|$ for matrix–matrix products.

Computing matrix norms can be harder than computing the associated vector norm. However, a number of matrix norms have relatively simple expressions:

1. $\|A\|_\infty = \max_i \sum_j |a_{ij}|$,
2. $\|A\|_1 = \max_j \sum_i |a_{ij}|$, and
3. $\|A\|_2 = \sqrt{\lambda_{\max}(A^T A)}$.

Note that $\lambda_{\max}(B)$ is the maximum real eigenvalue of B. Eigenvalues and eigenvectors form a more advanced part of linear algebra. See Appendix A on matrices and vectors for more information. However, a convenient bound is $\|A\|_2 \leq \|A\|_F$, where $\|A\|_F = \sqrt{\sum_{i,j} |a_{ij}|^2}$ is the Frobenius norm and is easily calculated.

Here is an example matrix to try it out on:

$$A = \begin{bmatrix} 1 & -2 & 1 \\ -2 & 3 & 4 \\ 5 & 1 & -2 \end{bmatrix}.$$

Then

$$\|A\|_\infty = \max(|1| + |-2| + |1|, \ |-2| + |3| + |4|, \ |5| + |1| + |-2|)$$
$$= \max(4, \ 9, \ 8) = 9.$$
$$\|A\|_1 = \max(|1| + |-2| + |5|, \ |-2| + |3| + |1|, \ |1| + |4| + |-2|)$$
$$= \max(8, \ 6, \ 7) = 8.$$

With some help from matrix computation systems like MATLAB^{TM} or Octave it is also possible to compute $\|A\|_2 \approx 6.695$. Also, we can compute

$$Az = \begin{bmatrix} 1 & -2 & 1 \\ -2 & 3 & 4 \\ 5 & 1 & -2 \end{bmatrix} \begin{bmatrix} 3 \\ -2 \\ 5 \end{bmatrix} = \begin{bmatrix} 12 \\ 8 \\ 3 \end{bmatrix}.$$

Note that $\|Az\|_\infty = 12 \leq 9 \times 5 = \|A\|_\infty \|z\|_\infty$, $\|Az\|_1 = 23 \leq 8 \times 10 = \|A\|_1 \|z\|_1$ and even $\|Az\|_2 \approx 14.7309 \leq 6.695 \times 6.1644 \approx \|A\|_2 \|z\|_2$.

The sensitivity of the solution of a system of linear equations to changes in the data is usually described through the error bound below (see [4, 18]). If $Ax = b$ and $(A + F)(x + e) = b + d$, then

$$\frac{\|e\|}{\|x\|} \leq \frac{\kappa(A)}{1 - \kappa(A)\|F\|/\|A\|} \left[\frac{\|d\|}{\|b\|} + \frac{\|F\|}{\|A\|} \right],$$

where $\kappa(A) := \|A\| \|A^{-1}\|$ is the **condition number** of the linear system. Provided $\kappa(A)$ is not very large, we say that the linear system $Ax = b$ is *well-conditioned*, as small (relative) changes in A and b result in small (relative) changes in the solution x. In general, you lose about $\log_{10} \kappa(A)$ digits in computing x.

If A is singular, then solutions might not exist, and if they do exist there are infinitely many. If A is close to being singular, then the linear system is sensitive to small changes in the data. This means that a general linear system solver cannot always be *forward stable*. But it can be *backward stable*. In fact, standard error bounds for using LU factorization or Gaussian elimination to solve a linear system (the standard method for general linear systems) say that the computed solution $\widehat{x}$ of a linear system $Ax = b$ is the *exact solution* of the linear system

$$(A + F)\widehat{x} = b,$$

where

$$\|F\| \leq c_1(n)\, \mathbf{u}\, [\|A\| + \|L\| \|U\|],$$

$\mathbf{u}$ is the unit roundoff, $c_1(n)$ is a modest function of n, and $A = LU$ is the LU factorization of A. Since $\mathbf{u}$ is small, $\|F\|$ is (usually) small, and so the computed solution

$\widehat{x}$ is the exact solution to a nearby linear system. This makes LU factorization a backward stable algorithm, at least if $\|L\| \, \|U\| \approx \|A\|$.

Note that if $\mathbf{u}\,\kappa(A)$ is small, then from the error bounds we see that

$$\frac{\|\widehat{x} - x\|}{\|x\|} \lesssim \kappa(A) \frac{\|F\|}{\|A\|} \lesssim 2\,c_1(n)\,\mathbf{u}\,\kappa(A) \ll 1,$$

so that the solution of *this* linear system is forward stable. This is one example of the principle that

$$\text{well-conditioned} + \text{backward stable} \quad \Rightarrow \quad \text{forward stable}.$$

Note that being well-conditioned is a property of the problem, but backward stability is a property of the algorithm used to solve the problem.

2.4 Numerical accuracy and reliability

Choose numerical algorithms which are numerically stable if at all possible. There is a wide literature on this, and you should have some idea of which algorithms are numerically stable in your area of interest. Have a look at numerical analysis textbooks like [4, 18], have a look in the library at the numerical analysis books (or books on your particular area of interest), and check the journals in numerical analysis, scientific computing, or computing in general. For more ideas, have a look at Chapter 11 on algorithm awareness.

The following suggestions give some additional information on problems that can occur due to floating point arithmetic, and ways of avoiding them.

2.4.1 Catastrophic cancellation

Catastrophic cancellation is probably the most common source of numerical trouble. This can occur when nearly equal quantities are subtracted: $c := a - b$ where $a \approx b$. The problem is that usually a is computed as $\widehat{a} = (1 + \epsilon_1)a$ and b is usually computed as $\widehat{b} = (1 + \epsilon_2)b$. Both ϵ_1 and ϵ_2 are small, typically $|\epsilon_1|, |\epsilon_1| \lesssim \mathbf{u}$ with $\mathbf{u}$ unit roundoff. Then the computed value of c is

$$\widehat{c} = (1 + \epsilon_3)\,[(1 + \epsilon_1)a - (1 + \epsilon_2)b]$$
$$= (1 + \epsilon_3)\,[a - b] + (1 + \epsilon_3)\,[\epsilon_1\,a - \epsilon_2\,b].$$

If $|a - b|$ is much less than $|a|$ and $|b|$ then $|\epsilon_1\,a - \epsilon_2\,b|$ can be larger than $|a - b|$ if ϵ_1 and ϵ_2 have opposite signs (so that the error *adds* instead of subtracts). The error in c is still small, but its relative error $|\widehat{c} - c|/|c|$ can be quite large. If we then divide by a small number, we can get large errors.

Here is a simple example. Suppose we want to compute the mean and variance of some test data in a list $a_1, a_2, \ldots, a_n$. (The variance is the square of the standard deviation.) The formulas for these quantities are:

$$\bar{a} = \frac{1}{n} \sum_{i=1}^{n} a_i \quad \text{(mean)}$$

$$v = \frac{1}{n-1} \sum_{i=1}^{n} (a_i - \bar{a})^2 \quad \text{(variance - two pass)}$$

$$= \frac{1}{n-1} \left[\sum_{i=1}^{n} a_i^2 - n\bar{a}^2 \right] \quad \text{(variance - one pass)}.$$

The second formula for the variance is very popular since we can use it to compute the mean and the standard deviation *in one pass through the data*. On the other hand, if we used the first formula for the variance we would need to compute the mean first, and then compute the variance on the second pass through the data.

However, the second formula has some hidden numerical problems if the input data is fairly large. For the input list

$$34\,124.75$$
$$34\,124.48$$
$$34\,124.90$$
$$34\,125.31$$
$$34\,125.05$$
$$34\,124.98$$

the computed results using single-precision were a mean of $34\,124.91$ and a variance of 38.5934 (standard deviation of 6.212). By comparison, using the two-pass algorithm gives a mean of $34\,124.91$ and a variance of $0.078\,778$ (standard deviation of $0.280\,67$). If you have a look at the data, you can see they don't differ from the the the mean by more than 0.42, so the variance from the one-pass algorithm can't be correct.

The reason is the catastrophic cancellation in $\sum_{i=1}^{n} a_i^2 - n\bar{a}^2$, where the sum of the squares has magnitude close to $n\bar{a}^2$. The squaring has also resulted in much larger numbers. To get a rough estimate of the roundoff errors, let's suppose that $\sum_{i=1}^{n} a_i^2$ and $n\bar{a}^2$ are computed exactly. Then the error we expect in the difference can be approximated by $\mathbf{u}\,n\bar{a}^2 \approx 6 \times 10^{-8} \times 6 \times (3.4 \times 10^4)^2 \approx 416$. This is then divided by $n - 1 = 5$ to give an error estimate for the variance of about 83, which is much larger than the true variance. This means that this estimate of the variance is almost entirely error.

But wait! The two-pass algorithm also has cancellation: doesn't computing $a_i - \bar{a}$ cause catastrophic cancellation? The answer is that it can, but the errors are much smaller because the a_is and $\bar{a}$ are much smaller than $\bar{a}^2$. The error in $a_i - \bar{a}$ can be roughly estimated by $\mathbf{u}\,|\bar{a}|$, so the error in $(a_i - \bar{a})^2$ can be roughly estimated by $2\,|a_i - \bar{a}|\,\mathbf{u}\,|\bar{a}|$. This gives an error in the variance which we can estimate by $2n \max_i |a_i - \bar{a}|\,|\bar{a}|\,\mathbf{u}$. So we get an error estimate of roughly $2 \times 6 \times 0.42 \times 3.4 \times 10^4 \times 6 \times 10^{-8} \approx 1.02 \times 10^{-2}$. This means that the computed variance 7.877×10^{-2} has one digit of accuracy.

The problem is not that there is cancellation, so much as increasing the size of the numbers in the computation (e.g., by squaring a_i to get a_i^2) before subtracting nearly equal quantities. Try to keep the numbers small, or at least prevent them from becoming much larger. Also, try to avoid dividing by especially small numbers.

Another example: Consider the problem of computing $(e^z - 1)/z$. The obvious code suffers from catastrophic cancellation for z small. On the other hand, for small z we have the rapidly convergent Taylor series expansion $(e^z - 1)/z = 1 + z/2! + z^2/3! + \cdots$. However, the number of terms needed depends on the accuracy desired, and the divisions can make for a slow routine.

It turns out that the problems with catastrophic cancellation can be dealt with by a remarkable little trick [63]:

```
w = exp(z);
/* exp(z) underflow */
if ( w == 0 ) return -1/z;
/* exp(z) == 1, special case */
if ( w == 1 ) return 1.0;
return (w-1)/log(w);
```

This gives full precision for any z, excepting z which give overflow. For small z, $w = fl(e^z) = fl(1 + z + z^2/2! + O(z^3))$. Assuming that this is computed to full precision, we have a loss of accuracy in adding $z + z^2/2$ to 1. For z in the range $\mathbf{u}$ to $\sqrt{\mathbf{u}}$, $z^2/2 < \mathbf{u}/2$, and so will not make any contribution to w. Instead, $w = fl(1 + z)$. So the numerator of the returned result is $w - 1$, while the denominator is $fl(\log(w))$. Now $\log(w) = (w - 1) - (w - 1)^2/2! + \cdots$. Since $w - 1$ is in the same range as z (but with less accuracy), $fl(\log(w)) = fl((w - 1) - (w - 1)^2/2) = (w - 1)[1 - (w - 1)/2](1 + \epsilon_1)$ with $|\epsilon_1| \le \mathbf{u}$. This means that the computed ratio is

$$\frac{w - 1}{(w - 1)[1 - (w - 1)/2](1 + \epsilon_1)}(1 + \epsilon_2), \qquad |\epsilon_1|, |\epsilon_2| \le \mathbf{u}.$$

Canceling the $w - 1$ factors, we get a result that is within unit roundoff of $1/[1 - (w - 1)/2] = 1 + (w - 1)/2 + O(w - 1)^2$. But $w - 1$ is within $\mathbf{u}$ of z, so our computed result is within unit roundoff of $1 + z/2! + z^2/3! + \cdots = (e^z - 1)/z$, as we wanted. We could carry out a similar analysis for different ranges of z and obtain similar results.

Another algorithm that works similarly, but is not quite as good is:

```
w = exp(z);   u = 1 + z;
if ( w == 1 || u == 1 ) return 1;
return (w-1)/(u-1);
```

Unfortunately, if $z \approx \sqrt{\mathbf{u}}$ the errors are approaching $\sqrt{\mathbf{u}}$ in size in this algorithm. The reason is that the computed value of u will be the same as the computed value of w, since $z^2/2 + \cdots$ will be smaller than $\mathbf{u}$. But then $(w - 1)/(u - 1)$ will be exactly one, not $1 + z/2 + O(z^2)$ as it should be.

The first modification is worthwhile as it provides full accuracy without having to determine what that accuracy is.

2.4.2 Numerical stability

Much bad numerical behavior can be traced to a single operation. But not all. Take for instance the problem of computing $I_k := \int_0^1 x^k e^{-x}\, dx$ for $k = 0, 1, 2, \ldots$. We can show that

$$I_k = k\, I_{k-1} - e^{-1}, \qquad k = 1, 2, \ldots, \qquad I_0 = 1 - e^{-1}.$$

From the first formula for I_k it is easy to see that $I_k > I_{k+1} > 0$. The following algorithm is *correct*, but *not stable*.

```
double  I[N];
I[0] = 1.0 - exp(-1.0);
for ( k = 1; k < N; k++ )
  I[k] = k*I[k-1] - exp(-1.0);
```

The trouble is that if there is an error of δ in I[k-1], then we get an error of $k\,\delta$ in I[k]. This amplifies the error, especially if k is large. Even if there is an error of only unit roundoff ($\approx 10^{-16}$) in I[0], we expect the error in I[20] to be about $20! \times 10^{-16} \approx 12$, while the true value is close to $e^{-1}/21$. When we run this code[3] we get the following results:

```
I[0] =    0.63212055882856
I[1] =    0.26424111765712
I[2] =    0.16060279414279
I[3] =    0.11392894125692
```

---

[3] We used the DJGPP version of the Gnu C compiler on a Windows XP computer.

```
I[4]   =     0.087836323856248
I[5]   =     0.071302178109799
I[6]   =     0.059933627487354
I[7]   =     0.051655951240039
I[8]   =     0.045368168748868
I[9]   =     0.040434077568367
I[10]  =     0.036461334512231
I[11]  =     0.033195238463104
I[12]  =     0.030463420385801
I[13]  =     0.028145023843975
I[14]  =     0.026150892644214
I[15]  =     0.024383948491768
I[16]  =     0.022263734696843
I[17]  =     0.010604048674894
I[18]  =    -0.17700656502335
I[19]  =    -3.7310041766152
I[20]  =   -74.987962973475
```

The numerical instability seems to appear very rapidly, but on close examination, we can see that I[17] is about half the value of I[16], and even I[16] is perhaps a bit too small. When the error is amplified by 16 or more with each iteration, even very small errors can become large in a few iterations.

This is an example of numerical instability that does not become apparent in one, two, three or even ten steps. But it does become apparent and eventually overwhelms the computed results. In this case, the problem can be fixed by reversing the iteration: use $I_{n-1} = (I_n + e^{-1})/n$ for $n = \ldots,$ 3, 2, 1. The trouble now is getting started. We don't know "I_∞", and even if we did, it would take an infinite amount of time to do the computations. But since the error is rapidly *reduced* we can start with a very rough value of (say) $I_{30} \approx e^{-1}/30$ which means that the error in I_{20} by this reverse method is about $e^{-1}/(30 \times 29 \times 28 \times \cdots \times 21) \approx 9 \times 10^{-16}$, which is almost full double-precision accuracy.

2.4.3 Speed and/or reliability

Speed and reliability are not necessarily mutually exclusive! Consider Newton's algorithm for solving a single linear equation with a single unknown and the bisection method.

The Newton method for solving an equation $f(x) = 0$ is an iteration

$$x_{k+1} = x_k - \frac{f(x_k)}{f'(x_k)}, \qquad x_0 \text{ given.}$$

This method can be extremely fast when it converges. But it is not guaranteed to converge. Consider first the equation $x = \cos x$. This can be represented by $f(x) := x - \cos x = 0$ whose derivative is $f'(x) = 1 + \sin x$. The iterates of Newton's method with $x_0 = 0$ are

$$x_0 = 0$$
$$x_1 = 1$$
$$x_2 = 0.750363867840$$
$$x_3 = 0.739112890911$$
$$x_4 = 0.739085133385$$
$$x_5 = 0.739085133215$$

and $|f(x_5)| \leq 10^{-16}$. On the other hand, if we apply this to the function $f(x) = \tanh(x)$ with $x_0 = 2$ we get

$$x_0 = 2$$
$$x_1 = -11.6449585986$$
$$x_2 = +3255536207.19$$
$$x_3 = -\text{Inf}$$
$$x_4 = \text{NaN}.$$

The code stopped at this point, because no comparison with a NaN is evaluated as true.

This bisection method solves the same equation, $f(x) = 0$, but uses a very different strategy. It takes an interval $[a, b]$ where $f(a)$ and $f(b)$ have opposites signs. That is, $f(a) > 0$ and $f(b) < 0$, or $f(a) < 0$ and $f(b) > 0$. This guarantees that there is a solution of $f(x) = 0$ for some $x \in [a, b]$.

```
bisect (f, a, b, ε),
    if sign f(a) = sign f(b) then return fail
    while |b − a| ≥ ε
        c ← (a + b)/2
        if sign f(c) = sign f(a)
        then b ← c else a ← c end if
    end while
end bisect
```

As long as our function f is continuous, the intervals $[a, b]$ must converge to a solution x of $f(x) = 0$. For example, if $f(x) = x - \cos(x)$, we can start with $a = 0$: $f(a) = 0 - \cos 0 = -1 < 0$, and $b = \pi/2$: $f(b) = \pi/2 - \cos(\pi/2) = \pi/2 >$

0. In 34 iterations the bisection method gets the interval down to $[a, b] = [0.739\,085\,133\,2,\ 0.739\,085\,133\,291]$.

The bisection method is guaranteed to work, but is relatively slow. Newton's method works most of the time and when it does it usually converges very, very quickly. So, which should you use? The tortoise or the hare?

The best answer is: both. There are algorithms which combine the speed of Newton's method (or get close to it) and the reliability of the bisection algorithm. There are several ways of doing this. One is to keep an interval $[a, b]$ where $f(a)$ and $f(b)$ have opposite signs. At each iteration of the hybrid method, we do a bisection step which halves the width of the interval $[a, b]$, and then do a Newton step using the mid-point c of $[a, b]$ as the starting point. Let w be the result of the Newton step. If w is outside the interval $[a, b]$ then we ignore the Newton step; if w is inside the interval $[a, b]$ then we compute $f(w)$ and replace the interval $[a, b]$ with $[a, w]$ or $[w, b]$ according to the sign of $f(w)$. Pseudo-code is given below.

```
hybrid(f, a, b, ε)
   while |b − a| ≥ ε
      // bisection step
      c ← (a + b)/2
      if sign f(c) = sign f(a)
      then b ← c else a ← c end if
      // Newton step
      c ← (a + b)/2;   w ← c − f(c)/f'(c)
      if a < w < b then
      if sign f(w) = sign f(a)
         then b ← w else a ← w end if
      end if
   end while
end hybrid
```

The best hybrid method is probably Brent's [15]. In designing this algorithm Brent took not only the number of iterations into account, but also the problems of rounding error. If you only have one variable and one equation, this is probably the algorithm of choice.

3

Priorities

Let's get this straight. Your priorities in writing scientific software should be, roughly speaking:

- correctness,
- numerical stability,
- accurate discretization (including estimating accuracy),
- flexibility,
- efficiency (speed and memory).

If your program is not correct, then nothing else matters. If the algorithm is not numerically stable, the results cannot be trusted (at least not unless you test them first). If the discretization or other approximations used are inaccurate we will still not be able to trust the results. Even better is to have a method that can estimate the errors in the discretization and approximations. The estimates don't have to be exact (if they were, we could compute the exact values), but good enough to give a reasonable idea of their size.

If the software is not flexible, then others probably won't use it, since they will have a hard time making it do something slightly different. Once we have a correct implementation of a numerically stable algorithm, *then* we can think about how to make it fast. Speed is still one of our priorities, but it comes last. Don't forget memory. If your algorithm needs more memory than your machine has, then it won't run. And sometimes this is more important than speed.

3.1 Correctness

Without correctness, we really can't expect any useful results. So we must first make sure that our programs bug-free. Since human beings make errors even for the simplest tasks (and programming involves a great deal of thought), the probability that someone can write a bug-free program of any significance without debugging is close to zero.

In addition, we should carefully check our logic when we are designing and writing the software. Catching mistakes early saves a great deal of pain later.

So we need to test and debug our programs. In fact, we should *design* our software *for* debugging and testing. There will be more to say on this later.

There is a caveat that should be mentioned here: since operations on floating point numbers are almost always only approximately true, we will not get answers that are *exactly* correct. For example, even trivial code such as z = x + y; in C will not necessarily make z exactly the sum of x and y if these are floating point quantities. However, if the operations were done in exact arithmetic we would get the exact answer.

Much has been made of "proof of correctness" methods, which make use of formal logic. There are even programs that automate part of this process. But for most programming tasks full-strength "proof of correctness" methods are impracticable. However, there are a number of features of these methods that we advocate.

"Proof of correctness" methods force the user to write down the explicit conditions that should be satisfied when a routine is called (*preconditions*), and the properties that are satisfied when the routine exits (*postconditions*). These are good habits. Writing down even informal preconditions and postconditions for your routines will help debugging and also testing later on. In fact, this is an example of a *contract*: provided the preconditions hold when the routine is called, the routine guarantees that the postconditions will hold on return. Some languages and systems provide automated support for "programming by contract".

Another technique that is worth using to help write loops is the idea of a *loop invariant*. A loop invariant is a logical statement at a point in a loop that should be satisfied every time the loop invariant is reached. A very simple example is a summation routine. In C this might look like this:

```
/* factorial
    -- precondition: n >= 0
    -- postcondition: returns n! */
int factorial(int n)
{
   int k, product;
   if ( n < 0 ) return 0;
   product = 1;
   for ( k = 2; k <= n; k++ )
      /* loop invariant: product = (k-1)! */
```

```
    product = k*product;
 return product;
}
```

The advantage of the loop invariant is that if we wish to check that it really does hold every time one goes through the loop, we only have to check the first time through the loop, and that if it was true the last time through the loop, it must be true this time through the loop. This works just like a proof using mathematical induction.

Support for these constructs is provided in some languages, such as C/C++, which have the *assert* macro. The macro evaluates its argument, and if the result is true then execution continues as if nothing happened; but if the result is false then execution is aborted with an error message identifying the failure of the assertion.

For more information on these topics, see [80].

3.2 Numerical stability

Catastrophic cancellation, overflow, and more gradual amplification of errors are all examples of numerical instability. Avoiding these, and finding ways of reducing the errors, are important aspects of designing numerical algorithms and their implementations. See Chapter 2 for examples of how these problems arise, and how to avoid them.

Knowing ways of identifying and handling numerical instabilities should be part of the background of everyone practicing scientific programming.

Choose your numerical algorithm with care. It will repay you later.

3.3 Accurate discretization

Not all computational tasks in scientific computing require a discretization of a "continuous" problem, but it happens very frequently. This should be done in a way that results in accurate solutions. This is a core topic in much of numerical analysis.

A related issue is estimating the error in the solution that is computed. This is done much less than it should be, but it gives crucial information to the user about how much the result should be trusted. (Read the story of the Sleipner A oil rig collapse in Chapter 4; this disaster could have been averted if error estimation had been used.)

We will consider error estimates for differential equations. The discretizations have some parameter which measures how refined the discretization is. For most ordinary differential equations, this parameter is the step-size; for the finite element method it may be the size of the largest element. Since we can usually control this parameter, we would like to know how large the errors are, and how to change these parameters to change the resulting errors.

One kind of error estimate is the *a priori* error estimate. This kind of error estimate depends on the discretization parameter and certain properties of the (unknown) exact solution. This kind of error estimate is usually of the kind that says that the size of the error is bounded by $C h^p$ where C is a number depending on the exact solution, h is the discretization parameter, and p is a fixed exponent that depends only on the discretization strategy. These error bounds usually assume that the exact solution is "sufficiently differentiable", meaning that the exact solution can be differentiated a certain number of times, typically $p + 1$ times. If this is violated, then the form of the error bound can be different.

A priori error bounds are very useful in determining the suitability of a particular discretization strategy – large values of p indicate that the error becomes small very rapidly as the discretization parameter h becomes small. Methods which have large values of p are called **high-accuracy methods**. High-accuracy methods can give extremely accurate solutions for modest values of the discretization parameter. However, their success often depends on the solution being very smooth, and any significant feature of the solution that has a size of about h can make high-accuracy method perform very badly. In short, high-accuracy methods often have a threshold behavior – if the discretization parameter is well below a threshold, the results are very accurate, but if they are significantly above this threshold, the results can be very inaccurate.

A different kind of error estimate is the *a posteriori* error estimate. This does not make any assumptions about the exact solution. Instead, the idea is to estimate the error in a given computed (approximate) solution. This may require the solution of some associated system of equations. This is the kind of error estimate that the designers of the Sleipner A oil rig did not have in their finite element software. If they did, then they would have realized that part of their solution was inaccurate. The development of *a posteriori* error estimates is not a simple task – substantial mathematical theory is needed to develop these kinds of error estimators. Part of this theory can be found in textbooks on finite element methods, such as [36] and [13].

3.4 Flexibility

Let's start with a slogan:

If users can't do what they want (easily) with your code, they will use something else.

While this is rather obvious, it should remind us that we can't easily tell what users will want to do with our code. (And users could include the very same programmer after a few months or years!) So we should try to design the code to allow users to do different (but legitimate) things with our code.

One way of making a lot of code flexible is to set up a library based on a particular mathematical abstraction with a specific data structure. The most successful libraries of this kind are **matrix libraries**. While MATLAB^{TM} is an interactive system and not a library, it is based around the abstraction of matrices with a consistent set of internal data structures; this is both very flexible and very successful. MATLAB users can use MATLAB's matrices in ways which the designers never dreamed of. But because the users and the designers of MATLAB have a common understanding of the mathematical abstraction of matrices, users do not have to know whether the designers had their problems in mind when they designed MATLAB.

This kind of approach can be used for many other kinds of problems. But we should be careful about trying to make the code too abstract. After all, we need to provide concrete implementations and, in general, users have great difficulty with software that uses abstractions they are not already familiar with.

Most of our applications will not just involve libraries of this kind, but will have to deal with the specifics of our particular problem. Nevertheless, it is usually possible to find suitable abstractions that handle the problem of interest.

One way in which programmers make their programs less flexible is by building assumptions into their code. Have a look at this Fortran function for computing Simpson's approximation to the integral $\int_a^b f(x)\,dx$ for a function f:

```
real function trapezoidal(a,b,n)
  real :: a, b, f, sum, h
  external :: f
  integer :: i, n
  h = (b-a)/n
  sum = 0.5*(f(a) + f(b))
  do i = 1, n-1
     sum = sum + f(a+i*h)
  end do
  trapezoidal = h*sum
end function trapezoidal
```

This builds in the assumption that the name of the function to be integrated is "f". If another function builds in the same assumption, but we want to apply it to a function called "g", we are in trouble. How can we get around this assumption? We can pass the function as a parameter. Then it doesn't matter what the function is called. Here is how to do that:

```
real function trapezoidal(f,a,b,n)
  real :: a, b, f, sum, h
  external :: f
  integer :: i, n
  h = (b-a)/n
  sum = 0.5*(f(a) + f(b))
  do i = 1, n-1
    sum = sum + f(a+i*h)
  end do
  trapezoidal = h*sum
end function trapezoidal
```

It is important to know how to pass functions and subroutines as parameters. While this tends to be relegated to the "advanced" section of most introductions to programming, it is basic to most scientific computing.

3.5 Efficiency: time and memory

Efficiency in time and memory may be the last priority, but it is still essential in design and development. Scientific computations are typically large, and any significant improvement in the execution time or the amount of memory required can be important. Fortunately, provided you are willing to suffer a small to modest loss of time for overheads, the pursuit of efficiency does not need to cause sacrifices in other areas (accuracy, flexibility, reliabilty, . . .) provided it is well-designed. And, in fact, good, flexible design will actually make efficiency much easier to attain.

The first area in which you should look for efficiency is in the data structures and overall algorithms you use. A "cheap" algorithm that is easy to implement but takes $O(n^2)$ time is likely to be a much bigger headache than a more complicated $O(n \log n)$ algorithm when n starts to become large. In fact, if you are interested in pushing n to the limits that your machine will allow, it is almost always the $O(n^2)$ algorithm that will limit the program.

If it is necessary, proper design will make it easy to first implement a simple $O(n^2)$ algorithm, and then to replace it later with a better $O(n \log n)$ algorithm for better performance. And you will be able to compare the results with the simple algorithm and the faster algorithm to check for bugs.

Other tools that you should consider in your quest for efficiency are the compiler's optimization options (in Unix or Linux, or if you are using a GNU compiler, add "-O" to your compilation command line) and profilers for finding how much time is spent in which routines (the Unix commands `prof` and `gprof` do this).

4

Famous disasters

Here are some stories of some famous disasters involving scientific or engineering software. Further details of these disasters can be found in [3] and in [57]. Original reports on these disasters can be found in [41] for the Patriot missile failure, [71] for the Ariane 5 crash, and [54] for the collapse of the Sleipner A platform.

4.1 Patriot missiles

On February 25th, 1991 a Scud missile launched by Iraq against Saudi Arabia hit a US Army base at Dahran in Saudi Arabia, killing 28 soldiers. The soldiers should have been protected by a Patriot missile which was meant to fire, hit and destroy the incoming Scud missile. It fired, but it missed the incoming Scud. While hitting a missile with a missile is a difficult task, it had a bigger difficulty: the software controlling the Patriot missile's guidance system did not have a very good idea of where the Scud missile actually was.

It turns out that the problem was a form of catastrophic cancellation. In order to predict the location of the Scud missile, the Patriot missile's guidance system needed a good estimate of the Scud's velocity. Positions of the Scud missile could be obtained via radar tracking at times separated by up to a few seconds; the velocity could be approximated by the ratio

$$x'(t) \approx \frac{x(t_2) - x(t_1)}{t_2 - t_1}.$$

To us, it should be clear that this expression is vulnerable to catastrophic cancellation. It turns out that the biggest problem is in the denominator: the error in the denominator could be roughly bounded by $\mathbf{u}(|t_1| + |t_2|)$, so that the relative error in the denominator is roughly bounded by

$$\mathbf{u}\frac{|t_1| + |t_2|}{|t_2 - t_1|}.$$

So if $t_2 \approx t_1$(they only differed by at most a few seconds), and t_1 and t_2 are large, then we can expect relatively large errors in the denominator. And consequently, we would expect poor velocity estimates.

So . . . if the Patriot missile guidance system had been running for a long time (and they ran for days on end) then they would become progressively less accurate at targeting Scud missiles.

Once the source of the problem was identified, they started to modify the software. In the meantime, there was a simple solution: regularly reset the Patriot missile software. It took a day to re-write and re-install the software to fix the problem once they realized what was wrong.

4.2 Ariane 5

On June 4th, 1996 the European Space Agency launched their latest spacecraft – the Ariane 5, larger and more powerful than its predecessor the Ariane 4 – from the coast of French Guiana in equatorial South America. However, 30 seconds after liftoff, it veered out of control and was destroyed before it could crash back to Earth. What went wrong?

This is a story of overflow, software re-use, and error handling. The navigation software on the Ariane 5 (and on its predecessor, the Ariane 4) was in two parts: one piece was for the pre-flight portion of the flight, another for the in-flight portion of the flight. The main task of the pre-flight navigation software was to get an accurate fix of its location at the start of its flight. This part of the software used fixed-point arithmetic. The in-flight navigation software used floating-point arithmetic. For a short while from just before take-off until a short while after take-off, both navigation systems were in operation in order to prevent transition problems.

Since these pieces of software had been working on the Ariane 4, the software was re-used. The trouble was that the Ariane 5 was a larger and more powerful rocket, and accelerated considerably faster than the Ariane 4. When the Ariane 5 took off, it reached the speed at which the fixed-point arithmetic unit in the pre-flight navigation software overflowed sooner – *before the pre-flight navigation software was turned off*. So an overflow error was generated. Because the software designers took the attitude that software was correct unless shown otherwise, *they did not write routines to handle fixed- or floating-point errors*. As a result the pre-flight navigation software crashed. Unfortunately, this crashed *all* the navigation software. Fortunately, they had a backup system . . . but it was loaded with the same software and so crashed as well (a fraction of a second earlier, in fact). With all navigation software out of action, the rocket soon started tumbling and had to be destroyed.

The final report from the inquiry into the disaster stated that "*It was the decision to cease the processor operation which finally proved fatal. . . . The reason behind this drastic action lies in the culture within the Ariane programme of only addressing random hardware failures. From this point of view exception- or error-handling mechanisms are designed for a random hardware failure which can quite rationally be handled by a backup system."* In other words, there was no allowance for systematic or software errors. Such arrogance should always be viewed with suspicion.

In the earlier section on fixed-point arithmetic, we saw that reducing errors using fixed-point arithmetic tended to push the fixed-point arithmetic to overflow. This makes fixed-point arithmetic particularly vulnerable to problems of this kind; each new situation needs to be checked to see if overflow is a possibility.

4.3 Sleipner A oil rig collapse

In August 1991, Norway's newest oil rig for drilling North Sea oil was in Gands-fjorden near Stavanger being assembled. During this process, the Sleipner A oil rig sprang a leak and sank to the bottom of the fjord, and the rest of the rig followed.

The problem wasn't in any of the software that was running at the time, and it wasn't due to roundoff error. Instead it was in the design software. Like most large structures it was analyzed by a finite element system, in this case it was a popular finite element program called NASTRAN. Finite Element software gives approximate solutions to the partial differential equations for elastic materials. This involves discretizing the equation by first decomposing the elastic bodies into small "elements". The smaller these elements are (provided they are not too slender), the more accurate the solution (the stresses and deformations) will be. The mathematical theory of finite element methods is well understood.

However, the finite element software used did not have any routines to compute the *a posteriori* error estimate. As a result the large errors in the stresses at a crucial part of the structure were not noticed. After the disaster, more refined analysis of the stress (using smaller elements) resulted in a much more accurate estimate of the stresses in this part of the structure. When this was done, it was clear that that part of the structure would collapse when it was fully loaded.

While this story does not involve floating-point arithmetic (or fixed-point arith-metic), it does illustrate the fact that most scientific software uses approximations, and so (almost) never gives the exact answer. Instead we need to understand how to estimate the errors in the answers produced because of the approximations made.

5

Exercises

1. Suppose that you are wanting to solve an ordinary differential equations $dx/dt = f(t, x)$, $x(0) = x_0$ where $x(t)$ is a three-dimensional vector. How could you present the solution? What if $x(t)$ is a three hundred-dimensional vector?

2. Compute $(1 - \cos x)/x^2$ for $x = 10^{-k}$, $k = 0, 1, 2, \ldots, 16$. Note that the limit of $(1 - \cos x)/x^2$ as x goes to zero is $1/2$. Estimate the roundoff error for small x by noting that $\cos x \approx 1$ for small x. Note that this is an example of catastrophic cancellation.

3. A common problem is to compute $\sqrt{x^2 + y^2}$. A standard implementation might be

```
double hypot(double x, double y)
{   return sqrt(x*x+y*y);   }
```

but this can suffer from overflow if x or y is very large. Re-write this to avoid overflow. Test your code with some large inputs (say $x \approx \pm 10^{200}$ and y a similar size). [**Hint:** If x is larger than y, note that $\sqrt{x^2 + y^2} = |x|\sqrt{1 + (y/x)^2}$. Now what should we do if y is larger than x?]

4. The standard formula for the solutions of a quadratic function $ax^2 + bx + c = 0$ is

$$x_\pm = \frac{-b \pm \sqrt{b^2 - 4ac}}{2a}.$$

If b^2 is small compared to ac and b is also positive, then $-b + \sqrt{b^2 - 4ac}$ is likely to result in catastrophic cancellation. Noting that $x_+ \cdot x_- = c/a$, and that one of x_- and x_+ can be computed without catastrophic cancellation, show how to compute the other accurately.

5. One way of computing the variance of a collection of values $x_1, x_2, \ldots, x_n$ is first to compute $\overline{x} = (1/n)\sum_{i=1}^{n} x_i$ and then $s^2 = (1/(n-1))\sum_{i=1}^{n}(x_i - \overline{x})^2$. But this is a two-pass algorithm – we need to store all the data before we can compute s^2. Now we will develop a one-pass algorithm to do the same. Let a_k be the average $(1/k)\sum_{i=1}^{k} x_i$ and $v_k = \sum_{i=1}^{k}(x_i - a_k)^2$. First show that $a_{k+1} = (1/(k+1))(ka_k + x_{k+1}) =$

39

$a_k + (x_{k+1} - a_k)/(k+1)$. Now we derive an update formula for v_k:

$$v_{k+1} = \sum_{i=1}^{k+1}(x_i - a_{k+1})^2$$

$$= \sum_{i=1}^{k}((x_i - a_k) + (a_{k+1} - a_k))^2 + (x_{k+1} - a_{k+1})^2$$

$$= \sum_{i=1}^{k}(x_i - a_k)^2 + 2(a_{k+1} - a_k)\sum_{i=1}^{k}(x_i - a_k)$$

$$+ k(a_{k+1} - a_k)^2 + (x_{k+1} - a_{k+1})^2$$

$$= v_k + k(a_{k+1} - a_k)^2 + (x_{k+1} - a_{k+1})^2.$$

Implement this method and check with the data that caused the problem with the original approach described in Section 2.4.1. You might like to expand $a_{k+1} - a_k$ in the above formula to avoid catastrophic cancellation problems for large k.

6. Suppose that your computer can perform about 10^9 floating point operations per second and has about a Gigabyte of memory (which is $2^{30} \approx 10^9$ bytes of memory). Since double precision numbers take up eight bytes of memory each, work out the size of the largest square matrix that could fit in memory. If we used LU factorization to solve a linear system, how long would this take, assuming that your LU factorization gets nearly peak performance? [**Hint:** LU factorization requires about $(2/3)n^3$ flops.]

7. For some kinds of mathematical problem, the solution can be checked in a finite number of arithmetic operations and standard function values. For some others, this is not possible unless we already know what the solution is. Identify which of the list below of kinds of mathematical problem belong to which category of problems. [**Note:** Sometimes extra information, such as gradients, can be useful.]
   (a) Solving linear systems of equations: solve $Ax = b$ for x.
   (b) Solving nonlinear systems of equations: solve $f(x) = 0$ for x.
   (c) Solving ordinary differential equation initial value problems: $dx/dt = f(t, x)$, $x(t_0) = x_0$.
   (d) Solving partial differential equation boundary value problems: $\nabla^2 u = f(x)$ in a domain Ω and $u(x) = g(x)$ on the boundary of Ω.
   (e) Solving optimization problems: $\min_x \phi(x)$.
   (f) Computing an integral: $\int_a^b f(x)\,dx$.

8. Run the following codes for computing $(e^z - 1)/z$ for $z = 1, 10^{-1}, 10^{-2}, \ldots, 10^{-16}$ in double precision and print out the results to 16 digits.
   (a) `return (exp(z)-1)/z;`
   (b) `w = exp(z);`
   ```
   /* exp(z) underflow */
   if ( w == 0 ) return -1/z;
   /* exp(z) == 1, special case */
   ```

```
    if ( w == 1 ) return 1.0;
    return (w-1)/log(w);
(c) w = exp(z);   u = 1 + z;
    if ( w == 1 || u == 1 ) return 1;
    return (w-1)/(u-1);
```

Compare with the results obtained from using the Taylor series $(e^z - 1)/z = 1 + z/2! + z^2/3! + \cdots + z^k/(k+1)! + \cdots$. Use 20 terms of the Taylor series for $|z| \le 1$; ideally these should be added from the smallest to the largest (that is, in reverse order).

Part II

Developing Software

6

Basics of computer organization

In this section we remind our readers of a number of things that are important to understand when developing scientific software. The first is how a Central Processing Unit (CPU) works. This is particularly important for getting the maximum performance out of your computer. The second is how variables are stored in memory. This is important not only for the performance of your code, but also whether it runs correctly or not. The third is what compilers, linkers, loaders and interpreters do to the code you write when they turn it into a program that actually runs on your computer. This is particularly important for people who write libraries of routines; these days that includes most programmers.

In this section we will not deal with the most advanced aspects of programming for performance. That will come in the next chapter.

6.1 Under the hood: what a CPU does

A CPU is the hardware that does the actual processing. The other hardware that makes up a computer – memory, input and output devices (keyboard, mouse, network connector, display, disk drives), support hardware – are there mainly to support the operations of the CPU.

So what does a CPU actually do? At the bottom level it is an electrical circuit containing many transistors, which we can consider to be electrically controlled switches carrying out logical operations ("and", "or", and "not"). The circuits form sub-systems of the CPU, as illustrated in Figure 6.1. Inside the CPU are a number of fast registers to store temporary data which are going to be operated on. The part of the CPU that does the actual computation is called the *Arithmetic-Logic Unit* (ALU). The program controls what computations the CPU does. This is read from memory into the CPU, which then decodes the instructions, switches the appropriate links connecting the registers and the ALU to take the input data from

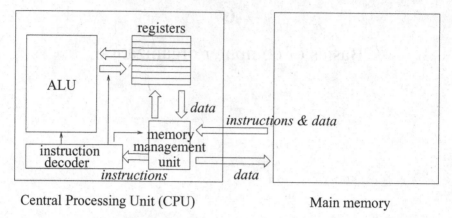

Central Processing Unit (CPU)   Main memory

Figure 6.1. Basic CPU architecture.

the appropriate register and to put the result in the appropriate destination register. If the CPU wishes to read or write some part of main memory, it activates the switches connecting the register to the main memory (or memory management unit) so that data can be transferred between them.

To keep track of where in the program we are, the CPU has a special register called the ***program counter***. Usually this increases with each instruction by the length of the instruction, so that it points to the next instruction to read in, decode, and execute. Sometimes, when the CPU executes a *branch* or *go to* instruction, the program counter is set to a new value which is where the CPU continues to execute. There are other special registers that contain ***condition codes*** which indicate if the result of the last arithmetic operation was zero, positive, or negative. Using these codes, when the CPU executes a *conditional branch* (such as a *branch if positive* instruction), the CPU will check the control code register, and if the appropriate condition code is set, the program counter will be set to the prescribed value; if the condition code is not set, the program counter will be incremented to the address of the next instruction.

Other instructions include *branch to subroutine* which implements calls to routines using the system stack. The use of stacks to call routines is described in the next section.

Some CPUs have very extensive instruction sets. These are often called *Complex Instruction Set Computers* (CISCs), which typically have instructions for loading and adding the contents of a register with the contents of the top of the stack and storing the location at the top of the stack. This makes writing in machine code or ***assembly language*** more convenient. However, it makes the hardware design more complex. In the past, this was dealt with by having a second level of software called **microcode** which implemented the machine instructions in terms of direct hardware operations.

Beginning in the mid-1980s, there was a strong move to reduce the complexity of the hardware by reducing the number and complexity of the machine instructions. CPUs designed this way were called *Reduced Instruction Set Computers* (RISCs). This began as an academic exercise, but later entered the marketplace through a company called MIPS (later acquired by Silicon Graphics). In RISC CPUs, instead of having many instructions that accessed memory, there were only two, *load* and *store*, for each size of data item (usually *byte* and *word*). RISC computers sometimes had shallow stacks implemented in hardware so that, say, *add* instructions applied to the top two stack entries and did not have to specify which registers to add.[1] RISC CPUs also introduced new ways of handling registers, that were often copied in other non-RISC CPUs. One of the advantages of RISC CPUs was that each machine instruction could be executed in one clock cycle. This often put them at the leading edge of performance.

The "RISC revolution" has now largely passed. While the Intel CPUs that now dominate the market are generally regarded as being CISC CPUs, many of the features of RISC CPUs have been incorporated into the Pentium architecture. Pentium CPUs are now described as having a load/store architecture, meaning that the complex memory access instructions have been dropped. The relentless advance of Moore's law (the number of transistors on a CPU double roughly every 18 months) has meant that simplicity is not a virtue for hardware designers. Instructions can still execute in an average of one clock cycle or even less by using a complex combination of pipelines, parallelism, and other techniques. Some of these issues will be dealt with in the next part on performance issues.

6.2 Calling routines: stacks and registers

Stacks (also known as *LIFOs* for *Last In First Out*) are basic data structures for modern computer systems. This was not always so. In the 1950s and 1960s, computers used different ways of storing variables and calling routines which made certain kinds of routines (like recursive routines) impossible. Now, virtually all CPUs are intended to work with stacks. We will refer to the stack that is basic to the system as the *system stack*.

The basic operations on a stack are *push, pull*, and *peek*. Push puts a data value onto the top of the stack; pull removes whatever is on the top of the stack, and peek

---

[1] This was the case for the Transputer developed by Inmos. The Transputer was an innovative approach to parallel computing: each Transputer had four serial links to communicate with other Transputers, and were programmed using a language called Occam which had message passing primitives built in.

			6			
	5	5	11			
2	2	2	2	22		
3	3	3	3	3	3	25

| push 3 | push 2 | push 5 | push 6 | 5+6 | 2 x 11 | 22+3 |

Figure 6.2. Expression evaluation using a stack.

tells us what is on the top of the stack. Pushing data onto the stack does not destroy any data, rather the data that was previously on the stack is pushed down, and can be accessed only after the newly pushed data is pulled from the stack.

Stacks are very useful for evaluating expressions which involve intermediate quantities. Consider evaluating the expression $3 + 2 \times (5 + 6)$. Here is how it is done using stacks (see also Figure 6.2):

- push 3 onto the stack;
- push 2 onto the stack;
- push 5 onto the stack;
- push 6 onto the stack;
- now pull 5 and 6 from the stack, add them to get 11;
- push 11 onto the stack;
- pull 2 and 11 from the stack, multiply them to get 22;
- push 22 onto the stack;
- pull 3 and 22 from the stack, add them to get 25;
- we could push 25 onto the stack, but that's the final answer.

This is not quite the most efficient way of doing this. We pushed things that we immediately pulled; in a CPU, these could be held in a register. But it gives you the idea.

To implement this data structure, we need a pointer into memory called the ***stack pointer***. This tells us where the "top" of the stack is. When we push an item of data, we increase the stack pointer, and put the new item in the new place pointed to by the stack pointer. This means that we can push the data without destroying the old data in the stack. To pull the data item from the stack we simply decrease the stack pointer by one data item. To peek, we simply fetch the data item pointed to by the stack pointer.[2]

---

[2] In actual computer systems, the system stack is usually thought of as growing *down* instead of *up*, so instead of increasing the stack pointer to push, they actually decrease the stack pointer; similarly to pull a data item, the

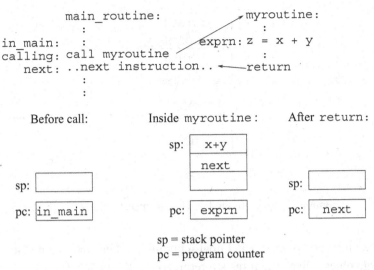

Figure 6.3. Function call using stacks.

6.2.1 Calling routines

Stacks are also vital for calling functions. Consider calling a function with no arguments first: (in Fortran)

```
call myroutine()
```

The function call is translated into an instruction that we will call *branch to subroutine* myroutine. This instruction increments the program counter and then pushes that value onto the stack; the program counter is then set to the memory address of myroutine.

Inside myroutine there may be some computation, but at the end there is a *return* instruction. This return instruction pulls the address from the top of the stack and puts it in the program counter. This way, the program returns to where it was before the call to myroutine was made. The whole sequence is illustrated in Figure 6.3.

If we are calling a function, then we need to return a value. There are two ways of doing this:

- the return value can be in a designated register;
- the return value can be stored on the stack.

Since the calling and called routines have to agree on which way to do it, there has to be a fixed rule, once and for all, for deciding how to do this. Generally small

stack pointer is increased instead of decreased. However, the idea is the same, and if it is confusing to think of stacks growing down, then don't worry about it – it works just the same way if you think of stacks growing up.

return address
return value
x
b
a

Figure 6.4. Stack frame for z = myroutine(a,b,x).

objects like integers, pointers, and floating point numbers are returned in registers, while large objects like structures are returned on the stack.

6.2.2 Passing arguments

What happens if myroutine needs arguments: myroutine(a,b,x)? There are two main ways of passing the arguments a, b, and x.

- We can copy the *value* of the arguments onto the stack. This is called *pass by value*. If the argument is an expression, the expression is evaluated (using the stack if necessary) and the result of the expression is left or put on the top of the stack.
- We can put the *address* of the arguments onto the stack. This is *pass by reference*. If the argument is the value of an expression, as **for example** myroutine(a,c*w+z,x), then we can put the value of the expression (c*w+z) into a memory location and pass the address to that location.

Note that if a variable is *passed by value*, then changing that value inside the called routine will not change it outside. But if it is *passed by reference* and changed inside, then it is changed outside as well.

In addition to the variables passed, it might be necessary to save some data in registers on the stack to be restored when the routine returns. This is often true of control codes mentioned earlier, which remember whether the result of the last operation was zero, positive or negative. Sometimes, if only a few small variables are passed, then this can be done through registers. However, since both the calling and called routines need to agree on this, there has to be a fixed rule for when this is done.

The data put on the stack for calling a routine is called the *stack frame*. Figure 6.4 gives an example of how a stack frame might look.

Note that passing arrays by value will take up a lot of memory on the stack. Since the stack is constantly changing size as expressions are evaluated and functions called, this can result in stacks becoming extremely large, which is not desirable. Many systems provide only a very limited amount of memory for the stack, and in older microcomputer systems there was no protection of other memory if the stack became too large. So it is usual to pass arrays by reference, even if all other variables are passed by value (as is the case in C). In Fortran, all variables are passed by reference. In Java, the standard types (int, char, float, double and bool) are all passed by value, but all others (including arrays) are passed by reference.

6.2.3 A cautionary tale

Sloppy programming practices can sometimes work on some hardware, and then suddenly fail. For example, in C the standard memory allocation function is called malloc. Also in C, if you do not declare the return type of a function, it is assumed to return an integer (int). The malloc function returned a pointer. This didn't matter because integers and pointers fit in the same registers, so many C programmers didn't declare the malloc function.

But a new microprocessor appeared in 1979 by Motorola called the 68000, which broke of a lot of code. What happened was that even though integers and pointers were the same size, they were stored in different registers. The 68000 had two sets of registers – one set of eight data registers and one set of eight address registers. Since malloc returned a pointer, its return value was put into the first *address* register. But any code that used malloc assumed it returned an integer, got the value in the first *data* register. And the value left in the first data register had nothing to do with the value returned by malloc.

6.3 Allocating variables

Variables need a piece of memory to store their value. There are three main choices for where this memory is

- *On the stack.* This is where local variables are usually stored. To create a local variable, simply update the stack pointer as if pushing that variable. The address of the local variable can be computed by adding a known constant to the stack pointer (these are details that the compiler works out). Unless the local variable is initialized, its value is whatever was left on the stack, which is usually not useful. Since the stack is usually overwritten by other data between calls, the value of a local variable between calls is typically regarded as undefined. It also means that you should (almost) never return the address of (or pointer to) a local variable.

Arrays can be allocated on the stack, but it is not done in most modern computing environments. It was done by Algol compilers and can also be done by Fortran 90 compilers, but it results in a number of complications – calculating the address of local variables depends on the size of the arrays allocated on the stack, and stack space is usually fairly limited. It usually doesn't take too many arrays on the stack to overflow the stack space.

- *In a fixed memory location.* In the first versions of Fortran, this was how everything was stored. It was efficient. No address calculations were needed. But it was restrictive. Array sizes had to be fixed at the time the program was compiled, and recursive routines are impossible with this approach. Since Fortran 77, local variables are allocated on the stack. Storing variables in fixed locations means that the value of the variable is "remembered" from one routine call to another, unlike storage on a stack where the value of the local variable is forgotten (and the stack is overwritten by other local variables and stack frames).

  Now, many languages provide this kind of storage allocation for selected local variables. In C or C++, declaring a local variable to be `static` means that it is stored in a fixed memory location. In recent versions of Fortran, variables declared with the keyword `save` are stored in this way. This is often used in routines that use *reverse communication*.

  Global variables are variables that are accessible by all routines. These are variables that must be stored in a fixed memory location, so that all routines know how to access them.

- *In the memory heap.* This provides permanent storage for variables and arrays, and can accommodate arrays whose size is not known when the program is compiled. However, the allocation has to be done explicitly in most programming languages. In C, this is done using a routine such as `malloc` or `calloc`; in Pascal, C++, and Java a `new` command is used and in Fortran 90 and later versions of Fortran the `allocate` command is used. The *memory heap* is a data structure that contains a list of blocks of memory along with information about them (if free, how big they are, etc.). What each of these routines (`malloc`) and commands (`new`, `allocate`) do is to call a routine to find a free block of memory from within a memory heap and return a pointer to the start of that block of memory.

  De-allocating memory allocated on the memory heap is equally important. Without this, repeated requests for memory allocations on the memory heap without returning memory will eventually cause the heap to run out of memory. This is an example of a *memory leak*. De-allocating memory on the memory heap involves re-inserting the block of memory into the heap. Do not de-allocate memory that was not originally allocated on the heap, or de-allocate the same block of memory twice. This can result in programs crashing. These problems can often be caught by using special libraries of "debugging" allocators which carry out a number of consistency checks in an attempt to ensure that inappropriate blocks of memory are not inserted into the heap. Alternatively, if a system supports *garbage collection*, all the de-allocation will be carried out by the system.

Here is a quick summary of the important differences between these ways of storing variables

- Storage in fixed memory locations is efficient, but limits what can be done with it. This prevents recursion, and if it is used as a global variable can cause complications in understanding, writing, and debugging code.
- Storage on the stack is almost as efficient as storage in fixed memory, but is much more flexible. However, stack space is often limited, so it is best not to use this for large arrays.
- Large objects, or objects that must keep their value beyond the end of the routine that creates them, are best stored in the memory heap. There is significant overhead in allocating and de-allocating memory, but the gain in flexibility in enormous.

6.4 Compilers, linkers and loaders

Most languages for scientific computing are *compiled* languages. That means that they are first compiled into a programming language that is closer to the machine's language. Usually it is the machine language (called *machine code*) – the language that the CPU can execute directly.

However, if we need to use some libraries (including the system's libraries), then we need to store some extra information with the machine code so that we can *link* the two pieces of software. This machine code with extra information is called *object code*. (In Unix systems this is usually identified by the "`.o`" extension, and in Microsoft Windows, by the "`.obj`" extension.)

Part of the extra information that object files contain is called *relocation* information, and the code in an object file is called *relocatable code*. Machine code is meant to start at a specific memory location, since otherwise the jump and branch instructions will go to the wrong places. But a routine in a library cannot guarantee that that block of memory will be free. What if another routine needs that block of memory? Then we need extra information so that the routine can be shifted to a block of memory starting at a different address.

Part of the extra information in object files is the names of the routines and global variables in the object file, the names of routines and global variables, and the (relocatable) addresses of those routines and global variables. The names are often called *symbolic addresses* or just *symbols*. These are needed if we want to link the routines to other routines. This process is called *resolving addresses*.

6.4.1 Libraries

Libraries are collections of routines that are ready to be linked with other routines. Libraries are extremely useful implementations of the idea of modularity: each routine in the library is expected to operate correctly whatever it is

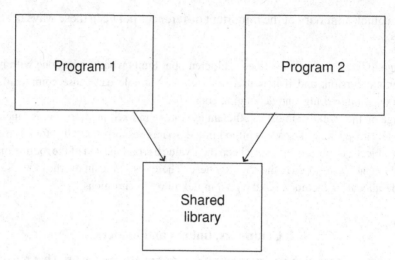

Figure 6.5. Shared libraries can be called by multiple programs.

linked to, provided the interface is implemented correctly and known preconditions hold.

The simplest libraries are **static libraries**, which are usually implemented as files containing the object code of the different routines together with an index showing which routines contain which symbols. In Unix systems these are usually ".a" files ("a" for "archive"); in Microsoft Windows these are usually ".lib" files. Library files are basically collections of object code files. These are linked with the routines that use them and the other libraries they use before we can execute the code. The resulting executable code can be sent to any other machine with the same operating system and machine code and run.

There are also **shared** and **dynamically linked libraries**. In Unix these are usually ".so" or ".sl" files, while in Windows these are ".dll" files. When these are linked with the main program and its routines, the executable code contains the unresolved symbolic names that are defined in the shared or dynamically linked library. When the executable code is run, the shared or dynamically linked library must be found, the library is then loaded into memory, and the symbolic addresses resolved. Usually the library can be shared by separate programs – only one copy of the library is needed, as illustrated in Figure 6.5.

Sharing the library is efficient in memory, but there is a cost that must be taken into account when you are programming routines for a shared or dynamically linked library: the code should be **re-entrant**. That is, while the code is being executed by one program, it can simultaneously be executed for another program. While separate programs have separate stacks so that variables stored on the stack are not shared, variables stored in fixed memory locations are shared by the two programs.

Shared variables are dangerous and should be avoided in shared libraries.

So if you are writing a shared or dynamically linked library, avoid `static` or `saved` local variables and avoid global variables.

6.4.2 Interpreted languages and variations

Most languages used for scientific computing are *compiled*. However, some programming languages are *interpreted* instead. Examples of this include Lisp, BASIC (*Beginners All-purpose Symbolic Instruction Code*), and MATLAB. Interpreted languages are most often used for their flexibility and the interactive environment that they provide. They can be excellent for quickly implementing an idea and seeing how it works. Users of Lisp, BASIC, and MATLAB can all attest to this.

But interpreted languages are typically very inefficient. Because code in the interpreted language must be parsed to determine what it means, there is a great deal of overhead. Typically this overhead slows down execution by a factor of anything from 20 to 1000. MATLAB is able to be more efficient for matrix computations since the basic matrix operations (dot products, matrix multiplication, LU factorization, etc.) are available as pre-compiled routines. But if you wrote your own MATLAB matrix multiply routine using MATLAB's `for` loops, you will notice that it is much, much slower than with a compiled language.

The inefficiency of interpreted languages can be mostly overcome by providing compilers for interpreted languages, and there are compilers for Lisp, BASIC, and MATLAB, for example.

An alternative to the purely compiled and purely interpreted languages is to use an intermediate language. Often this intermediate language is described as a "virtual machine code" – machine code for a hypothetical but plausible CPU. This intermediate language should be easy to interpret, but designed to fit the high-level language. Then compilation can be done quickly, so that often an interactive feel is maintained.

Java is an example which uses an intermediate language, although the reason for the intermediate language is portability rather than to maintain an interactive environment. The interpreter for the compiled Java "bytecode" is called the Java virtual machine (JVM). Other examples of languages or systems using an intermediate language include the P-code system for Pascal, and SmallTalk "bytecodes".

Sometimes hardware is actually built to directly execute the intermediate language –
implementing the "virtual" machine as hardware. This was the idea behind Lisp
machines (to execute Lisp directly) and other projects, such as Lilith to execute
M-code produced by Modula-2 compilers. Microsoft's .NET family of languages
(such as C#) are all compiled to a common intermediate language which is similar
to Java bytecode.

7

Software design

7.1 Software engineering

Software engineering is about the task of designing and implementing software. It is not about the specific algorithms or techniques to be programmed, but about how to organize both the software and the people who develop it. While many programmers have the attitude "Just do it!" and can cope with small programs just fine, large programs and, indeed, any programs that you expect other people to use, need careful attention and design.

There are many other books available to help programmers be more effective at their work. One of the first such books is *The Mythical Man-Month* [17], which is justifiably famous for its advice on avoiding software disasters. A book that many have found invaluable is *Elements of Programming Style* [65]. Recent books of this kind include books on trends such as Extreme Programming like [21], and *The Pragmatic Programmer* [58]. Many contain a great deal of wisdom, and have been written with considerable and deep experience. They usually generate a great deal of lively controversy. One of the especially good features of these books, as opposed to textbooks on software engineering such as [86], is their emphasis on practical aspects of programming and the words of experience with large systems and difficult situations.

7.2 Software life-cycle

Software is eternal. Once a program is written in a specific programming language, it is a valid program in that language and when compiled and executed will do essentially the same thing now and forever. Yet our software is ever-changing. Microsoft comes out with new versions of its operating system every few years, and sends out patches on a weekly basis. Computer programming languages have multiple versions coming out every few years. Why does "eternal" software change so rapidly?

- *New features*;
- *bug fixes*;
- *new hardware*;
- *reliance on other software*.

Since software keeps changing, we need to deal with **software maintenance**. In one sense, software does not need to be maintained. But we do need to find ways to handle new features, bug fixes, new hardware, and other software. But maintaining software is not like maintaining, say, a bicycle. If something goes wrong with a bicycle it is usually because something broke, and needs to be repaired or replaced. A burst inner tube means going to a bicycle store and buying a new inner tube, and then taking out the old and putting in the new. You don't have to change any of the *design* of the bicycle. And you wouldn't want to.

But with software, we aren't trying to repair "broken" statements or functions to make them like they were when the software was new. They haven't changed. What we have to do is *re-design* the software to work correctly, better, or work in a new environment. Re-designing something is always a risky proposition (riskier than just making it "like it was"), so we have to be careful about doing this. We need to ask ourselves, "Are our assumptions justified?", "Will this introduce a new bug?", etc. To make this easier and more reliable, we should design our software in the first place to make it easier to debug, test, and modify.

Bugs are a perpetual problem in software. Since even for simple tasks people make errors, perfectly bug-free software is a practical impossibility. However, we should be able to reduce the occurrence of bugs to a very low level by good design and testing. Once other people use our software (or we re-use our own software), problems and flaws usually become apparent, even if they are not "bugs". (When we write a piece of code that is what we wanted to write, but does something different from what we want because of a mistaken assumption or deduction, it is called **misimplementation**.) To fix these problems or flaws, we have to re-design the software. Then the software is again put to use, and perhaps, new flaws are found.

This is the basic idea of the lifecycle of software. Software is designed, tested and debugged, used, and from the results, the software is re-designed and the process continues. Skipping or skimping on part of the cycle doesn't mean that you have escaped from doing extra work. Instead, you find that you have to spend even more time later on in testing and debugging. In the mean time your users (which could include you!) might give up in disgust with the extra time this is taking.

If you have been involved in a few projects, you will start to get an idea of how the software lifecycle works. If you have made your software public, or incorporated it into some commercial software, then you probably have had feedback from users – bug reports, difficulties in using the software, ideas for future features, and occasionally praise for your efforts. Writing software is partly art and craft as well as science, so developing your own skills should become part of your day-to-day programming efforts. *The Pragmatic Programmer* [58] has some ideas about how to do this. Edward Yourdon, a long-time proponent of software engineering, has some as well [107, pp. 113–124].

7.3 Programming in the large

Programming in the large is about designing the overall structure of the software, and organizing people to write it. This is obviously very important for large-scale software efforts such as writing operating systems, where there are many different aspects that need to be properly co-ordinated (e.g., disk drives, displays, process managers, windowing systems, and network systems). When even a few people work on a common piece of software, effort must be spent on programming in the large.

Issues that should be considered for programming in the large are:

- Requirements specification.
  What exactly needs to be done? What is the form of the input? Form of the output? Are there time or memory performance objectives? The answers to some of these questions are well outside the domain of the programmer(s), but is something that the client (whoever he/she is) might or might not have clearly thought out. A clearly thought out specification should form the basis of a set of tests. And testing should be integrated throughout the software development cycle.
- Main data structures (or databases) to be used.
  For large software systems that will be put to many uses, this is perhaps the most important question of all. Deciding what data structures will be operated on then becomes the central design issue. Consider MATLAB again: the matrix is its essential data structure, but it also needs data structures to handle variable names and values, expressions, and MATLAB routines. Related questions are "What parts of the software can access which data structures or databases?", "What parts can modify which data structures or databases?", "What data needs to be stored in which data structure or database?" In object-oriented systems, the main objects must be designed: "What are the object's interfaces?", "How should it respond to its requests?"
- Software libraries to be used as a basis for work.
  Using other people's libraries is a common way to speed up development work, and allows programmers to concentrate on the relevant aspects of their programming. But

we need to make sure that the libraries really can do what we expect of them. We need to know what their *interfaces* are (i.e., how we communicate with the routines in these libraries). We might also need to know something about *how* they carry out their task, especially if we have strong performance requirements. And what if the library changes?

- How to co-ordinate programmers.

Programmers, being human, obviously need to be managed differently from software or computers. There is much to be said about managing people both in the context of software development and outside of it, but this is outside of our scope. Look up some books on the subject, for example *The Mythical Man-Month* by Frederick Brooks [17], and a standard text on software engineering, such as [86]. Many techniques for handling teams of programmers and ensuring the quality of the software written, such as code inspections and structured walkthroughs, are described in [86], along with results of quantitative studies of their effectiveness.

- How to co-ordinate software development.

If different people are developing different components of the same software system, they need to co-ordinate how to do things. The most important information that they need to know is about the *interfaces* between the different software systems. This might be as simple as knowing how to call the relevant routines in the different components, but it might also involve files and file formats. For example, a Finite Element package might use a file generated by a Computer-Aided Drafting (CAD) program to define the geometry of the region. (An example of such a file format is the Initial Graphics Exchange Specification, or IGES.) Any change to the file format would require changes to both the CAD program and the Finite Element package. Also note that any *assumptions* made by a component must also be considered as part of the interface. There are automated tools to support co-ordination between programmers, such as version control systems.

- Language specification.

What programming languages will we use? Will we use more than one language? If so, which? And how do we get them to communicate properly? How portable is the language? Are there requirements that force us to use a particular language? For example, real time systems may require a particular language/operating system combination. Some legacy systems will require a particular programming language. If there is some choice of languages, how would you decide which is most suitable for the task? Also, if you wish to use BLAS (which is written in Fortran), how will you interface to it? Fortunately there are a number of interfaces to BLAS for different languages such as C/C++ and Java. How will the system be built? Can changes be incorporated quickly and automatically?

- Software portability.

How portable will the software be? Will it run under Microsoft Windows? Under Linux? Under other versions of Unix? Under Apple OS X? Will it require other software to be installed? Will the user have to re-compile the software? What compilers are acceptable? These are all questions that you should consider. Even if you are the only user, you may need or want to change machines or operating systems and then you will have to face these issues.

To get an idea of what "programming in the large" is all about, sometimes it is worthwhile reading stories about particular large software development projects. One is the IBM OS360 project to write an operating system for IBM's System 360 in the 1960's. This experience was the starting point for Brook's book *The Mythical Man-Month* [17]. Another well-documented software project is the development of the SmallTalk programming language at the Xerox Palo Alto Research Center (also known as Xerox PARC). This is described in [67]. If you want to know more about SmallTalk itself, the classic reference is [44].

Do not think that these questions will be decided once for always. Later events and experiences will often force developers to re-think previous decisions. This is particularly true if Extreme Programming (XP) practices are used.

7.4 Programming in the small

Programming in the small is about the nitty-gritty details of programming. It covers the basics of programming, writing loops, declaring variables, accessing data structures, etc. It also covers many aspects of optimizing programs, especially for reducing the amount of time they take to execute. There are some aspects of this that are particularly important for programmers in scientific computation, especially those related to *memory hierarchies*. There will be more on memory hierarchies later.

However, you should keep in mind a quote of Donald Knuth (paraphrasing a quote of C.A.R. Hoare):

premature optimization is the root of all evil.[1]

Often the best approach to optimization is to wait until you have evidence of poor performance before trying to optimize. See the section on profiling tools on how to obtain this evidence. You should also be aware of the capabilities of the compiler's optimizer. Very often things that you do to improve performance would already be done by the compiler. For example, the C keyword `register` is now essentially obsolete. The idea was that you should declare a few key variables as `register` variables (syntax: `register int x;`) so that the compiler would know to keep them in registers, rather than in main memory. Optimizing compilers now are so good that they can work this out themselves. They also have the advantage of knowing how many registers it has available for this purpose.

---

[1] The full version of the quote is "We should forget about small efficiencies, say about 97% of the time: premature optimization is the root of all evil."

Another example of a useless optimization is to convert the following code from:

```
void copy_array1(double a[], int length, double b[])
{
  int i;
  for ( i = 0; i < length; i++ )
    b[i] = a[i];
}
```

to use C's pointer arithmetic:

```
void copy_array2(double a[], int length, double b[])
{
  int i;
  for ( i = 0; i < length; i++ )
    *b++ = *a++;
}
```

If there is an opportunity for optimization, an optimizing compiler will probably recognize what the first version does (using a[i] and b[i]) instead of the clever (but obscure) pointer-arithmetic version. The code it would produce for the first version would often be faster than the code produced for the second version. We've seen this in practice.

Optimizing compilers do a number of clever things that you don't need to worry about:

- *Register allocation.* Assign commonly used variables to registers for rapid access.
- *Common sub-expression elimination.* If an expression appears several times, evaluate it once and store the result.
- *Loop transformations.* Re-order loops to avoid inefficiencies.

There are things that you should optimize at a low level. Here is a quick summary of some of these.

- **Temporal locality**: Nearby memory accesses in time should be to nearby locations in memory. Accessing far-apart memory locations means that each time a new memory location is accessed, memory within the CPU has to be filled with values at and around that memory location.
- **Memory usage**: Try to re-use dynamically allocated memory. This is not only helpful for avoiding **memory leaks** (see later), but also avoids time allocating and freeing memory.

Here is an example of temporal locality in action. Consider computing a matrix–vector multiplication: $y = Ax$. In terms of components, $y_i = \sum_{j=1}^{n} a_{ij}x_j$ for

$i = 1, 2, \ldots, m$, where A is $m \times n$. When we write a routine for that, there are two ways of ordering the loops: should we do the i loop first, or the j loop? We can do it in either order:

```
for ( i = 0; i < m; i++ )
{
  y[i] = 0;
  for ( j = 0; j < n; j++ )
    y[i] = y[i] + a[i][j]*x[j];
}
```

or

```
for ( i = 0; i < m; i++ )
  y[i] = 0;
for ( j = 0; j < n; j++ )
{
  for ( i = 0; i < m; i++ )
    y[i] = y[i] + a[i][j]*x[j];
}
```

To see which results in better memory accesses, we have to realize that C stores its arrays in *row-major order*. That is, consecutive memory locations hold a[0][0], a[0][1], a[0][2], ..., a[0][n-1], a[1][0], a[1][1], ... To keep our memory references close together, we should make the j loop the inner loop.

Now Fortran does things differently. It stores arrays in *column-major order*. That is, in the array

```
double precision a(m,n)
```

the entries are stored in the order a(1,1), a(2,1), ..., a(m,1), a(1,2), a(2,2).... If we were writing a Fortran routine, we should put the loops the other way around, i.e., the loop on i should be the inner loop:

```
do i = 1, m
  y(i) = 0;
enddo
do j = 1, n
  do i = 1, m
    y(i) = y(i) + a(i,j)*x(j)
  enddo
enddo
```

We will talk about memory allocation and memory usage later in Chapter 14.

7.4.1 Zero-relative and one-relative indexing

In C, C++ and Java, array indexes start at zero. In Fortran, Pascal, Ada and MAT-
LAB, they are at one by default. So C uses *zero-relative indexing* and Fortran uses
one-relative indexing. Most pseudo-codes in numerical analysis books use one-
relative indexing with occasional use of zero-relative indexing for things like Fast
Fourier Transforms, where it is clearly more natural to use zero-relative indexing.

Of course, transforming from one to another is essentially a mechanical process.
But it is one you should be careful to get right.

An example is solving a lower-triangular linear system. First, here is an example
in Fortran to solve $Lx = b$ with L a lower triangular matrix[2] using one-relative
indexing:

```
do i = 1, n
   sum = b(i)
   do j = 1, i-1
      sum = sum - L(i,j)*x(j)
   enddo
   x(i) = sum / L(i,i)
enddo
```

To generate the equivalent zero-relative indexing code, any array index appearing
in a loop bound (like i in the second do loop) has one added to it, and the loop
bounds then have one subtracted from them. So the bounds for the first do loop are
replaced by $1 - 1 = 0$ and $n - 1$ respectively. For the second do loop, the bounds
are replaced by $1 - 1 = 0$ and $((i + 1) - 1) - 1 = i - 1$. This can be written in C
using the for loop

```
   for ( j = 0; j < i; j++ )
```

Here is the equivalent C code:

```
for ( i = 0; i < n; i++ )
   {
      sum = b[i];
      for ( j = 0; j < i; j++ )
        sum -= L[i][j]*x[j];
      x[i] = sum / L[i][i];
   }
```

Some people (e.g., the authors of *Numerical Recipes in C* [87]) avoid using zero-
relative indexing by making all arrays one bigger than necessary or using pointer

---

[2] A matrix L is lower triangular if $l_{ij} = 0$ for $i < j$.

arithmetic to make the pointer point to one place *before* the actual array; we believe this practice is unnecessary. Our advice is that when using C, C++, or Java, it is better to use zero-relative indexing, and one-relative indexing in Fortran, Pascal, and MATLAB. The transformation from one-relative indexed routines to zero-relative indexed routines (and vice versa) is not hard, and the resulting loops usually look more natural in the language you are writing in.

7.4.2 *Variables and function names*

The names of variables and functions are important, as well-chosen names can make code much easier to read and understand. Names do not have to be long, or give a complete description: something mnemonic will do. If we have some mathematical description, like

$$c_{ij} = \sum_{k=1}^{N} a_{ik} b_{kj}, \quad \text{or} \quad C = AB,$$

then it is sensible to use the same names rather than give complete descriptions.

```
int     i, j, k;
double A[N][N],  B[N][N],  C[N][N];
/* C = A*B */
/* code for matrix product */
for ( i = 0; i < N; i++ )
  for ( j = 0; j < N; j++ )
  {
    C[i][j] = 0;
    for ( k = 0; k < N; k++ )
      C[i][j] += + A[i][k]*B[k][j];
  }
```

If we tried more verbose names, we might not make it any more readable:

```
int index1, index2, index3, indexLimit;
double firstFactor[indexLimit][indexLimit],
  secondFactor[indexLimit][indexLimit],
  productMatrix[indexLimit][indexLimit];
for ( index1 = 0; index1 < indexLimit; index1++ )
  for ( index2 = 0; index2 < indexLimit; index2++ )
  {
    productMatrix[index1][index2] = 0;
    for ( index3 = 0; index3 < indexLimit; index3++ )
```

```
productMatrix[index1][index2] =
    productMatrix[index1][index2] +
        firstFactor[index1][index3] *
            secondFactor[index3][index2];
}
```

When you are dealing with more complex objects that don't have such a simple (mathematical) representation, a longer name is often better. For example, if the geometry of a problem is encapsulated into a single structure, then something like geometry or even geom should be fine.

The SmallTalk tradition of calling a variable aString does not seem to be more useful than calling the string s and having a comment like "write the comment string s to the log file" near the start of a routine or program.

Don't have a large collection of variables called ii, jj, kk etc., or i1, i2, i3, etc. When you declare variables in a routine, you should put a brief description of what that variable is for. But remember, the code is the final arbiter of what the code actually *does*, and these comments need to be updated if the purpose of variable changes.

Capitalized names and upper case names should be used for special things. In C, it is common to use all upper case names for things that are defined using the preprocessor (e.g., things that are #defined). If the object in question is represented by a capital letter in mathematics, then use that. In Fortran, upper and lower case are not distinguished, so aBcDEf is equivalent to abcdef. For historical reasons, Fortran programmers have tended to use all upper case. But these days, all upper case IS THE MORAL EQUIVALENT OF SHOUTING, and should generally be avoided.

7.4.3 Style and layout

Everyone has their own style. But if you are part of a team, you will need to make sure that your style fits with that of the other people on the team. One of the surest ways to waste time is to (continually) convert code from one style to another. Settle on a single, consistent style. Where possible, use an automatic system to keep to a particular style. For example, the emacs editor will automatically indent code in a particular way.

With Fortran, as long as you are using a Fortran 90 or later compiler, we would suggest that all new routines be written using the free format style rather than using the fixed columns of the pre-Fortran 90 dialects. Do indent Fortran code to highlight the structure of the code (e.g., indent the body of loops and if/then statements, with multiple spaces for loops within loops; indent the body of functions and subroutines).

Some programmers use all upper case for control words in Fortran. (In the language Modula-2, all key-words had to be in upper case.) This is perfectly acceptable, although it does tend to emphasize the control structure of some code more than the variables.

One of the main purposes of good style and layout is to make the structure of the code clear to the reader. Modern editors can help by coloring the text of the program to indicate control words (e.g., if, then, else), declarations, strings, and comments differently. This makes it easier to "see" the structure of the code and to find the part that you want to study.

7.5 Programming in the middle

Programming in the middle is about organizing the functions and files to carry out certain tasks. Often we need to break-down a single (large) function into smaller parts to avoid having hard-to-debug-and-test routines. Simplicity is best! But the pieces should also be more-or-less self-contained. If you can describe what a routine is intended to do in a short sentence or two, then you will be able to write it and test it fairly easily. If you need a long explanation of what a routine does, then it is a good candidate to break up.

Routines need to communicate with each other, usually by passing arguments. How you get the required information to a routine is that routine's *interface*. Programming in the middle has a lot to do with designing the interfaces. Simple interfaces are usually associated with functions which have a straightforward description of what they do. Complicated interfaces are hard to understand and hard to change when we have to. Part of this complexity can be reduced or hidden by using *data structures* to package the information needed. If these data structures are easy to describe in a high-level way (e.g., "a sparse matrix", or "an ordered binary tree", or "a description of the boundary of the domain") then the interface can be easy to understand, even if the underlying data structures are complicated.

Below we have an example of a suitable data structure for dealing with cubic splines. A *cubic spline function* s is a function that is piecewise cubic (that is, there are points $x_0 < x_1 < x_2 < \cdots < x_n$ where $s(x)$ is a cubic function of x on each interval $[x_i, x_{i+1}]$: $s(x) = A_i x^3 + B_i x^2 + C_i x + D_i$ for $x_i \leq x \leq x_{i+1}$) with the additional property that s is continuous and has continuous first and second derivatives. Typically we choose s so that $s(x_i) = y_i$ for given values y_i; that is, s interpolates the pairs of data (x_i, y_i). To store a cubic spline function we need to store the x_is, the y_is, and also $M_i = s''(x_i)$ for $i = 0, 1, \ldots, n$.

```
typedef struct {
  /* See Atkinson:
     Intro Numer Anal, 2nd Ed'n, pp. 166-173 */
  int     length;
  double *xlist;      /* list of knots */
  double *ylist;      /* values interpolated */
  double *Mlist;      /* 2nd derivatives at knots */
} spline;
```

Having settled on a data structure, we now want to decide which functions we need and what their interfaces will be. We should have routines to create this data structure so that it is ready to use. We need to construct different kinds of splines (natural splines, clamped splines, periodic splines, and "not-a-knot" splines). All of these different splines can be represented by this data structure without needing any extra information to say which type of spline we are representing. The differences are all contained in `Mlist`. We will assume that the knots are listed in `xlist` in increasing order.

In order to construct a spline we need to specify the knots (`xlist`) and the values to interpolate (`ylist`). Natural, "not-a-knot", and periodic splines need no extra information for their construction. Clamped splines, however, need the derivative values at the first and last knots. Construction of the different splines is probably best done by different routines, although they may share some common parts. (We might want to refactor the code and the design later.) Since we have the knots and values to interpolate in the data structure, we can have a routine that simply sets these values.

Here is a collection of interfaces written in C that seems as if it can work well with the task at hand:

```
/* spline_create -- allocates spline structure
      with the desired length */
spline *spline_create(int length);

/* spline_destroy -- frees spline structure memory */
void    spline_destroy(spline *s);

/* spline_print -- prints a representation of
      the spline s to the stream fp */
void spline_print(FILE *fp, spline *s);

/* spline_read -- reads a representation of
      a spline from stream fp and return the spline */
```

```
spline *spline_read(FILE *fp);

/* spline_setxy -- copies the knot and interpolation
        values into xlist and ylist */
spline *spline_setxy(spline *s,
                        double x[], double y[], int length);


/* spline_eval -- evaluates spline s at point t */
double spline_eval(spline *s, double t);


/* spline_make_natural -- constructs natural spline
        using knots and values (xlist & ylist resp.) in s */
spline *spline_make_natural(spline *s);


/* spline_make_periodic -- constructs periodic spline
        using knots and values in s;
        must have ylist[length-1] == ylist[0]
        for periodicity */
spline *spline_make_periodic(spline *s);


/* spline_make_clamped -- constructs clamped spline
        using knots and values in s, but with
        end-point derivatives dy0 at xlist[0] and
        dy_end at xlist[length-1] */
spline *spline_make_clamped(spline *s,
                        double dy0, double dy_end);
```

Put this into a header file, probably called something like `spline.h`. Then the implementations of these routines should be put somewhere like `spline.c`, which should contain the line:

```
#include "spline.h"
```

at the start of the file and all files that use these routines.

Once we have set up these interfaces, we should think about the major components we would need to implement these spline functions. The most important task is to solve a tridiagonal system of linear equations. (To compute the coefficients for a periodic spline function we need to solve a slight modification of a tridiagonal linear system.) It would probably be best to write a single tridiagonal linear system solver. It would not only be sharable amongst the different spline routines, but also usable elsewhere. Of course, you could short-circuit this if you already had a library available which did this already, such as LAPACK [5], or Meschach [92].

7.6 Interface design

In interface design, we need to decide how to pass information to routines, and get information back. In this section we will look at a number of issues and techniques for doing this.

7.6.1 Pass by value vs. pass by reference

The first issue here is whether to pass the value of a variable, or a *reference* or *pointer* to the variable. Variables passed by value are not changed outside the routine when they are changed inside; a variable passed by reference that is changed inside the routine will be changed outside. Variables used for holding the output from a routine must be passed by reference, and it is safer to pass inputs by value.

In C, variables and expressions are passed by value; to pass a variable by reference we have to explicitly pass a pointer, which we can get by applying the "&" operator in C.

```
main()
{
  double x, y;
  myroutine(x,&y);
  ...
}
void myroutine(double by_value, double *by_ref)
{
  ...
  by_value = ...;      /* x unchanged */
  *by_ref = by_value;  /* y is changed */
  ...
}
```

Although in Fortran all variables are passed by reference, it is possible to indicate whether an argument is an input or output argument using the `intent` property:

```
subroutine myroutine(x,y)
  real, intent(in) :: x
  real, intent(out) :: y
  ...
  x = y      ! not allowed !
```

```
  y = x      ! allowed !
  ...
end
```

So

```
real z
call myroutine(3+2,z)
```

is acceptable, but

```
real z
call myroutine(z,3+2)
```

is not.

Note that in Java, all the basic built-in types (int, float, double, char, bool) are passed by value, while arrays and objects are passed by reference. In C++, objects can either be passed by value (which requires a copy-constructor), by reference, or as a pointer (which is an explicit way of passing by reference).

Where pass by value is allowed, it should be used for passing small objects (integers, floating point numbers, complex numbers, etc.). However, for large or variable-sized objects (such as matrices and vectors) this can be very inefficient, as the data in the objects must be copied in order to pass them by value; large objects such as arrays should be passed by reference.

Any variable used to hold an output must be passed by reference.

What if you want to pass a variable by reference for efficiency, but you want to show that it is only an input variable? This is particularly important if you are passing arrays in C or C++, which are automatically passed by reference. In C or C++ you should use the keyword to indicate that it is not to be changed:

```
double another_routine(double x, const double y[])
{
  ...
  y[4] = 0.0;   /* illegal */
  ...
}
```

7.6.2 Scratch space

Often a routine working with arrays needs extra memory. If the amount of extra memory needed is not known at the time the routine is written, there are at least two ways of getting this memory. One is by passing an array (called a *scratchspace* or **workspace** array), the other is by allocating memory. (There is more on memory allocation in Chapter 14.)

Since allocating memory typically has some overhead and has not always been available, many routines are written requiring scratch space arrays to be passed. This is particularly true in Fortran routines as memory allocation was not available until Fortran 90. Users of Fortran numerical libraries have undoubtedly read documentation that gives formulas for how large the scratch space arrays should be. Sometimes the size of the scratch array needed could not be determined until after the routine is called, in which case there had to be an `ifail` argument (`integer, intent(out)`) which is set to some non-zero value to indicate insufficient scratch space.

Although memory allocation is available in all serious programming languages for scientific computing, scratch space arrays can still be useful for efficiency. This is appropriate for routines that are short and executed many times, and where the size of the scratch space array is computable before calling the routine. This avoids the cost of memory allocation (and de-allocation), and can greatly improve efficiency.

If you do not want to use scratch space arrays, you can allocate the memory you need. If your system does not have garbage collection (e.g., in Fortran or C/C++), then you should de-allocate the allocated memory at the end of your routine. Even if you do have garbage collection (e.g., in Java), you may want to find ways of re-using allocated memory. For more on this, see Chapter 14. In Fortran routines, arrays can be created with a size that is a simple expression of the input arguments. This is sufficient for most scratch space arrays.

An alternative is to use "scratch structures" – data structures that contain the desired memory and "know" how big they are and can be re-sized as needed. This relieves the caller of the routine from having to determine the amount of scratch memory needed before calling. It also relieves the called routine from having to de-allocate any memory. In C++, this can be done using More details of how to create these data structures can be found in Section 14.7.1.

If you are having difficulty in choosing between scratch space arrays (or scratch space structures) and allocating and (possibly) de-allocating memory, consider providing several interfaces: one where scratch space arrays (or scratch space structures) must be passed, and another which takes care of all the memory allocation and de-allocation as needed. Rationales for multiple interfaces are given in Section 7.6.4.

7.6.3 Returning values vs. output arguments

Outputs from a routine can be passed back to the caller by either setting the value of a variable passed by reference specifically to hold the output, or by returning the output as from a function. For small and built-in types, returning the output is usually the best practice.

If more than one value should be returned then output arguments are essential.

Consider a max function which returns the maximum of an array of floating point numbers. The maximum value should definitely be returned. But if you also want the index where the maximum occurs (which is often the case), then we need to have an output argument:

```
double mymax(double x[], int length, int    *index);
```

If we wish to return an array, for example, after computing a matrix–vector product, then we should use an output argument:

```
/* computes out <- A*x (A is n x n) */
void matrix_vector_prod(double **A, double *x,
        int n, double *out);
```

Sometimes it is worthwhile both to have an output argument and to return the output. This is often done in the Meschach matrix library. For example, the Meschach routine for computing matrix–vector products has the interface

```
VEC *mv_mlt(const MAT *A, const VEC *x, VEC *out);
```

This structure has the additional advantage that if out is NULL when mv_mlt is called, then out is allocated to be the correct size; if out is not the correct size for the product when called, then it is re-sized to the correct size. Thus this one routine can be used to allocate the output if needed, or use an output argument and re-use memory.

7.6.4 Multiple interfaces

A routine that requires a scratch space array of objects to be passed puts an additional burden on the caller of that routine. This makes it harder to use the routine and makes bugs more likely. This is also true when a routine has many parameters that "tune" the behavior of the routine, but do not otherwise change the results of the computation done by the routine.

In situations like this, it is often helpful to have several interfaces to a routine. Some libraries' documentation will refer to "expert" and "non-expert" interfaces to a routine. The expert interface will have all the scratch space and "tuning" arguments. The non-expert interface will have the tuning parameters set to default values, and can allocate the scratch space to pass to the expert routine.

If you create a non-expert interface, remember that the aim is to provide a simpler interface. The main computations should not be reproduced. Instead it is better for the simple interface to only set the "tuning" parameters and allocate the scratch space arrays before calling the "expert" interface. There is a small overhead for the additional function call, but if efficiency is the over-riding goal, the "expert" interface should be called directly. Making the "non-expert" routine call the "expert" routine avoids maintenance problems: bug fixes for the main operation only need to be done to one routine.

Here is how an "expert" interface routine might look (in C):

```
double expert(const double *array, int len, double
  tolerance,
            double *scratch)
{
  double val;
  val = 0;
  /* assume length of scratch is >= len */
  /* do operation with input array, using scratch */
  return val;
}
```

Now our "non-expert" interface simply allocates the scratch array, and calls the "expert" interface:

```
double non_expert(const double *array, int len)
{
  double val, tolerance;
  double *scratch;

  /* set default tolerance value */
  tolerance = 1e-6;
  /* allocate scratch */
  scratch = (double *)malloc((size_t)len);
  if ( scratch == NULL )
    /* error! */ ;

  val = expert(array,len,tolerance,scratch);

  /* de-allocate scratch */
  free(scratch);

  return val;
}
```

One way of creating multiple interfaces is to have optional or default arguments. Fortran allows named optional arguments; C++ has default arguments. Here is an example of how to use optional arguments; note that if an optional argument is not present, then that argument *cannot be assigned to*.

```
module my_ifaces
  implicit none
contains
  subroutine expert(array, len, abstol, reltol)
    real :: array(:)
    integer :: len
    real, optional :: abstol, reltol
    real :: abstol0, reltol0

    abstol0 = 1e-6
    if ( present(abstol) ) abstol0 = abstol
    reltol0 = 1e-8
    if ( present(reltol) ) reltol0 = reltol

    ! code using abstol0 and reltol0
    print *, 'abstol =', abstol0
    print *, 'reltol =', reltol0
  end subroutine expert

  subroutine use_iface
    real :: array(100)
    call expert(array, 100)
    ! uses abstol = 1e-6, reltol = 1e-8
    call expert(array, 100, 1e-3)
    ! uses abstol = 1e-3, reltol = 1e-8
    call expert(array, 100, reltol=1e-3)
    ! uses abstol = 1e-6, reltol = 1e-3
  end subroutine use_iface
end module my_ifaces
```

7.7 Top-down and bottom-up development

Top-down development of software was part of the ***structured programming*** movement, and was based on the idea of refining a high-level idea into more and more concrete steps, until the high-level idea is completely expressed in the programming language chosen. An interactive program like MATLAB might start with the high-level description

```
while ( not done )
{
    read command;
    execute command;
}
```

While this can be a good way to learn to program, it is not necessarily the best one for all circumstances. In fact, critics of the structured programming or top-down approach say that it tends to lead to monolithic systems: large programs with very little modularization. Structured programming seems to be most useful for writing a routine once responsibilities have been modularized.

In another approach, systems that are built around a particular data structure(s) may be best developed by starting with the data structures with their basic operations and working up. This is bottom-up development, which also has its proponents. Finally, there is the middle-out approach to development: pick a level of software somewhere in the middle, and start there. Refine the operations at the middle level in a top-down way, and then combine the middle level routines and structures in a bottom-up way. All of these are possible and useful.

Another feature of most large-scale software is that it tends to be *layered*. For example, we could have low-level operations handled by one set of routines. These are called by mid-level routines which implement intermediate operations, which are called by the high-level routines which implement the application. The number of layers does not have to be limited to three; there could be any number. Starting from the bottom layer, each layer should be tested and checked. Once basic functionality has been established for each layer, you should start implementing the next layer. Improved features, performance, etc., can be dealt with later.

If all these ways are possible, what should a programmer do? We would recommend the following.

- Identify the overall structure of the system at the highest level.
- Identify what components you would need to make a minimal system work.
- Start work on the minimal system components, identifying what you would need to build a minimal version of each component.
- Start building the components (or sub-components) from near the bottom level.
- Test as you build! Keep old tests and re-apply them when making changes.
- Once you have a minimal "end-to-end" system done, and you are ready to add new capabilities, repeat the above process recursively for the new capability.
- Don't be afraid to re-design data structures. Don't be afraid to throw code away and re-write it.

7.8 Don't hard-wire it unnecessarily!

Consider the problem of computing (approximately) $\int_0^1 e^x \, dx$. If we used the trapezoidal rule we might write something like this:

```
n = 100;
h = 1.0/n;
sum = (exp(0.0)+exp(1.0))*(h/2);
for ( i = 1; i < n; i++ )
    {
        x = i*h;
        sum = sum + exp(x)*h;
    }
```

But we aren't quite sure what error our answer has. There's an easy answer: just double the value of *n*. Let's set n = 200 and then we have to copy the code. But we have to change the name of the second variable, because we want to take the difference between the two.

```
n = 200;
h = 1.0/n;
sum2 = (exp(0.0)+exp(1.0))*(h/2);
for ( i = 1; i < n; i++ )
    {
        x = i*h;
        sum2 = sum2 + exp(x)*h;
    }
printf("Error is approximately %g\n", sum2-sum);
```

But later we will probably want to do this for another function, like $g(x) = x^2 \cos(\pi x)$. So we will write something like

```
n = 100;
h = 1.0/n;
sum = (0.0*0.0*cos(M_PI*0.0)+1.0*1.0*cos(M_PI*1.0))*(h/2);
for ( i = 1; i < n; i++ )
    {
        x = i*h;
        sum = sum + x*x*cos(M_PI*x)*h;
    }
```

This is starting to look a bit complicated, and easy to make errors. Instead, let's **re-factor** these codes to avoid repeating ourselves. (Re-factoring is re-organizing the internal structure of code without changing what it does.) First let's write a routine for handling the common parts: the trapezoidal routine:

```
double trapezoidal(double (*f)(double),
                   double a, double b, int n)
{
  double h, sum;
  int    i;
  h = (b-a)/n;
  sum = 0.5*((*f)(a)+(*f)(b));
  for ( i = 1; i < n; i++ )
    sum = sum + (*f)(a+i*h);
  return sum*h;
}
```

Then we can compute $\int_0^1 e^x \, dx$ like this:

```
sum  = trapezoidal(exp,0.0,1.0,100);
sum2 = trapezoidal(exp,0.0,1.0,200);
printf("Error is approximately %g\n", sum2-sum);
```

For $\int_0^1 x^2 \cos(\pi x) \, dx$ we need a function

```
double x_sqr_cosx(double x)
{   return x*x*cos(M_PI*x);   }
```

and then pass it like this:

```
sum = trapezoidal(x_sqr_cosx,0.0,1.0,100);
```

Now the trapezoidal rule code is all in one place (instead of being repeated lots of times), and we can use it for other things very easily. The code is simpler, and easier to understand. It's shorter, too. We don't have to look through three different implementations of the trapezoidal method checking them all for bugs. By re-factoring the code in this way, *debugging and testing adds instead of multiplying* as we add features and capabilities to the code. So remember the slogan:

> *don't hardwire special choices unless you are willing to re-do the wiring.*

7.9 Comments

Programmers are taught to put comments in their code. Generally this is a good idea. Reading completely undocumented code is difficult. But you should be careful about what kinds of comments you should put in; some are very helpful.

- *Comment your interfaces* In C it is common to use header files to contain information about the types of variables that are passed to a collection of routines. This is also a good place to put comments about the meanings of the variables passed and what the routine does, and any special cases or behavior the user should know about. For example:

```
/* sum_array -- returns sum(i=0 to n-1) a[i]
     a -- input array to be summed
     n -- length of array (zero returned if n <= 0) */
double sum_array(double a[], int n);
```

Since header files may be available where the source code is not, this is a useful form of documentation. In other languages the C/C++, the source code should contain this kind of documentation.

This kind of comment is more than an ordinary comment – it is a ***contract*** with any software that calls this routine. Provided the preconditions hold (a is a valid array of length n), then the postcondition (the sum of a[i], for i going from zero to n-1, is returned) holds on return.

- *Loop invariants and assertions* If you have some statement that is guaranteed to be true (assuming that the pre-conditions for the routine are satisfied) at a particular point in the code, then put that into a comment. (See the previous discussion of ***loop invariants***.)
- *Warnings about unusual behavior* Some code behaves in a way that is difficult to see from the source code. This should be rare. But if you have unusual behavior, then you should definitely warn the reader about what is happening where it is happening. Of course, it is always better to have the behavior of code obvious by inspection!
- *Descriptions of what is done, not how* To help others navigate a complex piece of code, it can be very useful to have headings describing what the code is trying to do, such as:

```
/* use binary search to find i where
        xlist[i] <= t < xlist[i+1] */
```

before an implementation of the binary search algorithm. Of course, if the code is re-organized to use a different method, then the comment should be removed or modified.

Some comments should be avoided. Simply re-stating what is obvious from the code is bad practice:

```
/* increment i */
i = i+1;
```

It seems harmless. Why not? The trouble is that when code is modified, the comments don't always get changed to reflect this. The code itself after all is the most authoritative description of what the routine actually does. For example, if the code was changed to go backward through an array instead of forwards, after the change you might read

```
/* increment i */
i = i-1;
```

Confusing or incorrect comments are worse than useless.

One of the slogans of the Extreme Programming movement is

once and only once!

There should only be one authoritative description of the behavior of the code. This should be the code itself. Comments that give meaning to the code that is not evident from the code itself are good, but you will need to modify these if you modify the code!

7.10 Documentation

A purist might hope that the code itself is all the documentation that you would need. But as users, we all need extra information that tells us how to use the software, not just how it works inside. Large systems also need documentation in order to "navigate" the software source code in order to understand how it works. Ideally this should be kept small. As mentioned above regarding comments in header files, it is important to document interfaces as others will need this and will not necessarily be able (or willing!) to read through the source code to find this out.

There are two kinds of documentation.

- *User documentation* This focuses on how to use the system, not on how it works. Information about the kinds of algorithm used can be included, but is usually kept to a minimum. Interfaces (whether function calls, file formats, or *Graphical User Interfaces (GUIs)*) are what you should describe here.
- *Developer documentation* This is for other programmers so that they can change or re-use your software for other purposes. This should outline the structure of the software (e.g., what routine calls what), the data structures used, and conventions about how the system should be used (e.g., "Always call function init_XYZ() before any other calls to the library").

Documentation should be kept in sync with the actual software. When things change in the software, the documentation should change with it. Some systems (e.g., the javadoc system for Java) provides for the automatic generation of certain kinds of documentation from the source code and its comments. Simple versions of this can be easily implemented for other languages provided users adopt a standard for inserting documentation in comments. For example, in C++ you could extract all lines that begin with "// **" as being comments to be included in external documentation. Extracting these comments can be easily done with a tool like `grep` or `sed` in Unix (see Chapter 17 for more information about `grep` and `sed`):

```
grep '// **' < file.cpp >> documentation
sed -n -e 's/^ *\/\/ \*\*//p' < file.cpp >> \
    documentation
```

Readers familiar with `perl` could use it to create similar, and also more sophisticated, documentation generators. Users will still need documentation targeted at their concerns, which the programmer may have to write. However, this additional documentation should not change often the way a user uses the software should be fairly stable. Unix man (short for manual) pages provide concise, direct documentation. Programmers or those needing information only about simple commands, will find this is usually all they need. This kind of documentation shows how to use the software, the interfaces, the assumptions built into the software, special cases, data formats, and bugs (or misimplementations). More complex systems (like compilers and editors, for example) need more extensive documentation. Often "tutorial" documentation giving fairly extensive examples of how to use the software are very valuable for users. For graphical user interfaces, screen shots are often useful, especially for users with less programming experience. Example driver programs and input files are also excellent ways of showing how to use a routine or library.

Our advice: keep your documentation simple and direct. Large documents are an obstacle to the use of the software, and will probably not be read (which is a waste of paper and a waste of time).

Document only what is necessary for others to understand, use, and modify the software.

There is one area in which you should not forget to include comments: in your data! This should be so for both your test data and for serious problems. You should especially have comments in any configuration files. A simple way to implement this is to pick a "comment character" to indicate the start of a comment, which goes to the end of the line. In many systems (MATLAB, LaTeX, PostScript) the percent sign (%) is the comment character, while many Unix shells or command line interpreters use the hash character (#). Comments like this can be stripped out by using a Unix tool like `sed`:

```
sed -e 's/#.*$//' < data-file > stripped-file
```

which makes the data file ready to be read by a program. Alternatively, you can make sure that the program can read the data file with comments. The main change needed is to call a routine like `skipcomment` below before calling the routines to read in the data:

```
void   skipcomment(FILE *fp)
{
  int        c;

  c = getc(fp);
  while ( c != EOF && isspace(c) )
    c = getc(fp);

  while ( c == COMMENT_CHAR )
    { /* skip to end of line or end of file */
      while ( c != EOF && c != '\n' )
        c = getc(fp);
      /* skip over any further white space */
      while ( c != EOF && isspace(c) )
        c = getc(fp);
      /* put back non-white-space character */
    }
  if ( c != EOF )
    ungetc(c,fp);
}
```

If the comment character is a "#", then the following code

```
skipcomment(stdin);   scanf("%d", &num_gnus);
skipcomment(stdin);   scanf("%d", &num_llamas);
skipcomment(stdin);   scanf("%lf", &weight_llama);
```

can read a data file like this:

```
# Data for the gnus and llamas problem
# See Drofnats et al., Journal of Gnus & Llamas
# volume 37, number 5, pages 77-87 (2001)
36 # number of gnus
27 # number of llamas
# llama weight in kilograms
227.5
```

7.11 Cross-language development

Since the 1980s there has been interest in using more than one programming language to construct programs, often combining Fortran and C or C++. An example is PLTMG, which was written mainly in Fortran 77 with some code written in C to interface with systems routines and graphics libraries. On the other hand, more scientific software is being written in C/C++ than before, but using the BLAS which is based on Fortran.

Combining programming languages in a single program has been a tricky task because it has been almost completely outside the standards for programming languages. This meant that combining languages was not portable and relied on some "tricks" to make sure that routines compiled in one language could call routines compiled in another. There has been a trend to accommodate cross-language development in the development of programming language standards. This was first evident in the development of C++, where the extern "C" feature was included to allow C++ programmers to call routines compiled in C. Java provides standard mechanisms for calling "native" libraries, which could have been compiled from almost any language. The recent Fortran 2003 standard incorporates standards for intermixing Fortran 2003 and C and C++. The Microsoft .NET system provides a family of languages which can be used together to produce single programs. However, all these languages fit into the same .NET framework, and calling routines compiled from outside the .NET framework is considerably more difficult.

7.11.1 Obstacles to cross-language development

In the past, each compiler would have its own way of determining how one routine calls another. Provided all the routines are compiled by the same compiler, all the routines have consistent conventions about how data is stored in data structures, and how stack frames are organized. Over time, standards have been set for many of the basic issues, such as how stack frames are organized for each family of CPUs.

In order to link routines compiled from different languages, the compiled routines have to be in a common, standardized format for linkable object code, and there must be a linker that understands this standardized format. Assuming that this is the case, in order to link the routines, the symbolic names that the linker sees must match the routines to be linked. But the names that the linker sees are not necessarily the same as the names given in the source code. A well-known example of this is the different behavior of the Fortran and C compilers in Unix. Under Unix, Fortran compilers typically append an underscore "_" to the names of routines, while C compilers do not. This made it difficult for Fortran routines to call C library routines even if they were linked to the C library; for example, if the Fortran routine had a line

```
returncode = printf(formatstring)
```

the compiled object file would contain the string "`printf_`" which did not match the string "`printf_`" used in the standard C library.

Even if the linker names can be made to match, there are additional sources of difficulties, especially with more sophisticated languages. Between C and C++, for example, care must be taken regarding the different systems for input/output (`printf` in C, for example, versus the "`<<`" operator in C++), memory allocation (the `malloc` function in C versus the `new` operator in C++), and error and exception handling (the `setjmp/longjmp` functions in C versus the `try/throw/catch` mechanism in C++). In each case there is a different mechanism used to carry out the associated operation, and these are potentially incompatible. In C++ there is also the matter of overloaded functions (several functions with the same name) and the associated "name mangling" that the compiler does to create unique names for each function that the linker has to deal with. If a C routine calls a C++ routine, it has to know what name the compiler has created for the specific function called. This can easily lead to non-portable code which can be broken even by using a new version of a compiler.

Another area where there are dangers of miscommunication across languages (or even different compilers) is the layout of data structures. Consider a data structure in Fortran 90:

```
type my_type
   integer :: i1, j1, i2, j2
   real, allocatable, pointer, kind(0d0) :: A(:,:)
   real(kind(0d0)) :: entry
end type my_type
```

The Fortran 90 standard does not require the compiler to put all these entries into contiguous memory locations, and often pointer and data alignment needs will prevent this from happening. For example, integers and pointers may need to be stored in memory locations with addresses divisible by four and double-precision floating-point numbers stored in locations with addresses divisible by eight. In this case, the compiler would probably put in four bytes of padding between the end of A and the start of `entry`. In fact, there is no requirement to keep these fields *in this order*. Also, whereas in C we might represent A as a pointer to point to doubles, a Fortran 90 compiler is more likely to represent A as a pointer to an array of double-precision numbers and possibly two integers for the dimensions of A. These potential incompatibilities would make it unlikely to match the obvious structure in C, even after noting that C uses row-major order and Fortran uses column-major order:

```
struct {
    int      i1, j1, i2, j2;
    double   **A;
    double   entry;
};
```

Another issue that can complicate cross-language development is the way in which arguments are passed to routines. In Fortran arguments are always passed by reference, in C arguments are almost always passed by value (passing by reference in C is done by passing pointers). This means that when a C routine calls a Fortran routine, it must pass pointers; when a Fortran routine calls a C routine, the C routine must take pointers for arguments.

7.11.2 Strategies for general cross-language development

In general, cross-language software development is system dependent. In keeping with good software engineering practices, the system dependent part of the software should be isolated from the other software. Sometimes this can be done (for example, in C/C++) by having one or two header files which contain the interface details.

In general, more sophisticated programming language features (class hierarchies in object-oriented systems, dynamic memory allocation and de-allocation) are likely to be implemented in incompatible ways. For example, new/delete in C++ will in general be incompatible with malloc/free in C; the class hierarchy in Java is incompatible with those in C++. Input/output systems are often also incompatible. There are too many different design choices to expect these things to be compatible at the object code level. This means that cross-language calls should be as simple as possible, passing only simple data structures: integers, floating point numbers, and arrays of these. Even strings in Fortran and C behave differently and may be implemented differently and incompatibly.

We need to deal with differences in how arguments are passed. For example, since Fortran expects arguments passed by reference, and C/C++ uses pass by value, to call a Fortran routine from C, *pointers* to the C/C++ variables containing the data must be passed. Similarly, calling C from Fortran, the C routine must expect pointers.

Java routines can call non-Java routines by using the native modifier for a Java method. The javah program can then generate header files for C as well as C code to be used as a skeleton for implementing an interface to a routine in C, or some other language. The *Java Native Interface* (JNI) [98, search for "JNI"] standard should be used where possible; this means that the javah program should be used with the -jni option. The JNI works by passing an env (for "environment") argument which contains the arguments passed as well as other information. Accessing the value of an argument requires a function call through the env argument.

Fortran 2003 has a number of features to allow interoperability with C and C++ [89]. This includes a number of new types such as C_INT, C_FLOAT and C_DOUBLE which are guaranteed to be interoperable with the C types int, float and double. There are also C_PTR and C_FUN_PTR types which correspond to C general pointer types and C function pointer types respectively. It is also possible to specify how Fortran 2003 and C derived types (data structures) can be made to correspond to C structs. The technical report [89] gives the following example:

```
typedef struct {
    int m, n;
    float r;
} myctype
```

is interoperable with

```
USE ISO_C_BINDING
TYPE, BIND(C) :: MYFTYPE
    INTEGER(C_INT) :: I, J
    REAL(C_FLOAT) :: S
END TYPE MYFTYPE
```

The report also states that *no Fortran type is interoperable with a C union type, struct type that contains a bit field, or struct type that contains a flexible array member*. This is not surprising as unions and bit fields and the more advanced parts of the recent C99 standard (e.g., flexible array members) are not part of the Fortran 90/95/2003 standards. Fortran 2003 can also call C functions that require items passed by value directly as long as an INTERFACE is set up in Fortran where the arguments passed by value have the VALUE attribute. For more details see the Fortran 2003 standard and/or the technical report [89].

In summary: cross-language development is system dependent. If possible, write the interface code according to published standards (if any). Keep the interface code isolated from the rest of the system. After all, standards do change (and standards for cross-language development are especially volatile), which typically requires changing the interface code. Unless the two languages are very tightly coupled, it can be useful to have interface routines that turn the data structures in one language into a form compatible for the other language. Avoid advanced data structures and concepts in the actual interface.

7.12 Modularity and all that

7.12.1 Mathematical abstractions

Mathematical software has an advantage over many other kinds of software because mathematicians have been dealing with specific kinds of abstractions for a long time. There is a well-established terminology and set of operations that mathematicians deal with. Matrices and vectors, for example, have been used as self-contained objects for over a hundred years now. So it is often easy to identify central mathematical abstractions that can form basic building blocks for scientific software. Other software developers (e.g., for computer games or databases) have had to develop and refine their own terminology and concepts.

Abstraction is a key tool in dealing with software complexity. Abstractions that can be "packaged" into a software system can be dealt with on a high level, without needing to go into the details of how things are implemented. The abstractions can then be operated on as independent objects, as long as we understand that abstraction. We have already seen the usefulness of the abstractions of "matrix" and "vector" in MATLAB.

It should be noted that it is not just the data structure itself that makes up the mathematical abstraction, but also the *operations* that you can perform on it. This was one of the key insights that led to ***object-oriented programming***.

7.12.2 Information hiding

The principle of information hiding is that routines should be allowed to access only the data that they need to do their job. All the rest should be kept out of sight. Conversely, the data that one part of the system needs only for its own internal purposes should be hidden from the other parts of the system. Why?

Because if that internal data is not hidden, then routines could be written to take advantage of the internal data of other routines and processes. Then when another part of the system is changed, the routine accessing it would also have to be changed or the system would (probably) break. This makes the process of debugging much harder, because you not only need to look at the routines that had legitimate access to the data that changed, but also all the other routines that could possibly rely on this data. Redesigning the broken routine would also be a much more difficult task.

This principle has become deeply incorporated into object-oriented programming: access to data is controlled by the ***class*** that contains it.

7.12.3 Flexibility via abstraction

Abstraction is the process of distilling the minimal essence of a concept, removing it from the context we usually use to think about that concept. For example, we usually think of an $m \times n$ matrix A as a rectangular array of numbers. Another way of thinking about a matrix is as a linear operator $A : \mathbf{R}^n \to \mathbf{R}^m$. That is, we can treat A as a function, albeit satisfying certain requirements: $A(\alpha x + \beta y) = \alpha A(x) + \beta A(y)$ for any numbers α and β and vectors $x \in \mathbf{R}^n$ and $y \in \mathbf{R}^n$. It can be difficult to enforce or test these requirements in general, but it does lead to a very flexible (and efficient) way of dealing with many situations. This approach uses *functional representation* of matrices, and is discussed in Section 8.4.

Abstraction occurs continually in mathematics, and we can use mathematical descriptions to create abstractions suitable for implementing as software. However, this does not work well for all applications. Using functional representation of matrices can result in efficient ways of representing addition, subtraction, and scalar multiplication of matrices. However, it cannot be used to implement an efficient transpose operation. To do that we need to resort to the concept of a matrix as an array of numbers.

7.12.4 Procedural and object-oriented programming

Packaging data into data structures is a good step, but object-oriented programming goes further, by also packaging the *routines* that operate on the data into an object. This has been implemented in numerous languages, beginning with Simula, SmallTalk, and then in the C-like languages C++, Java, C#, and also in a number of other languages such as Eiffel [77] and Sather [94]. Now most new languages have many object-oriented features, including the Fortran 2003 standard [1].

Object-oriented languages extend the idea of modularity by controlling access to the underlying data. Getting a piece of the underlying data should be achieved by a routine in the object (that is, by a member function of the object) rather than by directly accessing it. Similarly, modifying the underlying data should be via a member function, which can ensure self-consistency of the data in the object. This extra layer of function calls can have a performance impact. This overhead can be removed in C++ and other object-oriented languages by *inlining* functions. Inlining puts a copy of the function (renaming variables if necessary) in place of the function call.

7.12.5 Layered software

Layered software is very important for large software projects. Different parts of a large project can be split into two distinct kinds of software, usually in terms of whether the software is "high-level" or "low-level". For example, LAPACK is built on top of the BLAS. Here the BLAS deals directly with the matrices and this is where most of the inner loops belong. Most machine-dependent efficiency concerns can be dealt with at the level of the BLAS, freeing the implementors of LAPACK to concentrate on algorithmic issues. In the spline function example in Chapter 18, the components of the software that deal with tridiagonal matrices form a layer which the spline routines can call.

Layering is a large-scale version of modularity, where whole aspects of a piece of software are assigned to a particular collection of routines and data structures. To make this work effectively, programmers need a certain discipline. Getting around problems in the "lower level" layer, by going directly to the underlying data structures, should be avoided wherever possible. Conversely, this means that bugs and misimplementations in the "lower level" layer must be fixed quickly. The responsibilities of the "lower" layer should be simple and easily stated. Adding features to the "lower" layer should be done rarely and be carefully considered.

8

Data structures

8.1 Package your data!

Data structures with heterogeneous elements (i.e., elements of different types) have been incorporated into almost all serious programming languages: records in Pascal and Modula-2, structs in C/C++, classes in Java, and most recently type structures in Fortran 90. These are useful in packaging together data, even if you don't have a nice abstract interpretation of the data. Combining data used for a common purpose into a single data structure can provide some level of abstraction which can simplify interfaces and other routines.

For example, if you are working with spline functions, the basic function to evaluate a cubic spline function might have an interface that looks like this:

```
/* eval_spline -- returns spline function value at t,
    where spline is determined by
      xlist, ylist, & Mlist as given in
      Atkinson's Intro Numer Anal, 2nd Ed'n, pp. 166-173
    This represents the spline function s(x) where
    xlist[i] is the i'th knot, i = 0, 1, ..., length-1
    ylist[i] = s(xlist[i]),
    Mlist[i] = s''(xlist[i]). */
double eval_spline(double xlist[], double ylist[],
                   double Mlist[], int length, double t);
```

If we set up a suitable spline data structure

```
typedef struct {
  /* See Atkinson:
    Intro Numer Anal, 2nd Ed'n, pp. 166-173 */
  int     length;
  double *xlist;    /* list of knots */
```

```
    double *ylist;      /* values interpolated */
    double *Mlist;      /* 2nd derivatives at knots */
} spline;
```

then the interface becomes much simpler and easier to understand:

```
/* eval_spline -- returns cubic spline function s at t */
double eval_spline(spline *s, double t);
```

What is even better is if we change the implementation of the spline functions (and the internals of `spline`), we don't have to change the interface! We would have to re-compile our functions that use `spline` and re-link, but that would be all.

8.2 Avoid global variables!

Suppose that we had a function `fred` whose behavior depended on a global variable `foobar`, which could have one of two values: FOO or BAR. Then `foobar` would be part of the interface for `fred`. But it is a *pathological connection,* and not to be trusted. Suppose we called `fred` on two different occasions like this:

```
foobar = FOO;
answer1 = fred(...);
/* lots of code in between */
...
answer2 = fred(...);
```

Then we will be using the FOO version. Now we need to call another routine called `george` in between:

```
foobar = FOO;
answer1 = fred(...);
...
answer3 = george(...);
...
answer2 = fred(...);
```

This is fine so far. But maybe things go faster if `george` calls `fred`!

```
double george(...)
{
    /* now call fred() */
    foobar = BAR;
    fred(...);
    ...
}
```

Now we have a problem. Something will be wrong with the call to fred. You might check all the arguments passed to the second call to fred, but they are what they should be. What's wrong? You won't know until you get around to checking the global variable.

Of course you can fix this problem by always remembering to set foobar just before you call fred. The better strategy is to pass foobar like the other parameters. That way the compiler will tell you if you forget!

8.3 Multidimensional arrays

In most programming languages the model of a simple linear array is essentially the same. There are some differences: in some languages the length of the array is part of the data structure (e.g., Java and Common Lisp), while in most languages the length is implicit and the user must keep track of it (e.g., C/C++). Apart from this difference, the models of linear arrays with one subscript are essentially the same.

However, multidimensional arrays such as $m \times n$ matrices are interpreted in different ways. In some languages a two-dimensional $m \times n$ array is treated as a single data structure (e.g., Fortran and Pascal), while in others a two-dimensional $m \times n$ array is treated as an array of length m of arrays of length n (e.g., C/C++ and Java).

In languages that treat a two-dimensional array as a single data structure, the entries can be laid out in either ***row-major order*** or ***column-major order***. In row-major order the last index changes fastest as one goes through memory, while for column-major order the first index changes fastest. For example, in Pascal, which uses row-major order, the entries of a matrix

```
real A[3,3];
```

appear in the order A[1,1], A[1,2], A[1,3], A[2,1], A[2,2], A[2,3], A[3,1], A[3,2], and A[3,3]. In Fortran, which uses column-major order, the entries of

```
real A(3,3)
```

appear in the order A(1,1), A(2,1), A(3,1), A(1,2), A(2,2), A(3,2), A(1,3), A(2,3), A(3,3).

In languages where two-dimensional arrays are treated as arrays of arrays (such as C/C++ and Java) the layout in memory is somewhat more complex. However, in any such language the ordering of entries in memory is like the row-major case since changing the last index by one will give adjacent entries in memory.

In Fortran, to declare a two-dimensional array of double-precision numbers that can be allocated (i.e., created), use

```
real(kind(0d0)), allocatable :: A(:,:)
```

To actually allocate an $m \times n$ array, we use an allocate statement:

```
integer :: errno
allocate(A(m,n), stat=errno)
if ( errno /= 0 ) then ! allocation failed
```

If we don't use the "stat=errno" part, then the program aborts if the allocation fails. For higher-dimensional arrays in Fortran, we simply use more indexes:

```
integer :: errno
real(kind(0d0)), allocatable :: A(:,:,:)
! now the actual allocation...
allocate(A(m,n,p), stat=errno)
if ( errno /= 0 ) then ! allocation failed
```

Now consider C and C++. We need to make a careful distinction between the two-dimensional array

```
double A[4][3];
```

which has the sizes fixed at compile time, and the more flexible data structure

```
double **B;
```

In the case of A[4][3], the size determined by the compiler, and space is allocated for the correct number ($4 \times 3 = 12$) of entries. Also, the compiler will convert any reference to A[i] to a pointer to the start of the ith row of A[4][3] (zero relative), which is $i \times 3$ doubles after the start address of A. An element reference A[i][j] will access the double-precision number located $i \times 3 + j$ doubles after the start address of A.

By comparison, double **B does not allocate any memory. After memory has been properly allocated, B will point to an array of pointers to arrays of doubles, as shown in Figure 8.1. Although we can access the entry B[i][j], it happens by a different mechanism to A[i][j]. This time B[i] refers to the ith pointer in the array of pointers starting at B. Then B[i][j] refers to the jth pointer in the array of doubles starting at B[i].

To allocate the pointer-to-pointer structure we need to first allocate the memory for the array of pointers, and then allocate the memory for each array of entries. The obvious way of allocating an $m \times n$ array takes $m + 1$ calls to malloc or new to create the structure, as shown in Algorithm 1: however, this is inefficient

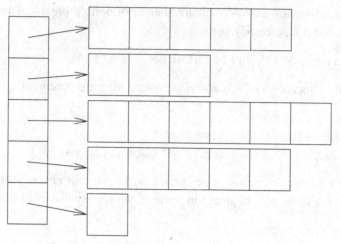

Figure 8.1. Example of pointer-to-pointer structure.

Algorithm 1 Naive matrix allocation method

```
B = (double **)malloc(m*sizeof(double *));
if ( B == NULL ) return NULL;
for ( i = 0; i < m; i++ )
  {
    B[i] = (double *)malloc(n*sizeof(double));
    if ( B[i] == NULL ) { free(B); return NULL; }
  }
```

Algorithm 2 Fast matrix allocation method

```
B = (double **)malloc(m*sizeof(double *));
if ( B == NULL ) return NULL;
B[0] = (double *)malloc(m*n*sizeof(double));
if ( B[0] == NULL ) { free(B); return NULL; }
/* now set the other pointers */
for ( i = 1; i < m; i++ )
  B[i] = B[0] + i*n;
```

---

in both time and memory. A more efficient way of doing this is to allocate a single $m \times n$ block of memory for the entries and then set up the pointers into this block of memory, as shown in Algorithm 2.

There is a temptation to grab the memory in a single call to `malloc`. However, this is dangerous and is not portable unless you use the *open array* syntax. Code

---

Algorithm 3 Dangerous matrix allocation method

```
/* dangerous due to misalignment problems */
B = (double **)
      malloc(m*sizeof(double *)+m*n*sizeof(double));
if ( B == NULL ) return NULL;
B[0] = (double *)(B[m]);
/* now set the other pointers */
for ( i = 1; i < m; i++ )
  B[i] = B[0] + i*n;
```

---

is shown in Algorithm 3. The reason is that mixing different types in a single call to `malloc` can create problems for data alignment. If a computer system requires that pointers are aligned on 4-byte boundaries (i.e., the address of a pointer is a multiple of four) but `doubles` should be aligned on 8-byte boundaries, then odd m can result in program termination.

Note that a de-allocation routine must match each allocation routine – the calls to `free` must match the calls to `malloc`, or in C++, the `delete` operations must match `new` operations. Note that in C++, it is not possible to use `new` to allocate different types in one call.

Higher-dimensional arrays can be created in similar ways to two-dimensional arrays. The analog of Algorithm 2 for allocating a three-dimensional array is shown below.

```
/* creates m x n x p array */
B = (double ***)malloc(m*sizeof(double **));
if ( B = NULL )
  return NULL;
B[0] = (double **)malloc(m*n*sizeof(double *));
if ( B[0] == NULL )
  { free(B); return NULL; }
B[0][0] = (double *)malloc(m*n*p*sizeof(double));
if ( B[0][0] == NULL )
  { free (B[0]); free(B); return NULL; }
for ( i = 0; i < m; i++ )
  {
    B[i] = B[0] + i*n;
    for ( j = 0; j < n; j++ )
      B[i][j] = B[i][0] + j*p;
  }
```

In Java, two-dimensional arrays are really arrays of arrays, and each array implicitly carries its own length. Because Java does not allow pointer arithmetic, unlike C and C++, the method of Algorithm 2 is not possible in Java. Instead we use the method of Algorithm 1; here is code for this:

```
double B[][];
B = new double[m];
for ( int i = 0; i < n; i++ )
  B[i] = new double[n];
```

Since Java and C++ are object oriented languages, it is possible to have a different underlying representation of an array and design a suitable interface for accessing entries. For example, a matrix can be a one-dimensional array internally, but the class can have access functions get(i,j) and set(i,j,value) for getting and setting entries in the matrix. There are overheads in terms of programmer convenience and in terms of speed, although in C++ it is possible to have these access functions inlined for greater efficiency.

8.4 Functional representation vs. data structures

The most general representation scheme is the use of a function to define the object. This is a valuable idea for matrices. One way of thinking about this is that a matrix can be thought of as a two-dimensional array of numbers $A \in \mathbb{R}^{m \times n}$, or as a linear operator $A : \mathbb{R}^n \to \mathbb{R}^m$. So we can represent a matrix as a function like this:

```
/* operator -- returns with y = A*x */
void operator(double x[], double y[]);
```

The matrix–vector multiply can be implemented in the most efficient means possible (it might involve using a Fast Fourier Transform, for example, or be defined by a multigrid algorithm). It is an extremely general way of describing a matrix.

This generality has drawbacks. You can't do LU decomposition or even modify any entries in a functionally defined matrix. In this case, you can't even compute $y = A^T x$ given this representation of a matrix without a lot of work. You can, in principle, extract A as a two-dimensional array from the functional representation: set $x = e_i$, then $y = Ae_i$ is the ith column of A. However, this is an inefficient thing to do unless A is small.

Another example of functional definition is the idea of *iterator* that is used in object-oriented programming for describing lists. An iterator is a class (think: a data structure plus associated functions) for which the allowed operations are getting the current item, going to the next item, and testing if we are at the end of the list.

In the C++ Standard Template Library (STL), these are `iterator` classes, and the container classes in the STL can produce iterators on request. For example, if we have linked list `list<double> x` then we can go through the items in the list like this:

```
list<double>::iterator i;
for ( i = x.begin(); i != x.end(); ++i )
    cout << "Found number " << *i << endl;
```

Note that in C++ a number of the operations are overloaded, particularly `*i` (for accessing the current item), and `++i` (for going to the next item). This provides a general and efficient way of handling lists of general objects through a functional representation. In Java this is done using the standard `Enumeration` class, which can be created by a Java `Vector` or `Hashtable` for instance.

8.5 Functions and the "environment problem"

Functional representation is the most memory efficient representation of "read-only" data structures possible. It is almost, but not quite, the most flexible.

The problem is that when we talk about a function, we are almost always talking about it in some context. For example, we might talk about a quadratic function

$$f(x) = px^2 + qx + r.$$

This is clearly a function of one variable (x), and we can integrate, differentiate and do other things to the function $f(x)$ as a function of x. However, to complete the definition of f, say to evaluate $f(3)$, we need to know what p, q, and r are. This we will call the *context* or *environment* of f. The problem is that we need to explicitly pass the information about what p, q and r are to the code that evaluates $f(x)$. This is particularly important if we are using a general purpose routine to integrate a function f over an interval $[a, b]$:

```
double integrate(double (*f)(double),
                 double a, double b);
```

There are a number of ways of doing this.

- *Global variables.* The quantities p, q, and r can be made global variables which are set before calling f. This is not recommended since passing information through global variables is not. This is discussed in Section 8.2.
- *Reverse communication.* In this approach (a favorite in Fortran 66 and 77), the `integrate` routine would not be passed a function, but would rather return to the caller with a flag set to indicate that the function should be evaluated (and where). The caller would

then do the evaluation before again calling the `integrate` routine with the flag set to say that the function had been evaluated. At the end of the process, the `integrate` routine would return with the flag set to a value to indicate that the computation was complete and one of the variables would contain the final (returned) value.

Reverse communication is difficult to implement, and difficult to use. We do not advise its use where there are better approaches (see below). Nevertheless, this technique is still in use, so we explain how to implement it, and how to use it.

- *Passing pointers.* An approach that works in C-like languages is to pass a pointer to an indeterminate type (`void *`) which points to whatever data structure(s) the function passed needed. This can also work in Fortran provided you ignore the Fortran type-checking system.

  This approach is easy to implement, but care should be taken in using it. The routine that calls `integrate` and the routine defining the function to integrate must be consistent and should be written together. They therefore become tightly-coupled routines, and should come with appropriate warning labels!

- *Classes contain the environment.* In object-oriented languages the class (or object) that does the function evaluation can contain the environment. This can be done most efficiently using multiple inheritance or a similar mechanism, such as Java's `interface`. It is straightforward to implement and striaghtforward to use. This is the most recommended approach for object-oriented systems.

8.5.1 Reverse communication

Reverse communication is a complex method to implement. Here we will consider computing $\int_a^b f(x)\,dx$. Below is a Fortran 90 interface for a reverse communication version of the one-dimensional integration routine `integrate`:

```
subroutine integrate_rc(state,iflag,x,fx,a,b,n,val)
   type(internal_state), intent(inout):: state
   integer, intent(inout):: iflag
   integer, intent(in)    :: n
   real, intent(inout)    :: x, val
   real, intent(in)       :: a, b, fx
   ! code goes here
end
```

Note that the internal state of the `integrate_rc` routine is maintained in the variable `state` which must be passed to `integrate_rc`. This type (which is described below) should be defined somewhere in the interface declaration or close to it. The main controlling argument is `iflag`. The required behavior could be described through a table:

iflag	On entry...	On exit...
0	Initialize	Successful exit
1	fx = $f(x)$	Evaluate fx:= $f(x)$
−1	Error	Failure

Any other value of iflag should be treated as an error. So the code to use this routine would look something like this:

```
integer:: iflag
real    :: x, fx
type(internal_state):: state

iflag = 0
call integrate_rc(state,iflag,x,fx,a,b,n,val)
do while ( iflag /= 0 )
  if ( iflag == 1 ) then
    ! code for evaluating fx = f(x)
    fx = f(myparam,x) ! or something horribly complicated...
    call integrate_rc(state,iflag,x,fx,a,b,n,val)
  else ! if ( iflag /= 0 ) then
    exit        ! exit do while loop
  end if
end do
! val is now the computed integral if iflag == 0
```

As you might suspect, the code inside integrate_rc is even more complex! However, to generate a reverse communication routine from a more conventional routine with passed functions is essentially a mechanical translation. Here is a conventional Fortran routine for the integration problem (for the trapezoidal rule).

```
subroutine integrate(f,a,b,n,val)
  real, intent(in)  :: a, b
  real, intent(out) :: val
  real, external    :: f      ! function
  integer           :: i, n
  real              :: h, sum
  h = (b-a)/n
  ! position 1
  sum = 0.5*f(a)
  ! position 2
  sum = sum + 0.5*f(b)
```

```
  do i = 1, n-1
    ! position 3
    sum = sum + f(a+i*h)
  end do
  ! position 4
  val = sum*h;
end subroutine integrate
```

To convert this to a reverse communication routine we need to note all the points at
which a function call occurs. (These are positions 1, 2, and 3.) We need to construct
a data structure that contains the state information for this routine, which consists
of the local variables together with the position within the routine. We only need
to record which of positions 1, 2, or 3 we are at; more refined information is not
needed. So we will have a data structure that will look like this:

```
type:: internal_state
  integer:: position
  integer:: i, n
  real::    h, sum
end type internal_state
```

Note that we don't really need to include `val`, since that is only computed at the
end, and so is not really needed as a local variable.

When we write the reverse communication routine, we need to remember that
we have to update the state of the system as if we were tracing the execution of the
conventional routine.

```
subroutine integrate_rc(state,iflag,x,fx,a,b,n,val)
  type(internal_state), intent(inout):: state
  integer, intent(inout):: iflag
  integer, intent(in)    :: n
  real, intent(inout)    :: x, val
  real, intent(in)       :: a, b, fx

  if ( iflag == 0 ) then
    ! Initialization
    state%position = 1
    state%n = n
    state%h = (b-a)/n
    x = a          ! evaluate function at a
    iflag = 1
  else if ( iflag == 1 ) then
```

```
   select case ( state%position )
   case ( 1 ) ! position 1
      state%sum = 0.5*fx
      x = b         ! evaluate function at b
      iflag = 1
      state%position = 2
   case ( 2 ) ! position 2
      state%sum = state%sum + 0.5*fx
      state%i = 1        ! start of loop
      x = a + state%i*state%h
      iflag = 1
      state%position = 3
   case ( 3 ) ! position 3
      state%sum = state%sum + fx
      state%i = state%i + 1
      x = a + state%i*state%h
      iflag = 1
      if ( state%i == n-1 ) then
         state%position = 4
      end if
   case ( 4 ) ! position 4
      state%sum = state%sum + fx
      val = state%sum*state%h
      iflag = 0     ! That's all folks!
   case default
      iflag = -1    ! Error !
   end select
else
   iflag = -1      ! Error !
end if
end subroutine integrate_rc
```

Note that we had to split the initial function calls $f(a)$ and $f(b)$. That way we could correctly identify whether we had to compute $f(b)$ next, or go on to the loop.

In spite of the fact that constructing reverse communication routines is essentially a mechanical process, it is a fairly involved and tedious one.

Note that it is more traditional not to have an explicit data structure holding the state. Instead, the local variables and a "position" variable are kept between function calls. In Fortran, declaring them using the save keyword will keep the values between function calls. This appears simpler than passing a "state" parameter, but it means that if the function f is itself defined in terms of `integrate_rc`, then `integrate_rc` will fail. Passing an explicit state parameter avoids this problem. Passing an explicit state parameter also makes the routine **threadsafe**; that is, the routine can be used with threads.

8.5.2 *Passing pointers*

If you are using a language with pointers, then an attractive alternative is to pass the environment or context via a pointer. This is particularly easy in C with the `void *` pointer type, which could point to any type of data or data structure.

We will do a C version of the integrate routine passing a `void *` pointer to some (user-defined) data structure.

```
double integrate_pp(double (*f)(void *,double),
    void *params, double a, double b, int n)
{
  int i;
  double sum;
  sum = 0.5*((*f)(params,a) + (*f)(params,b));
  for ( i = 1; i <= n-1; i++ )
    sum = sum + (*f)(params,a+i*(b-a)/n);
  return sum*(b-a)/n;
}
```

Now to integrate a quadratic function, we set up the appropriate data structure and function:

```
struct quad_params {
  double p, q, r;   /* coefficients of quadratic:
                        p*x*x+q*x+r */
};
```

```
double quadratic(void *params, double x)
{
  struct quad_params *qp;
  qp = (struct quad_params *)params;
  return x*(qp->p*x+qp->q) + qp->r;   /* Horner's rule */
}
```

So, if we wished to compute the integral $\int_0^1 (x^2 - 7x + 3.5)\,dx$, we would use the following code:

```
struct quad_params qp = { 1.0, -7.0, 3.5 };
val = integrate_pp(quadratic, &qp, 0.0, 1.0);
```

This is much more convenient than reverse communication.

What if we want to integrate the sin function? There is a simple trick for that which doesn't involve much more work as long as we don't mind an extra layer of function evaluations:

```
double func_eval(void *params, double x)
{
    double (*f)(double);
    f = (double (*)(double))params;
    return (*f)(x);
}
```

That is, we make the function pointer itself the parameter of this universal function func_eval. To use it, we now call

```
val = integrate_pp(func_eval,sin,a,b);
```

to approximately compute $\int_a^b \sin x \, dx$.

Fortran 2003 introduces *procedure pointers* which have much of the same syntax as other pointers in Fortran 90/95, and can be used much like pointers to functions in C and C++. These can be passed and assigned to a specific procedure or function using pointer assignment, and can be set to null. Each procedure pointer has an explicit or implicit interface showing how it can be used as a function or subroutine. This interface can be taken from a pre-existing function or subroutine, or specified via an `abstract interface`.

8.5.3 Classes contain the environment

The most natural way of handling the environment problem goes to object-oriented languages. However, to implement this in a properly general way requires *inheritance* from an abstract base class, or a similar mechanism. Java has the `interface` mechanism for implementing a strictly limited kind of inheritance from an abstract base class, which is suitable for our purposes.

For example, in Java, we would use an interface class of the form:

```
public interface Func {
    public double eval(double x);
}
```

Then, if we want to set up a function like $x \mapsto ax^2 + bx + c$, we create a class that contains the environment of the function. So our class must contain the values of a, b and c. This would be a class like this:

```
public class Quadratic implements Func {
   private double a, b, c;
   public Quadratic(double _a, double _b, double _c)
   { a = _a; b = _b; c = _c; }
   public double eval(double x)
   { return (a*x+b)*x+c; }
}
```

To use it to evaluate the function $x \mapsto 3x^2 + 2x - 5$ at $x = -1.5$ we would use code like this:

```
public class FuncTest {
   public static void main(String args[])
   {
      Quadratic q = new Quadratic(3.0,2.0,-5.0);
      double x = -1.5;
      System.out.println(q.eval(x));
   }
}
```

A more serious use of the `Func interface` would be for writing a general routine for integration via the trapezoidal rule, for example:

```
public class Trapezoidal {
   public static double
      integrate(Func f, double a, double b, int n)
   {
      double sum = 0.5*(f.eval(a)+f.eval(b));
      double h   = (b-a)/n;
      for ( int i = 1; i < n; i++ )
         sum += f.eval(a+i*h);
      return sum*h;
   }
}
```

Then to evaluate the integral $\int_0^1 (3x^2 + 2x - 5)\,dx$ we create a `Quadratic` object with the correct coefficients and pass this to the `Trapezoidal integrate` routine:

```
Quadratic q = new Quadratic(3.0,2.0,-5.0);
System.out.print("Integral is (n=10) ");
System.out.println(Trapezoidal.integrate(q, 0.0, 1.0, 10));
```

If we were using C++, we would use inheritance from an abstract base class
to achieve the same thing. The key to this is to note that a Java interface is essentially an abstract class, and implementing a Java interface is like inheriting
an abstract class in most other object-oriented languages. Here is our quadratic
example:

```
class Func {
 public:
   virtual double operator()(double x) const = 0;
};
```

The class defining the quadratic function would look like this:

```
class Quadratic : public Func {
 private:
   double a, b, c;
 public:
   Quadratic(double _a, double _b, double _c)
   { a = _a; b = _b; c = _c; }
   double operator()(double x)
   { return (a*x+b)*x+c; }
};
```

Then the trapezoidal integration routine would look like this:

```
#include          "trapezoidal.h"

double trapezoidal(Func &f, double a, double b, int n=100)
{
   double sum = 0.5*(f(a)+f(b));
   double h = (b-a)/n;
   for ( int i = 1; i < n; i++ )
      sum = sum + f(a+i*h);

   return sum*h;
}
```

If we already have a large and complex class C, we could create a function class
from C using multiple inheritance:

```
class C_func : public C, public Func {
 public:
  double operator()(double x) const
  {
    double val = 0;
    /* code to compute val = function(x) goes here */
    return val;
  }
};
```

The only difficulty is that we need to create a new class for each new function. But, as we see above, this need not be a major problem: there is only a small amount of extra code needed to create the class – most of the code is for computing the function.

8.6 Some comments on object-oriented scientific software

The benefits of object-oriented programming for software development have become firmly entrenched in the minds of many, especially for developing "component-based software". This has happened to the extent that there are courses on "object-oriented software design" without a comparable course for non-object-oriented languages or systems. Almost all current textbooks on software engineering have at least a chapter on software engineering for object-oriented languages. Most have more.

One of the more recent developments is the use of ***design patterns*** as a major tool in object-oriented software development. An excellent starting point for understanding these patterns is the book *Design Patterns* [40], which not only gives design patterns and their rationales, but also describes a good many of their uses and pitfalls.

Most scientific software is not (yet) developed in object-oriented languages, and there have been some important concerns about the ability of object-oriented programs to provide the performance desired for high-performance computing. Java, for example, is strongly object-oriented in its design, but this seems as much a hindrance as a help for producing high-performance software. (See [11] and the notes above on Java.)

Yet, object-oriented systems offer a great deal of value to the development of scientific software. The problem is how to incorporate them into the standard ways of programming scientific software to gain the flexibility they promise, but without losing the performance that we want.

In this section we will concentrate on C++ as the object-oriented language of choice. This is because, more than in almost any other object-oriented language, the features of C++ were designed with efficiency in mind.

8.6.1 *The performance implications of object-oriented design techniques*

There are three areas in which object-oriented design tend to result in poor performance:

1. excessive time spent in object creation and destruction;
2. loss of control of placement of objects in memory;
3. excessive function call overhead as member methods and virtual methods (that is, methods that can be overridden through inheritance) replace direct access to data structures and fixed functions.

Object creation and destruction is particularly important in dealing with overloaded operators. For example, in C++, we can create a class of vectors, and overload the addition and subtraction operators. When we use the operators, in code such as

```
Vector x(10), y(10), z(10), w(10);
w = x + y + z;
```

then the naive implementation will result in a new vector being created after forming x + y and another new vector when this is added to z, which is then copied to w. Another area where object creation tends to occur is in passing objects *by value*. C++ provides reference types to mitigate this problem, while other object-oriented languages like Java use a *pass by reference* model throughout for objects.

Replacing direct access to data structures with member functions is needed in object-oriented design for **encapsulation** – with member functions the object controls access to its internal data. Virtual methods provide flexibility in how objects respond to requests while providing a consistent interface.

8.6.2 *Avoiding constructors and destructors*

Object creation and destruction can be major costs in object-oriented codes and can often be avoided. One source of object construction is the passing of objects by value; then a *copy* of the object should be passed, which results in the *copy constructor* being called to create the copy. In C++, consider a Vector class with a dot product

```
class Vector {
   Vector(Vector &); // copy constructor
   ...
   double dot(Vector y) { ... }
   ...
};
```

The trouble with this interface is that y is passed by value, so that the copy constructor must be called whenever the dot member function is called. The local copy inside dot must also be destroyed when the dot function returns. This results in $O(n)$ overhead (where n is the dimension of the vectors) for an $O(n)$ operation, which can be substantial.

It is better to use the interface

```
double dot(const Vector &y) const;
```

The interface shows that a reference (or pointer) to y is passed to dot, which is more efficient; y cannot be changed by dot; neither can the implicit current object (this in C++).

Syntactically, the member function is called the same way: x.dot(y), but because only a reference is passed, there is no call to the copy constructor on entry to the routine, and no call to a destructor when the routine dot returns.

Avoiding unnecessary object creation and destruction is harder in the context of operator overloading, but still possible if we use some of the features of C++. This is outlined in *The C++ Programming Language* [96, pp. 675–677]. From the point of view of object-oriented programming, the trick is to create objects which contain all the data needed for the operation, and delay carrying out the operation itself until it can be done efficiently. These objects are called "composition objects", or **compositors**. These hold the data necessary for carrying out one or more operations. When values are needed, a low-level routine that carries out the operation is called (e.g., a *saxpy* operation $y \leftarrow y + \alpha x$, or a matrix–vector multiply and add $z \leftarrow Ax + y$).

Here are some examples of how to do this with matrix and vector data structures. The basic data structures are classes MyMat and MyVec. The low-level routines we use are as follows:

```
MyVec &add_assign(const MyVec &v1, const MyVec &v2,
                MyVec &out);
MyVec &mul_assign(const MyMat &A, const MyVec &x,
                MyVec &out);
MyVec &mul_add_assign(const MyMat &A, const MyVec &x,
                const MyVec &y, MyVec &out);
```

When we define the matrix–vector product operator, the result should not be a MyVec, but rather a structure that holds the matrix and the vector, or rather, pointers or references to the actual matrix and vector. This structure is the MVmul class:

```
struct MVmul {  // represents m*v
  const MyMat *m; // use pointers
  const MyVec *v; // to avoid copying
```

```
MVmul(const MyMat &_m, const MyVec &_v)
{ m = &_m; v = &_v; }

operator MyVec(); // This computes m*v
};
```

Similarly, we create that `Vadd` class for holding a pair of vectors for addition:

```
struct Vadd {  // represents v1+v2
  const MyVec *v1, *v2;

  Vadd(const MyVec &_v1, const MyVec &_v2)
  { v1 = &_v1; v2 = &_v2; }

  operator MyVec(); // This computes v1+v2
};
```

We can create classes to hold the results of more than one operation, but this must be done using the previous "one operation" compositors. Here is a matrix–vector multiply and add class `MVmuladd`:

```
struct MVmuladd {  // represents m*v1+v2
  const MyMat *m;
  const MyVec *v1, *v2;

  MVmuladd(const MVmul &mv, const MyVec &_v2)
  { m = mv.m; v1 = mv.v; v2 = &_v2; }

  operator MyVec(); // This computes m*v1+v2
};
```

These are created out of the basic `MyMat` and `MyVec` objects through the usual arithmetic operators:

```
inline MVmul operator*(const MyMat &mm, const MyVec &vv)
{ return MVmul(mm,vv); }

inline MVmuladd operator+(const MVmul &mv, const MyVec &vv)
{ return MVmuladd(mv,vv); }

inline MVmuladd operator+(const MyVec &vv, const MVmul &mv)
{ return MVmuladd(mv,vv); }

inline Vadd operator+(const MyVec &v1, const MyVec &v2)
{ return Vadd(v1,v2); }
```

These compositors are only "evaluated" when they are converted to the MyVec
class throught the MyVec() conversion operators. These conversion routines call
the low-level operation routines.

All this is declared before we define the MyMat and MyVec classes:

```
class MyMat {
  string name;  // for our test code
 public:
  friend class MyVec;
  friend MyVec &mul_assign(const MyMat &A,
                            const MyVec &x, MyVec &out);
  friend MyVec &mul_add_assign(const MyMat &A,
     const MyVec &x,
                               const MyVec &y, MyVec &out);

  MyMat(string _name) : name(_name)
  { cout << "Creating MyMat " << _name << "\n"; }
 ~MyMat() { cout << "Destroying MyMat " << name << "\n"; }
  friend ostream &operator<<(ostream &s, const MyMat &x)
  { return s << x.name; }
};

class MyVec {
  string name;
 public:
  friend class MyMat;
  friend MyVec &add_assign(const MyVec &x, const MyVec &y,
                           MyVec &out);
  friend MyVec &mul_assign(const MyMat &A, const MyVec &x,
                           MyVec &out);
  friend MyVec &mul_add_assign(const MyMat &A, const
     MyVec &x,
                               const MyVec &y, MyVec &out);

  MyVec(string _name) : name(_name)
  { cout << "Creating MyVec " << _name << "\n"; }
 ~MyVec() { cout << "Destroying MyVec " << name << "\n"; }
  MyVec(const Vadd &vv)
  { add_assign(*vv.v1,*vv.v2,*this); }
  MyVec(const MVmul &mv)
  { mul_assign(*mv.m,*mv.v,*this); }
```

```
MyVec(const MVmuladd &mv)
{ mul_add_assign(*mv.m,*mv.v1,*mv.v2,*this); }
MyVec &operator=(const Vadd &vv)
{ return add_assign(*vv.v1,*vv.v2,*this); }
MyVec &operator=(const MVmul &mv)
{ return mul_assign(*mv.m,*mv.v,*this); }
MyVec &operator=(const MVmuladd &mv)
{ return mul_add_assign(*mv.m,*mv.v1,*mv.v2,*this); }

friend ostream &operator<<(ostream &s, const MyVec &x)
{ return s << x.name; }
};
```

We use these classes to perform the following operations:

```
cout << "operation: w = u+v;\n";
w = u+v;
cout << "operation: z = A*u+v;\n";
z = A*u+v;
cout << "operation: z = A*(A*u+v)+z;\n";
z = A*(A*u+v)+z;
cout << "operation: z = A*u + A*v + w + z;\n";
z = A*u + A*v + w + z;
cout << "operation: A*(u+v) + w + z\n";
z = A*(u+v) + w + z;
```

With diagnostic code to indicate when vector objects are created and destroyed, we get the following output:

```
Creating MyVec u
Creating MyVec v
Creating MyVec w
Creating MyVec z
Creating MyMat A
operation: w = u+v;
add_assign(u,v,w)
operation: z = A*u+v;
mul_add_assign(A,u,v,z)
operation: z = A*(A*u+v)+z;
Creating MyVec (A*u+v)
mul_add_assign(A,u,v,(A*u+v))
mul_add_assign(A,(A*u+v),z,z)
```

```
Destroying MyVec (A*u+v)
operation: z = A*u + A*v + w + z;
Creating MyVec (A*v)
mul_assign(A,v,(A*v))
Creating MyVec (A*u+(A*v)) .
mul_add_assign(A,u,(A*v),(A*u+(A*v)))
Creating MyVec ((A*u+(A*v))+w)
add_assign((A*u+(A*v)),w,((A*u+(A*v))+w))
add_assign(((A*u+(A*v))+w),z,z)
Destroying MyVec ((A*u+(A*v))+w)
Destroying MyVec (A*u+(A*v))
Destroying MyVec (A*v)
operation: A*(u+v) + w + z
Creating MyVec (u+v)
add_assign(u,v,(u+v))
Creating MyVec (A*(u+v)+w)
mul_add_assign(A,(u+v),w,(A*(u+v)+w))
add_assign((A*(u+v)+w),z,z)
Destroying MyVec (A*(u+v)+w)
Destroying MyVec (u+v)
Done!
Destroying MyMat A
Destroying MyVec z
Destroying MyVec w
Destroying MyVec v
Destroying MyVec u
```

As can be seen from the output, more complex expressions can be handled this way, but objects will be created. Furthermore, since the operations are inlined, the decisions about what temporary objects to create and destroy is made at compile time. If no objects are created or destroyed, then there is no run-time penalty! This code does not check for bad *in situ* operations such as $z \leftarrow Az + u$ that overwrite the output. This can be done by means of checks within `mul_add_assign` and `mul_assign` that the output pointer is not equal to the pointer to the vector being multiplied. If the `MyVec` and `MyMat` structures do not share memory, then we would need only to check the addresses of the structures in order to avoid *in situ* operations.

8.6.3 *Granularity of routines*

In order to encapsulate the data inside objects, direct access to the internal data structures is usually disallowed. Instead, accessor member functions are usually defined which provide the necessary access, but in a controlled way. This impacts performance because using an accessor function means that there is some function call overhead. Also, there may be checking code inside an accessor function (e.g., to check that an array index is within bounds), which may be redundant when the larger context is understood. Consider, for example, a `Vector` class

```
class Vector {
 private:
   double *array; // vector entries stored here
   int      dim;   // dimension of vector
 public:
   Vector(int _dim);
   // ...
   double &operator[](int i)
   {
      if ( i < 0 }} i >= dim )
         throw new VectorError("Outside array bounds");
      return array[i];
   }
   // ...
};
```

We can avoid the overhead of the function call by using inlining. Defining the function inside the class declaration like this makes this function available for inlining in C++. However, we still have the overhead for the array bounds checking code. This can have an excessive impact on code such as this:

```
Vector x(10);
double sum;
sum = 0.0;
for ( int i = 0; i < 10; i++ )
   sum = sum + x[i];
```

since the array bounds checking is done for each value of i, unless the compiler has a particularly powerful optimizer. While [11] (from 1998) reported that, for at least one Java system, array bounds checking only added 20% to the total time for accessing an array entry, the extra code may disrupt other optimizations, such as using fused multiply-adds. This is an area where known compiler optimization techniques can be applied; it is mostly a matter of the capabilities of the compiler used and the optimization level requested.

Note that member functions have direct access to the underlying data, so that these should not have any performance handicaps. This also means that member functions involving significant computation should be preferred to writing equivalent code via accessor functions. For example, it is better for a `Vector` class to provide a `dot` function for computing dot products, and a `sum` function for summing entries, than for the user of the class to write new functions to do this.

Note that in the C++ Standard Template Library the `vector` template classes have two access operators: `x[i]` that does *not* do bound checking, and `x.at(i)` that *does* do bound checking.

8.6.4 Template programming

Since its beginning, C++ has been designed for efficiency. Although templates were a relatively late addition to C++ (coming after Ada's `generic` features), these continue the tradition of C++ providing efficient features.

Templates are one mechanism for providing **generic programming** where one piece of source code can be used for different types without requiring or forcing conversions. Consider, for example, the following template for computing the maximum of two objects:

```
template <class T>
T max(T a, T b)
{ return ( a > b ) ? a : b; }
```

This can be used to compute the maximum of two integers, floating point numbers, or any other class where the "<" operator is overloaded.

```
#include  <iostream>
#include  "max-generic.h"

int main(int argc, char *argv[])
{
   std::cout << "max(3,7) = " << max(3,7) << std::endl;
}
```

Not only are there template functions, but also template classes (or types).

Templates are processed directly by the compiler. As a result there is no run-time overhead to templates, unlike the use of `virtual` functions which are heavily used in inheritance-based polymorphism. In addition, the modern C++ template mechanism supports **partial and complete specialization**. This means that specific cases for which there are especially efficient implementations can be handled more efficiently without the template user being aware of the different implementation(s).[1]

---

[1] This means that if you use the template specialization mechanism, you need to be especially vigilant that the different implementations are correct and consistent.

Here is an example of how templates can be used for implementing fixed-dimension vectors, and then specializing for two-dimensional and three-dimensional vectors with loop unrolling "by hand". First, here is an outline of the general template for these fixed-dimension vectors:

```
template <int dim>
class FDVec {
 private:
   double e[dim];
 public:
   FDVec()
   {
      for ( int i = 0; i < dim; i++ )    e[i] = 0.0;
   }


   // Member function: x.sum(y,out): returns out <- x + y
   ...


   // Member function: x.mult(s,out): returns out <- s*x
   ...
};
```

Here is how the sum function can be implemented in general:

```
FDVec<dim> &sum(const FDVec<dim> &y, FDVec<dim> &out)
{
   for ( int i = 0; i < dim; i++ )
      out.e[i] = e[i] + y.e[i];
   return out;
}
```

Since these are defined inside the class, these routines can be inlined, which will eliminate the function call overhead, and make for more efficient code.

In spite of this, for two- or three-dimensional vectors, these loops are too short to be efficient. The amount of code that is executed is too little to justify the expense of setting up the loop. This is especially true on pipelined CPUs like the Intel CPUs, where the pipeline must be flushed when the loop exits. It would be much more efficient to have "straight through" code. We do not need to write new classes D2Vec and D3Vec for two- and three-dimensional vectors. Instead we specialize the FDVec template for dim = 2.

```
// Specializations of FCVec template for 2-dim'l vectors
template<>
class FDVec<2> {
  private:
   double e[2];
  public:
  FDVec() { e[0] = e[1] = 0.0; }
  FDVec<2> &sum(FDVec<2> &y, FDVec<2> &out)
  {
    out.e[0] = e[0] + y.e[0];   out.e[1] = e[1] + y.e[1];
    return out;
  }
  FDVec<2> &mult(double s, FDVec<2> &out)
  {
    out.e[0] = s*e[0];   out.e[1] = s*e[1];
    return out;
  }
}
```

An alternative that avoids re-writing a lot of code for each specialization to one, two, and three dimensions is to use ***template recursion***. Here is an example of how you can use it for adding vectors:

```
// Example of use of recursive templates for loop unrolling
template<typename T, int len>
struct AddOp {
  static void add(const T *a, const T *b, T *out)
  {
    AddOp<T,len-1>::add(a,b,out);
    out[len-1] = a[len-1] + b[len-1];
  }
};
```

```
// Specialization to act as base case for recursion
template<typename T>
struct AddOp<T,0> {
  static void add(const T *a, const T *b, T *out)
  { }
};
```

The recursion is mainly handled by the first declaration of the AddOp template. The specialization takes care of the base case in the recursion (in this case zero). Then adding, for example, three-dimensional vectors can be done with loops unrolled at compile time by

```
AddOp<double,3>::add(x,y,z);
```

We compiled this using the DJGPP C++ compiler with the -O2 optimization switch. Careful inspection of the assembly code generated showed that it was equivalent to the desired code:

```
z[0] = x[0] + y[0];
z[1] = x[1] + y[1];
z[2] = x[2] + y[2];
```

Template recursion and template specialization have been particularly important in systems such as Blitz++ [102] which give performance that can match, and in some cases exceed, optimized Fortran without giving up the benefits of object-oriented programming.

There is a cost to sophisticated template programming. Firstly, there are limits on how deeply compilers can expand recursive templates. Often it is possible to control this limit by means of compiler options or pragmas embedded in the code. There is a similar limit to the depth of inlining that a compiler can carry out. Secondly, in large programs that use a great deal of template expansion, this can result in *much* longer compilation times, sometimes taking hours to compile.

9

Design for testing and debugging

This section is about how you should design your software so it is easy to test and debug. Bugs are inevitable. But we should try to eliminate them as quickly and thoroughly as we can. To do this, we need to test the code thoroughly. The best way to do this is to automate the testing. When bugs are uncovered, the situation that revealed the bug should be added to the set of (automated) tests. When changes are made, re-do the tests. This is known as *regression testing* and is how many software companies ensure the quality of their software.

Memory allocation and the associated debugging issues are dealt with in Chapters 14 and 15.

9.1 Incremental testing

This is perhaps the most crucial single technique in designing for debugging. Test as you go. Make sure each piece is working correctly before you put them together. Don't try to construct a full-featured program from the beginning, but make sure that you can get a "bare bones" version going. For any feature you want to add, first devise a test for what this feature does. Then start building the feature, checking it against the test you devised. This way you can test each new addition while having confidence that the base system is behaving correctly.

The Extreme Programming approach [21] is even stronger: *Before* you start writing code, write the test code and data. Furthermore, you should automate the tests, and add new tests as you refine, debug, and test the code. Whenever you feel that you have things working, run the complete set of tests. This ensures that you haven't broken anything that you thought was fixed. If *any* of the tests fail, you have to find out why and fix it.

A version of this approach is not uncommon in commercial software companies. Typically, the software is built each night and the automated tests are run. If some change breaks the "nightly build", then the author of that change is notified. At

Microsoft, for example, software development is not allowed to begin until the testers have OK'd the specifications. The specifications are the basis for the tests. Furthermore, every programmer is teamed up with a tester to carry out basic tests on new modules before they are made part of the "nightly build" [107, pp. 269–272].

Many scientific software systems are large and need many parts in place and operational before the whole can work. Incremental testing can still work here. Take, for example, a finite element program. There are many parts to this: geometry specification, mesh generation, matrix assembly (forming the linear system to solve), the linear solver(s), postprocessing, and visualization. We want to start testing well before all of these pieces (even very simplified ones) are put together. Many of these parts are going to be built around their own data structures or databases. Start with these parts. Write tests to see that these data structures are built properly and represent what they are intended to represent. Put the routines into libraries (or sub-libraries) so we can link test programs against the routines. Remember: keep the old tests to make sure that we haven't broken anything that was working before.

Another aspect of large-scale software systems is *integration*. That is, we need to be able to put all the parts together, so that they will be able to communicate with each other correctly. To do this we need to put together a minimal *end-to-end* system. How can we do that quickly? Perhaps we could start with just the linear solver and the matrix assembly parts. The linear solver can be just a standard dense LU factorize and solve routine(s), like the LAPACK routines SGETRF and SGETRS – there are lots of versions of this that are easy to code or use directly (but you will test it separately first, of course). The matrix assembly part could take a hand-written triangularization of a very simple domain (a square, or even just an interval in one dimension) and produce the matrix (just a simple dense matrix to start with; no fancy sparse matrix data structures yet) for a simple differential equation (like $d^2u/dx^2 = f(x)$). With this we can start integrating the system early on. Later we will modify the interfaces between these to pass sparse matrices, or perhaps even more sophisticated data structures, and use more sophisticated linear solvers. Note that the interfaces that we have may have to be changed later if we need, say, mesh information in the linear solver, as might happen with multigrid types of methods. But this can be handled when you get to it, and when you do, you can be confident that the rest of the system works as it should.

A word of warning about memory bugs: to catch some memory bugs, such as modifying array elements that are actually outside the array, you might need a debugging memory allocation library. So this should be part of the test set-up. You should also set any compiler or program switches to maximum testing of inputs and operations, such as array abounds checking where this is available. These bugs can be insidious and difficult to locate, so find them early when it is relatively easy. Don't trust a program that seems to run fine one time but crashes mysteriously another time. There may be memory bugs that are causing the problems both times, but only cause crashes when the right combination of circumstances appear.

Some bugs show up as slow convergence, for example if you are using Newton's method, or a variation of it. Newton's method normally converges very quickly when you are close to the solution (and the Jacobian matrix is not nearly singular). If you find that convergence is linear or worse even though it is converging, check that the code for computing the Jacobian matrix is consistent with the code for computing the function whose zero you are computing. A bug here might not stop Newton's method from converging, but it is likely to converge slowly.

Similar things can happen in other kinds of scientific software. For example, in Ordinary Differential Equation (ODE) solvers, the computed results may converge to the correct limit. But if they do so slower than the asymptotic rate predicted by the theory, then there may be a bug. (You might also have a stiff ODE, for example, and the "stiff order" may be different from the conventional order of the ODE solver.)

9.2 Localizing bugs

The hardest part of debugging is to find where the bug is. Once you have identified the section of code where the bug is to within a few lines, you can check the variable values, parameters passed to any routines and the returned values. If the bug occurs in a function call, and you have the source code you can debug that function – find out where the error occurs in that function, and repeat if necessary. If you don't have the source code, you can check the documentation you have (if writing C/C++, start with the header file) about that routine to see what it needs and what assumptions it makes.

Debuggers can help with localizing errors, especially if the program crashes. The most straightforward use of the debugger is to determine where the program crashed via a *stack backtrace* or possibly identifying the source code lines where the program crashed. This way you can at least find out the routine where the program is crashing.

Bugs that involve over-writing memory outside of an array do not necessarily cause the program to crash there. The program could crash later on. This makes these bugs much harder to localize. To track these down, see Chapter 15 on debugging memory problems.

9.3 The mighty "print" statement

While it is often derided, there is truly no better way to get started with debugging than with "print" statements. While debuggers are powerful tools, generating human-readable information is invaluable (and can often be used inside debuggers).

And since most of the time what we want to do is to localize the bug, information should be printed out about where we are. We used to write statements (in C) like

```
printf("Checkpoint A\n");
...
printf("Checkpoint B\n");
...
printf("Checkpoint C\n");
```

In C this can be automated rather better with a macro:

```
#ifdef DEBUG
#define  checkpoint() \
  printf("Checkpoint at line %d in file \"%s\"\n",\
  _LINE_, _FILE_)
#else
#define  checkpoint() /* no printing */
#endif
```

A similar macro can be implemented in C++. Thanks to the built in C macros _LINE_ and _FILE_, this *checkpoint* macro will tell you exactly where you are in the source code. We can use this macro in our code like this:

```
/* some code */
checkpoint();
/* some more code */
```

and it produces output like this:

```
Checkpoint at line 8 in file "checkpt-eg.c"
```

Next you will need to print out results from your code at selected places. This you will need to check. Usually you will do this with small problems so you are not overwhelmed. But sometimes, problems only become noticeable with larger problems. How do you avoid getting overwhelmed with data? First use the computer to do most of the checking for you. If you can check that a data structure is self-consistent, you can print out a message when it first discovers an inconsistency. Or perhaps the results are not consistent with the inputs.

Suppose we are trying to solve a linear system $Ax = b$. For now, let's suppose that A is a small matrix, so we can store it in main memory without difficulty. However you solve it, keep the matrix. Then when the computer tells you that the answer is x, print out the norm of the residual $\|Ax - b\|$. (Use your favorite norm; if you are writing things from scratch, just use the infinity norm: $\|r\|_\infty = \max_i |r_i|$, which is easy to compute.) If the number is of the order of unit roundoff ($\approx 2 \times 10^{-16}$ for double precision) times the norm of A ($\|A\|_\infty = \max_i \sum_j |a_{ij}|$) then all is well. It can even be bigger by 10 or even 100 times this value without problems. But if it is much bigger than this, you have a problem. It may be hard to solve a system of equations, but it is almost always easy to check a system of equations.

Loops can result in a *lot* of print out; there can be megabytes of output which can be overwhelming. How can we reduce this? One way is by getting the computer to give us summary information, like the residual *norm* $\|Ax - b\|$ instead of the vector $Ax - b$. Even so, we might get megabytes of print out. One way to get a handle on this is to periodically print out headings, and (on Unix) to pass this through the filters `more` or `less`, or use a text editor. (Note that `less` is actually better than `more` because it gives you the ability to go *backwards* through the output.) Both `more` and `less` allow you to search for text strings. Use this to go to headings in the output, skipping over the uninteresting material in the middle. This way you can check individual numbers and operations even in many megabytes of output. If it is small enough (e.g., only a *few* megabytes) you can send the output to a file and use your favorite editor to do the same thing: scan through the file for the heading strings that tells you where the important information is.

9.4 Get the computer to help

There are other ways in which you can get the computer to help you with testing and debugging. One of the simplest ways is to print out easy-to-understand (***human-readable***) information contained in your data structures. In fact, whenever you create a new data structure, one of your first tasks should be to write an output routine so you can see what is inside your new data structures. It is often helpful to have a second version which prints out essentially everything in your data structure (replicated data, scratch area, pointer addresses, etc.) so that you can check that the internal data structures are at least self-consistent.

9.4.1 Print routines

For printing the spline function data structure, you should have something like this:

```
void spline_print(FILE *fp, spline *s)
{
    int        i;
    fprintf(fp,"Spline: ");
    if ( s == NULL )
    {
        fprintf(fp,"NULL\n");
        return;
```

```
}
fprintf(fp,"length: %d\n", s->length);
fprintf(fp,"xlist: ");
for ( i = 0; i < s->length; i++ )
  fprintf(fp,"%20.14g ", s->xlist[i]);
fprintf(fp,"\n");
fprintf(fp,"ylist: ");
for ( i = 0; i < s->length; i++ )
  fprintf(fp,"%20.14g ", s->ylist[i]);
fprintf(fp,"\n");
fprintf(fp,"Mlist: ");
for ( i = 0; i < s->length; i++ )
  fprintf(fp,"%20.14g ", s->Mlist[i]);
fprintf(fp,"\n");
}
```

The output of this print routine looks like this:

```
Spline: length: 5
xlist:         0          1          3        4.5          5
ylist:         2         -1        0.5          3          1
Mlist:         0          0          0          0          0
```

Then we can write a function spline_dump which also prints out the address of the pointers s->xlist, s->ylist and s->Mlist. This will help to make sure that you have really allocated these arrays properly. Null values or repeated values, or values that are too close together are a sign that there is a bug in the way the data structure is constructed. Here is typical output from such a routine:

```
Spline: @ 91a10 length: 5
xlist @ 91a28:         0          1          3        4.5          5
ylist @ 91a58:         2         -1        0.5          3          1
Mlist @ 91a88:         0          0          0          0          0
```

Note that current debuggers allow the user to call routines interactively; calling a print routine can give useful human-readable information about the data structures under investigation.

9.4.2 Input routines

If you want to do interactive testing, then you should definitely write an input routine. This should read in data in the same format as your print routine outputs.

In fact, if you are careful, you can read in exactly what was printed out. This is a useful design rule in general, although not everyone follows it. MATLAB does not, for example. You cannot cut and paste MATLAB's output to use as input.

For the code below we use some macros to simplify the memory allocation calls in C:

```
#define NEW(type)  ((type *)malloc(sizeof(type)))
#define NEW_ARRAY(num,type) \
        ((type *)calloc((size_t)(num),sizeof(type)))
```

Note that we use `malloc` and `calloc` to allocate memory as needed. But we need to check the returned value to see that it is not NULL before proceeding, in case the memory wasn't allocated. Also, these macros ensure that the correct types are passed and that the type of the returned pointer matches the type used for the `sizeof` operation.

Here is how to program an input routine `spline_read` that reads the data printed by `spline_print`:

```
spline *spline_read(FILE *fp)
{
  int        i, length;
  spline *s;

  /* read header */
  if ( fscanf(fp," Spline: length:%u",&length) < 1)
    return NULL;
  s = spline_create(length);

  /* read xlist */
  fscanf(fp," xlist:");
  for ( i = 0; i < length; i++ )
    if ( fscanf(fp,"%lf",&(s->xlist[i])) < 1 )
      spline_error("spline_read: fscanf error");
  /* read ylist */
  fscanf(fp," ylist:");
  for ( i = 0; i < length; i++ )
    if ( fscanf(fp,"%lf",&(s->ylist[i])) < 1 )
      spline_error("spline_read: fscanf error");
  /* read Mlist */
  fscanf(fp," Mlist:");
  for ( i = 0; i < length; i++ )
```

```
if ( fscanf(fp,"%lf",&(s->Mlist[i]))) < 1 )
    spline_error("spline_read: fscanf error");

    return s;
}
```

We should also check that the `fscanf` calls were successful in finding the numbers we put into the arrays. We can do this with the following lines:

```
if ( fscanf(fp,"%lf",&(...)) < 1)
    /* error return */ ... ;
```

The above routine returns NULL if there has been an error. There are other ways of handling errors, and different languages have different support for error and exception handling. (More on that in the next section.)

Once you have these routines, you should of course test them. Set up some input data, and then print it out. Once you have it going properly, you can save the output in a file so you have a quick (and automatic) test that the input and output routines are working correctly. Now we have a routine that produces output that is both human *and* machine readable. Note that interactive input requires a different routine which will be considerably more complex. If is often said that the most complex part of any program is its **user interface**. But user interfaces are a topic for another book.

9.4.3 Testing mathematics

Now let's set up a test to see if the spline function *evaluation* routine is working correctly. First we need to have an evaluation routine to test:

```
/* spline_eval -- evaluates spline s at point t */
double spline_eval(spline *s, double t);
```

This can be tested by using the formulas that define the spline function (say from a numerical analysis text like Atkinson [4, pp. 166–173] or Burden and Faires [18, pp. 141–152]). Since our data structure uses M_i from Atkinson's presentation, we use the formulas that he gives directly in terms of these: let $h_i = x_{i+1} - x_i$. Then for $x_i \leq x \leq x_{i+1}$,

$$
s(x) = \frac{(x_{i+1} - x)^3 M_i + (x - x_i)^3 M_{i+1}}{6h_i} + \frac{(x_{i+1} - x)y_i + (x - x_i)y_{i+1}}{h_i}
$$
$$
- \frac{h_i}{6}[(x_{i+1} - x)M_i + (x - x_i)M_{i+1}].
\tag{9.1}
$$

Remember that even textbooks occasionally have mistakes, so we should verify this formula for ourselves if we can. If we fix some values we can compute a few values "by hand" and then write a short routines that tests these few values. Here is an example in C:

```
double t1_xlist[] = { 0.0,   1.0, 3.0, 4.5, 5.0 },
       t1_ylist[] = { 2.0,  -1.0, 0.5, 3.0, 1.0 },
       t1_Mlist[] = { 0.0,   1.0, 3.0, 0.0, -1.0 },
       t1_points[] = {    1.0,       1.5,      1.7,
                          2.3,       4.6 },
       t1_values[] = {   -1.0, -1.3125, -1.3395,
                      -0.9805,    2.608 };
spline *s;
int     length = 5, n_points = 5;


s = spline_create(5);
spline_setxy(s,t1_xlist,t1_ylist,5);
for ( i = 0; i < s->length; i++ )
  s->Mlist[i] = t1_Mlist[i];
fail = 0;
for ( i = 0; i < 5; i++ )
  if ( fabs(t1_values[i] -
       spline_eval(s,t1_points[i])) > 1e-12 )
  {
    printf("Spline eval'n test failed for test point %g\n",
           t1_point[i]);
    fail = 1;
  }
```

You should note some things about the test set used. The spline itself does not have equally spaced knots, and the spacings are not all integer. It is good to avoid places of symmetry for tests: the test points are not all at the knots (one is, but the others aren't). The test points are also not at the midpoints; however, they are integer multiples of 0.1. This means that we can actually represent the true values exactly once we know these values to an accuracy of 10^{-4}. The true values were computed interactively using MATLAB. Even though we have the exact values, we don't test for exact equality – remember we shouldn't test floating point numbers for equality!

Now we can test the spline *construction* routines. There are a number of different ones depending on the kind of spline you wish to construct: natural splines, periodic splines, clamped splines (derivatives at the end points are specified), or "not-a-knot" splines. We can construct a piecewise cubic function that has continuous second derivatives, and then work out the input to generate this function and its representation as a `spline` structure. Since natural splines have zero second derivatives at the end points, we will start with one of those. As a cubic spline is piecewise cubic, its second derivative is piecewise linear. Then we can integrate twice to get the spline function itself. So let's start with something like:

$$s''(x) = \begin{cases} x, & 0 \le x \le 1, \\ 1 - \frac{3}{2}(x-1), & 1 \le x \le 3, \\ -2 + 2(x-3), & 3 \le x \le 4. \end{cases} \tag{9.2}$$

Integrating once with $s'(0) = 1$ gives

$$s'(x) = \begin{cases} 1 + \frac{1}{2}x^2, & 0 \le x \le 1, \\ \frac{3}{2} + (x-1) - \frac{3}{4}(x-1)^2, & 1 \le x \le 3, \\ \frac{1}{2} - 2(x-3) + (x-3)^2, & 3 \le x \le 4. \end{cases} \tag{9.3}$$

Integrating again with $s(0) = -1$ gives

$$s(x) = \begin{cases} -1 + x + \frac{1}{6}x^3, & 0 \le x \le 1, \\ \frac{1}{6} + \frac{3}{2}(x-1) + \frac{1}{2}(x-1)^2 - \frac{1}{4}(x-1)^3, & 1 \le x \le 3, \\ 3\frac{1}{6} + \frac{1}{2}(x-3) - (x-3)^2 + \frac{1}{3}(x-3)^3, & 3 \le x \le 4. \end{cases} \tag{9.4}$$

This is the sort of calculation that should be double-checked, of course. You could try using Maple or Mathematica or MATLAB's symbolic toolbox to do these computations, or just to check them. We can then set the `xlist` and `ylist` arrays in the `spline` structure, and get the natural spline function construction function to compute `Mlist`. We know what `Mlist` should be: $M_i = s''(x_i)$. We can automatically check the resulting `Mlist`.

```
double t2_xlist[] = {  0.0,       1.0,        3.0,        4.0 },
        t2_ylist[] = { -1.0,  1.0/6.0,  19.0/6.0,       3.0 },
        t2_Mstart[] = {-1.0,      -1.0,       -1.0,      -1.0 },
        t2_Mlist[] = {  0.0,       1.0,       -2.0,       0.0 };
spline t2_dat;
t2_dat.length = 4;              t2_dat.xlist = t2_xlist;
t2_dat.ylist = t2_ylist;      t2_dat.Mlist = t2_Mstart;
spline_make_natural(&t2_dat);
for ( i = 0; i < 4; i++ )
  if ( fabs(t2_dat.Mlist[i]-t2_Mlist[i]) > 1e-12 )
  {
    printf("Error in computed Mlist[%d] = %g ",
           i, t2_dat.Mlist[i]);
    printf("Exact value: %g\n", t2_Mlist[i]);
  }
```

Note that we have specified to high precision what we expect from the test. For every test you should have a clear way of determining if the test was successful; the more precise and more stringent these conditions are, the better. Often you can check your computations against other ways of computing the same thing, but at the bottom level, we need to do some calculations by hand. We can test various properties of what we compute, but these tests can be fooled unless we do some hand-checking as well.

We are testing a class of implementations of cubic splines – those that compute `Mlist[i] = ` $s''(x_i)$. If we used the approach of Burden and Faires [18] where the spline is represented as a cubic function $a_i x^3 + b_i x^2 + c_i x + d_i$ on $[x_i, x_{i+1})$, these tests would not be applicable.

Which tests would be applicable for any algorithm? We can't computationally test directly for equality of functions in general. While it is not possible to write a guaranteed computational test for equality of functions, we *can* write computational tests for certain kinds of functions. For example, we can test if two cubic polynomials are the same by checking that they have the same values at any set of four distinct points. In fact this is part of a more general result that if two degree n polynomials agree at $n + 1$ points, then the two polynomials are the same. This is a consequence of the theory of polynomial interpolation [4]. Since a cubic spline is cubic polynomial on each interval $[x_i, x_{i+1}]$ we can check four spline values on each interval $[x_i, x_{i+1}]$ to see if the spline is a specific piecewise-cubic function.

But can we tell if a given function f is a cubic polynomial? No matter how many function evaluations $f(z_j)$ we compute, even if all of these match a cubic polynomial $p(z)$ there could be a point z^* where $f(z^*) \neq p(z^*)$. In spite of this, we can develop stringent computational tests that catch most, but not all, functions that are not cubic polynomials. If a function passes the test, but is *not* a cubic polynomial, it is a *false positive*. Such a test could be based on divided differences [4], which is also related to polynomial interpolation. For a cubic polynomial, all 4th- and higher-order divided differences should be zero. Some allowance should be made for roundoff error. How large should this allowance be? This requires careful analysis of the divided difference algorithm. If η_0 is a bound on the error in the function evaluations, then the error in the kth-order divided differences (assuming no further roundoff) for equally-spaced points $x_0, x_1, \ldots, x_k$ is $2^k(h^k k!)$ where the spacing is $h = x_1 - x_0 = x_2 - x_1 = \cdots = x_k - x_{k-1}$.

When you are designing initial test cases for numerical algorithms, don't use very large or very small (or "very extreme") values for your inputs. Since we always have roundoff errors, even if nothing else, we have to ignore small levels of error. If you use extreme values for your inputs, then these values could mean that some errors that are due to bugs will be smaller than our threshold for recognizing an error. Use modest values so that, for example, all terms in a sum are of similar sizes.

In selecting general test values, avoid "special" cases such as zero, or all values the same, or symmetrical inputs, etc. It may be worth creating tests for these special cases to make sure that they are handled correctly. But do not consider tests for special cases as any kind of substitute for general tests. Special case tests often conceal the effects of parts of the routine, and so conceal bugs in those parts.

Later you will want to "stress test" your code. Then large, extreme, and degenerate cases will be important, but the results will require more interpretation. For now we are focusing on correctness – removing basic bugs and misimplementations. For more on stress testing, see Section 9.10.

For methods like Newton's method it is particularly important that the Jacobian matrix computed is consistent with the function whose zeros we are trying to find. One of the most common bugs is computing an incorrect entry in the Jacobian matrix. How can we use the computer to help identify errors here? The Jacobian matrix can be approximated by using finite differences. You should consider writing a routine for computing approximate Jacobian matrices via finite differences for testing (exact) Jacobian matrix code. The error threshold will usually be much higher than unit roundoff, but you will be able to catch most common bugs this way. A routine like this might already be available; if so, use it.

9.5 Using debuggers

Debuggers are very useful for localizing bugs. One of the more popular debuggers in Unix environments is the GNU debugger gdb. There are also a number of GUI interfaces to gdb. One that is popular under Linux is ddd.

Debuggers can be most useful when the debugging information is incorporated into the executable file at compile time. For most Unix compilers this means using the -g compiler switch. For many compilers this is incompatible with the optimization (-O) switches, although not for the GNU compilers (gcc, gpp, etc.). Be warned, however, that optimization typically re-arranges code, and often strips the information that debuggers use.

One of the most important uses of a debugger is to find where (and why) a program crashed – to do this the debugger must be loaded with the executable file and the file containing a dump of the program's memory and status. In Unix the dump files are called *core files* and are usually called core or core.* where "*" is the process number. Once the files are loaded, a *stack backtrace* shows what routines were active when the crash occurred, and often the line in the source code where it occurred. Usually local variables can be printed, and routines called. Programs can also be run directly under the debugger's control, with *breakpoints* selected where the debugger will stop execution. This neither needs nor uses a core file. When this happens the value of variables can be viewed and the status of the program checked (again by looking at the stack backtrace). Provided the program has been compiled with debugging information included (-g for Unix compilers and gcc), debuggers can identify the line of source code where the event happened.

9.6 Debugging functional representations

In this section we will look at some of the issues in testing consistency of objects represented as *functions*. These approaches are **black box** approaches that just looks at how the input and output are related. You should also do **white box** testing that tracks *how* the function computes its values.

If we are using a functional representation of a matrix, we need to be careful that we really are representing a matrix and not something else. What we are really representing is a linear operator, which must satisfy the equation

$$A(\alpha x + \beta y) = \alpha \, Ax + \beta \, Ay \qquad \text{for all } x \text{ and } y \text{ and real } \alpha, \, \beta.$$

While we cannot possibly test this for all vectors x, y and real numbers α and β, we can test randomly generated vectors x, y and randomly generated values of α and β. For repeatability these vectors and values should be pseudorandom (that is, generated by some deterministic process), and the seed of the (pseudo)random number generator should be fixed before the test. We should automate these tests by writing a routine to compare $A(\alpha x + \beta y)$ and $\alpha \, Ax + \beta \, Ay$ for a number of pseudorandomly generated x, y and pseudorandomly generated α, β. Of course, we cannot expect these to be exactly equal because of roundoff errors. The size of the errors should be a modest multiple of $n \, \|A\| (|\alpha| \, \|x\| + |\beta| \, \|y\|) \, \mathbf{u}$; recall that $\mathbf{u}$ is the roundoff error. Here "modest" would be something like 10 or 20. If we had a buggy nonlinear function, the nonlinearities may depend on the size of x and y. So we should be able to vary the sizes of x and y. Using Java with the Jama matrix library [11, 10] we might write the body of a test function like this:

```
for ( int i = 0; i < 3; i++ )
{
double alpha = r.nextDouble() - r.nextDouble();
double beta  = r.nextDouble() - r.nextDouble();
Matrix x = Matrix.random(dim,1).minus(Matrix.random(dim,1));
Matrix y = Matrix.random(dim,1).minus(Matrix.random(dim,1));
Matrix Az1 = A.times(x).times(alpha).
    plus(A.times(y).times(beta));
Matrix Az2 = A.times(x.times(alpha).plus(y.times(beta)));
if ( Az1.minus(Az2).normInf() > eps )
   return false;
}
```

Note that r is a pseudo-random number generator. Other situations that can be handled in a similar way are tests comparing a matrix with its transpose where both represented by functions A and Atransp respectively. The crucial property is that

$$y^{\mathrm{T}}(Ax) = x^{\mathrm{T}}(A^{\mathrm{T}}y) \qquad \text{for all } x \text{ and } y.$$

Another example is comparing a nonlinear function f and its gradient ∇f. We can compare $(f(x_0 + \epsilon d) - f(x_0))/\epsilon$ with $\nabla f(x_0)^{\mathrm{T}}d$. Since the errors in this approximation are more than just roundoff errors, we have to be careful in how we choose the tolerance. The choice of this tolerance depends on the problem involved. There are two sources of error: one is due to the error in computing function values, including roundoff error; the other is due to the error in the linear approximation. Suppose the error in computing the function values is $\le \eta$ (for example, $\eta = 10\,\mathbf{u}\,\max_x |f(x)|$ would usually work). Then the error in $(f(x + \epsilon d) - f(x))/\epsilon$ would be at most $(2\eta + \mathbf{u}\,\max(|f(x + \epsilon d)|, |f(x)|))/\epsilon$. The error in $(f(x + \epsilon d) - f(x))/\epsilon$ due to the linear approximation is $\frac{1}{2}\epsilon d^{\mathrm{T}}\nabla^2 f(z)\,d$, where z is some point on the line between x and $x + \epsilon d$, and $\nabla^2 f(z)$ is the matrix of second derivatives. Adding these two error bounds gives a suitable tolerance. If you don't know the second derivatives, use an estimate multiplied by a modest "fudge factor" as the tolerance.

When designing tests of this kind, a good guiding principle is that of **scale invariance**. Ideally, scaling a function and its inputs should not alter the results of a test like this. Dealing with scaling of the inputs may mean making d an input to the routine, so we will first consider scaling the function itself:

$$f(x) = \alpha \, \widetilde{f}(x), \qquad \alpha > 0.$$

Then $\nabla f(x) = \alpha \, \nabla \widetilde{f}(x)$, and $f(x + \epsilon d) - f(x) = \alpha(\widetilde{f}(x + \epsilon d) - \widetilde{f}(x))$. This means that

$$\frac{f(x_0 + \epsilon d) - f(x_0)}{\epsilon} - \nabla f(x_0)^{\mathrm{T}}d = \alpha \left[\frac{\widetilde{f}(x_0 + \epsilon d) - \widetilde{f}(x_0)}{\epsilon} - \nabla \widetilde{f}(x_0)^{\mathrm{T}}d \right].$$

However, since $\|\nabla f(x_0)\| = \alpha \, \|\widetilde{f}(x_0)\|$, we note that $\|\nabla f(x_0)\| \, \|d\|$ does *not* scale with α:

$$\frac{\| f(x_0 + \epsilon d) - f(x_0) - \epsilon \nabla f(x_0)^{\mathrm{T}}d \|}{\epsilon \|\nabla f(x_0)\| \, \|d\|} = \frac{\| \widetilde{f}(x_0 + \epsilon d) - \widetilde{f}(x_0) - \epsilon \nabla \widetilde{f}(x_0)^{\mathrm{T}}d \|}{\epsilon \|\nabla \widetilde{f}(x_0)\| \, \|d\|}.$$

This approach would work well in most situations, but it is vulnerable to $\nabla f(x_0) \approx 0$. To deal with this there are some possibilities depending on how much user control is expected. The first is to have the user input a rough estimate of the scaling of the function α_0 and report

$$\frac{\| f(x_0 + \epsilon d) - f(x_0) - \epsilon \nabla f(x_0)^{\mathrm{T}}d \|}{\epsilon \, (\|\nabla f(x_0)\| + \alpha_0) \, \|d\|}.$$

Alternatively, for a non-expert, it may be best to avoid requiring a guess of the scaling of f and instead report

$$\frac{\|f(x_0 + \epsilon d) - f(x_0) - \epsilon \nabla f(x_0)^{\mathrm{T}} d\|}{\epsilon \left(\|\nabla f(x_0)\| + 1\right) \|d\|}.$$

9.7 Error and exception handling

Errors happen no matter what you do. What you do *when an error happens* is (in part) up to you.

Ideally you should check all the preconditions needed for a piece of software to work correctly. This is not always possible, especially when you have efficiency in mind. But if you at least do "sanity checking" to make sure that the data is self-consistent before continuing, you are likely to signal bugs close to their source and make testing and debugging much easier. This sort of checking usually has little impact on efficiency. If there is an impact on efficiency, then the checking code can be included inside if (debug) statements (or #ifdef/#endif in C/C++) so that the checking code can be removed by the compiler.

What should you do when the data passed to a routine are not self-consistent or clearly not appropriate? This will depend on the software environment in which you are working.

If you are using a C-type language, and the function you are in returns a pointer, then passing a NULL pointer is one way of signaling a major failure. This is what malloc does when it can't allocate memory. The user has to remember to check for this before continuing. This is the approach taken in the spline function spline_create above. This approach is not appropriate for functions returning ordinary scalar values. For example, for spline_eval to return zero on an error will mask the fact that an error has occurred, making it hard to find the bug that would follow.

A traditional Fortran approach is to pass (by reference) an integer variable called ifail, which is set to a particular value according to the error that occurs (usually negative), or some other value to indicate success (and perhaps some other information about the results of the routine). This should be checked by the calling routine, and the calling routine should probably pass ifail back to *its* calling routine. This can result in a cascade of returns in a Fortran program, and you can then decide what to do. If there is print out by the routines just before doing their returns, you can get an effective stack backtrace.

```
subroutine george(x, y, z, ifail)
  double precision x, y, z
  integer ifail
```

```
  ! some computation here
  call fred(x,y,ifail)
  if ( ifail < 0 )
    print *, 'Error detected in george, ifail =', ifail
    return
  endif
  ! more computation here
end
```

If necessary, consult the documentation of the routine generating the error to determine what kind of error has occurred.

Another approach is to set up an error handler, which might do something like print an error message and abort the program. Here is one way of setting up an error handler through a header file `error.h` and an implementation file `error.c` which allows each file to set up its own error handler. Here is `error.h`:

```
#ifndef ERROR_H
#define ERROR_H
void std_error_handler(char *file, int line, char *mesg);
void (*error_handler)(char *file, int line, char *mesg)
     = std_error_handler;
#endif /* ERROR_H */
```

The first two lines are to ensure that the definitions are not repeated (which compilers would flag as an error). While we normally don't intentionally include the same file more than once, if this file is basic to the system, it can be included many times over.

Here is `error.c`:

```
#include        <stdio.h>
#include        "error.h"

void std_error_handler(char *file, int line, char *mesg)
{
  fprintf(stdout,"Error in file \"%s\", line %d: %s\n",
          file, line, mesg);
  fprintf(stderr,"Error in file \"%s\", line %d: %s\n",
          file, line, mesg);
  exit(1);
}
```

The first `printf` sends a message to the standard output device, which may be a file as well as a terminal. The second `printf` sends the same message to the user's terminal.

Another approach is to raise an error or exception. This is partly language dependent; Ada, Common Lisp, C++, Java, SmallTalk and many other languages have a built-in error and exception handling mechanism. C has the routines `setjmp()` and `longjmp()` which can be used for this purpose – see Meschach [92] for an example of how they can be used – but they are not as flexible as C++ and Java which use `throw`/`catch` mechanisms. The `setjmp()`/`longjmp()` approach to error handling in C is also inconsistent with the `throw`/`catch` mechanism in C++, so if you are combining both C and C++ in a single program, you should be aware of this.

We start by creating an error class in C++, which holds the information that we want to pass back to whatever routine wants to handle the error. It can be trivial if you want:

```
class Error { };
```

At the point where an error occurs, we use the `throw` command to raise or throw an exception:

```
int harry(int x)
{
   if ( x < 0 )
     throw Error();
   else
     return 5*x;
}
```

This routine can be called by another (which might not know anything about errors):

```
int george(int x)
{
   return harry(1+2*x);
}
```

And this can be called by another routine (which might know something about errors):

```
int fred(int x)
{
   int y;
   try
```

```
    {
        y = george(x-2);
    }
    catch (Error e)
        {
            print_err_notice();
            throw; // re-throw error
        }
    return y;
}
```

We can try to execute the code in the braces following `try`. After the error is thrown before the completion of the code. After the error is thrown, control passes to the code following `catch`. Any data about the error that was `thrown` is in the `Error` object e. We can print out our location in the source code using a suitable macro:

```
#define print_err_notice() \
(cout << "Error caught in file \""<< \
            _FILE_ << "\" at line " << _LINE_ << "\n")
```

Then the error is re-thrown by "`throw;`". If an error is not caught, the program is aborted, and some summary information may be printed out.

9.8 Compare and contrast

Having a program that you can trust to compute what you want (even if it is slow, works in a different environment, on a different operating system, or avoids copyright issues) can still be used to test improved code. We can even write code ourselves for two different systems – say for MATLAB and for C or Fortran – and compare the results we get. This cross-referencing can help us to find bugs, and possibly numerical instabilities as well. Bugs are usually immediately evident by different outputs. If the systems use the floating-point system differently, numerical instabilities can become evident by divergent results, either immediately or gradually, but this is not guaranteed.

There may be other reasons for comparing codes. With MATLAB code we can do interactive testing quicker than we could using C of Fortran, while for very large problems, the C or Fortran version would run much faster than MATLAB. With interactive testing, repeatability can become a problem. Use the MATLAB diary command to record what you do. This record can be turned into a MATLAB script that be used repeatedly. Just don't forget to set the seed for the pseudorandom number generator interactively and in the script!

Often it is desirable to create a first implementation using a system such as MATLAB, and then re-implement the algorithm in a faster language. Then the new version can be tested against the same data as the MATLAB version, checking the intermediate values to identify if and where the new implementation diverges from the old to locate bugs.

9.9 Tracking bugs

In one-person software development it is tempting not to have any formal mechanism for tracking bugs – what they are, the code that is responsible for them, attempts to fix the bugs, and the results of these attempts. However, when a project starts getting larger or more complex, a more formal approach to tracking bugs becomes necessary. All version control systems have some level of support for bug tracking: every change has an associated description which can be printed out as part of the "log" for each file. The more recent systems such as Subversion and Bitkeeper have improved support for this. For example, with Subversion several related changes (which are commonly required for fixing a single bug) can have a single description, and it is possible to "roll-back" the source files to before the related changes.

While version control systems allow the description of changes, bugs should be described as they are discovered. This could be done using something as simple as using a text file for the bug description. Tracking the bug will require keeping this documentation synchronized with the actual code as modifications are made to fix the bug.

There are a number of bug-tracking software systems available. The *Bugzilla* system is an open-source system used for the Mozilla web browser project. All of these tracking systems are based on a database system and have bug reporting and updating components. Bug reports are entered into the system from users or developers saying what the problem is, and the context in which it occurs. Bug reports need to be specific about what is going wrong, the version of the software which goes wrong, the environment in which it goes wrong (operating system, compiler – if that is an issue, any data or files involved), and any error messages observed. Saying *"Bad answer for 10 × 10 matrix"* won't work; but saying *"Solving linear system with 10 × 10 Hilbert matrix and got zero correct digits in the solution instead of 2 or 3 correct digits as expected for double precision; see attached file containing input data and output"* is much more helpful. (Perhaps one of the variables was actually declared single precision?) With this information, the bug can be assigned to a person, who would receive notification of it along with information about its priority, severity, and the bug report(s). When a fix for the bug is found, a patch is created (say, by using the Unix command `diff -u old-version new-version` on all the changed files and concatenating the results) and passed to the bug control system. There may be an extra layer of quality assurance to make sure that the bug really is fixed before the modified version is shipped and the bug declared dead.

Often bug-tracking systems have a Web interface which allows developers to be distributed far and wide. There are a number of issues that bug-tracking software handles (or should handle) that go beyond what is needed for single-user development. We do not endorse any products here, and they may be over-kill for many small programming projects. But if your project is becoming decidedly large or complex, or you need to work with more than one other person (or even more than zero!), then you may need to use one of these.

9.10 Stress testing and performance testing

Stress testing is testing to see how well the algorithm behaves with large, extreme, or degenerate inputs. The key quantity to watch with stress testing is accuracy. Performance testing is about determining how the algorithm behaves with large-scale problems. The key quantities to watch with performance testing are time and memory usage.

9.10.1 Stressors: extreme inputs and degeneracy

Underflow and overflow can obviously be a problem for numerical algorithms. For example, computing the 2-norm

$$\|x\|_2 = \sqrt{\sum_{i=1}^{n} x_i^2}$$

in the obvious way can fail if $\sum_i x_i^2$ overflows. This can happen even with $n = 1$ if $|x_1| > \sqrt{\mathrm{fl}_{max}}$ where fl_{max} is the maximum real floating-point number (not Inf). This can be remedied by first dividing each x_i by $scale = \max_i |x_i|$, or a power of two close to this, computing the 2-norm in the usual way, and then multiplying the result by $scale$. Other examples can be found in Chapter 2 on floating-point arithmetic.

Degenerate situations, where some quantities are nearly equal, can also cause severe problems. Since degeneracies don't require extreme input values, they can be more subtle and less obvious at first. But they are at least as important as

Table 9.1. *Gaps in smallest two eigenvalues for Wilkinson example*

n	gap	n	gap	n	gap
4	5.85×10^{-1}	10	4.14×10^{-4}	16	5.28×10^{-9}
6	1.02×10^{-1}	12	1.33×10^{-5}	18	7.09×10^{-11}
8	8.53×10^{-3}	14	3.06×10^{-7}	20	7.63×10^{-13}

extreme inputs. Here are some examples of degenerate situations that require special consideration:

- matrices that are singular or nearly singular;
- geometric objects (such as polygons) that touch at a corner;
- repeated eigenvalues, or nearly repeated eigenvalues, of a matrix.

It is tempting to argue that since degenerate (and nearly degenerate) situations are rare, there is no need to write software to handle these situations. But this would be wrong. Sometimes, near degeneracy happens where it can be proved that degeneracy cannot happen. One example comes from computing eigenvalues of symmetric tridiagonal matrices:

$$
T = \begin{bmatrix}
\alpha_1 & \beta_1 & & & \\
\beta_1 & \alpha_2 & \beta_2 & & \\
& \beta_2 & \alpha_3 & \ddots & \\
& & \ddots & \ddots & \beta_{n-1} \\
& & & \beta_{n-1} & \alpha_n
\end{bmatrix}.
$$

If $\beta_i \neq 0$ for all i then this matrix *cannot have repeated eigenvalues*. But they can be *nearly* repeated. Consider the case where $\beta_i = -1$ for all i, and $\alpha_i = n/2 - |i - (n+1)/2|$. A table of these gaps for various n according to GNU Octave is shown in Table 9.1. This example was originally devised by Wilkinson [106, Chap. 5, §45, p. 308]. Note how rapidly the gaps go to zero! It can be shown that the gaps go to zero at a faster-than-exponential rate.

Stress testing can not only help to determine the robustness and limits of correctly implemented algorithms, it can also help identify the existence of bugs. However, this is a matter of judgment – implementations that would be correct under exact arithmetic might fail due to roundoff error in extreme situations. Sometimes small changes in how an operation is implemented can avoid these problems. Sometimes lack of robustness is intrinsic in the problem. In that case, you will have to think carefully about what your objective truly is for a numerical algorithm.

9.10.2 Performance testing

Performance of numerical codes has three parts: speed, memory, *and* accuracy. For direct methods (which should produce an accurate answer with one application) the three components are more-or-less independent: for given input data the algorithm runs once, uses a certain amount of memory, and produces its answer – the accuracy of the answer and the time and memory used to achieve it should then be measured. The point then is to see how the time, memory and accuracy behave as the problem changes. Typically, for speed, it is only the size of the input that matters; for accuracy, it can depend on the kind of input, and here it is important to consider stress testing to reveal problems with accuracy.

On the other hand, methods that rely on iteration have a trade-off between the time taken and the accuracy obtained. This is particularly true of iterative methods for large linear and nonlinear systems [7] and methods for ordinary differential equations [48, 49]. To display this trade-off it is often worthwhile to have a work–accuracy diagram, plotting the error obtained against the work required. Usually this requires a logarithmic scale for the error, and possibly for the work required as well, depending on the relationship between work and accuracy. For iterative methods, the error typically decreases exponentially or even faster in the number of iterations, so the work should be plotted in a linear plot; on the other hand, an ordinary differential equation solver typically has an error of $O(h^p)$ where h is the time-step, and the work is proportional to $1/h$. This gives an algebraic relationship between work and accuracy: error $\propto$ work^p. In this case, using logarithmic scales on both axes is better.

When doing performance testing there is also the question of *what* to measure. While time is the ultimate measure of speed of an algorithm, it can change depending on the compiler, the compiler options (especially the optimization options), the CPU, the clock speed, the type and amount of main memory, the operating system, and even how many people are using the system. Also, times can be misleading on interpreted systems such as MATLAB, since re-writing a for loop in terms of an intrinsic operation can result in *much* better performance[1] – re-writing in a compiled language could make a poorly performing algorithm in MATLAB an excellent algorithm in Fortran 90 or C++. Often it is better to measure some quantity that is more intrinsically related to the algorithm, such as the number of iterations or the number of steps, than the raw time taken. For proper comparisons, of course, if you are comparing between two substantially different iterations, you should measure comparable quantities, such as the number of function evaluations in a differential equation solver, or the number of matrix–vector multiplies in an

---

[1] Computing the product of two random 100×100 matrices using for loops took roughly 1000 times as long as the intrinsic matrix multiply in GNU Octave (a MATLAB work-alike).

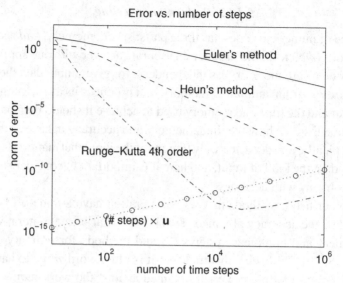

Figure 9.1. Work–accuracy diagram for the Kepler problem.

iterative linear equation solver. Record this information for later comparison. It can
also be used for debugging!

Here is one example of a work-accuracy diagram for solving the Kepler problem:

$$\frac{d^2\mathbf{x}}{dt^2} = -\frac{\mathbf{x}}{\|\mathbf{x}\|^3}, \qquad \mathbf{x}(0) = [1, \ 0]^T, \qquad \frac{d\mathbf{x}}{dt}(0) = [0, \ 1]^T,$$

corresponding to the motion of a planet about a much more massive sun. The above
initial conditions have the exact solution $\mathbf{x}(t) = [\cos t, \ \sin t]^T$. Using three methods:
Euler's method (error $= O(h)$), Heun's method (error $= O(h^2)$), and the standard
Runge–Kutta 4th-order explicit method (error $= O(h^4)$), the authors obtained the
work–accuracy diagram in Figure 9.1; the error is given by $\|\mathbf{x}(T) - \mathbf{x}_N\|$ where
$Nh = T$; we took $T = 10$. Since Euler's method uses just one function evaluation
per step, $N =$ number of function evaluations, but for Heun's method there are
two function evaluations per step so $N = \frac{1}{2}$(number of function evaluations), and
for the 4th-order Runge–Kutta method there are four function evaluations per step,
so $N =$ (number of function evaluations)/4. All computations were done in double
precision.

The slopes of the curves (where they are roughly straight) are close to -1
for Euler's method, -2 for Heun's method, and -4 for the 4th-order Runge–
Kutta method, reflecting the order of the methods. The first time we tried this,
we obtained a slope of about -2.9 for the "4th-order Runge–Kutta method", indicating 3rd-order accuracy (rather than 4th order). This did not seem right, and
investigating further revealed a bug in the code. The accuracy of the 4th-order

Runge–Kutta method bottoms out at about 10^{-13} for 1.2×10^4 function evaluations. Since 10^{-13} is getting close to $\mathbf{u} \approx 2.2 \times 10^{-16}$ for double precision, roundoff error is a likely explanation for this "bottoming out" of the accuracy. Indeed, since round-off error seems essentially random, summing N numbers of about equal size without cancellation would result in an error of size about $\mathbf{u}\sqrt{N}$. Setting $N = 1.2 \times 10^4$ would give a probable error of about 2.4×10^{-14}. If we used the upper bound of $\mathbf{u}\,N$ we would get an error bound due to roundoff error of 2.6×10^{-12}, which is substantially larger than the true error. If the errors in the function evaluations are more like $5\mathbf{u}$ instead of $\mathbf{u}$, we would get a probable error of $5\mathbf{u}\sqrt{N} \approx 1.02 \times 10^{-13}$, which is very close to the true error. This is not to say that the estimate of $5\mathbf{u}$ is very accurate for the relative errors in the function evaluations. But it does indicate that a substantial part of the error is roundoff error. Increasing the number of steps only makes this contribution from roundoff larger.

9.11 Random test data

Often random, or more accurately pseudo-random, test data are used to test numerical and other algorithms. For such problems, the solution is not known directly, but the results of an algorithm can often be tested against the input. For example, given an algorithm to compute the LU factorization of a matrix and an input A then the resulting L and U can be checked by computing the norm of $A - LU$. If the norm is a modest multiple of the unit roundoff $\mathbf{u}$, then the algorithm is likely to be correct.

In the following discussion, the term "random" is used to mean "pseudo-random". While the two terms are often confused, it is important to remember than any deterministic method for computing numbers cannot, by definition, be considered random. As John von Neumann said,

anyone who considers the arithmetical generation of random digits is, of course, in a state of sin.

Random test data can be useful as a check against most kinds of bugs. However, if a bug is found using random test data, it is important that the random number generators can produce repeatable results – say by using a seed for the random number generator. Without this, bug fixes cannot be checked.

Remember that

testing with random data is no substitute for careful stress testing!

Many bugs occur with special or extreme values or data sets. Problems with floating point arithmetic often occur with integers plus $\frac{1}{2}$, $\frac{1}{4}$ or $\frac{1}{8}$, since the choice of whether to round up or round down can cause difficulties in some cases. Random matrices are usually not ill conditioned. To test for ill-conditioned matrices, try Hilbert matrices [4], or other examples if you want non-symmetric matrices. For ill-conditioned matrices we do not expect full accuracy in the solutions, but we should aim for small residuals. Random matrices have other properties [34], which can make them much less useful for stress testing.

For non-numerical problems as well, random test data is a poor substitute for carefully designed stress tests. Consider, for example, quicksort. It is well known that quicksort with random data takes $O(n \log n)$ time on average, and with high probability. But its worst case time is $\sim c n^2$. You would have to do a very large number of random tests to see this worst case behavior. To see it, a carefully constructed data set would be needed.

10

Exercises

1. We wish to design in C++ a complex number system C++ allows operator overloading, so we can create code that looks like this:

```
complex z1, z2, w;
z1.set(1.0,2.0);   // z1 = 1  +  2i
z2.set(4.5,-1.2); // z2 = 4.5-1.2i
w = z1*z2;
cout << "w = " << w << "\n";
```

To do this we create a complex class:

```
public class complex {
   private:
      double  re, im;
   public:
      complex(double re_val=0.0, double im_val=0.0)
      { re = re_val; im = im_val; }
      complex operator+(complex z)
      { return complex(re+z.re,im+z.im); }
      ...
}
```

How are the arguments passed? By value or by reference? Is it efficient? When complex variables are created, are they created on the stack, or in the memory heap? How would you change this so that you could (automatically) get complex arithmetic with single precision or extended precision real and imaginary parts?

2. Now let us consider a similar C++ class for vectors. We should be able to use it like this:

```
Vector  x(10), y(10);   // create two 10-vectors
double  alpha, beta;
Vector  z = alpha*x+beta*y;
```

The class to implement this would look something like this:

```
public class Vector {
  private:
    int       dim;
    double *array;
  public:
    Vector(int n)
    {  array = new double[n]; dim = n; }
    int dimension() { return dim; }
    Vector operator+(Vector y)
        {  Vector sum(y.dimension());
           for(int i = 0; i < y.dimension(); i++ )
               sum.array[i] = array[i]+y.array[i];
        }
        ...
}
```

How are the arguments passed? Is it efficient? Is there a better way of passing the arguments? Re-write the above code with any improvements you have identified.

3. Read and discuss Sections 1 and 2 of the paper *Developing numerical libraries in Java* [11] by Boisvert, Dongarra, Pozo, Remington, and Stewart. Is it worth developing a VectorDouble class specifically for vectors of double precision numbers? Can you think of any alternatives?

4. An idea that has become important in software design is *composability*. That is, it should be possible to combine (compose) a software design technique with other techniques or with itself. Here we explore this idea in a particular context.

   A two-dimensional integral over a rectangular region with edges aligned with the axes can be written as a nested double integral

$$\int_a^b \int_c^d f(x, y) \, dx \, dy = \int_a^b \left(\int_c^d f(x, y) \, dx \right) dy.$$

So, in principle, a routine for doing a one-dimensional integral should be usable for computing two-dimensional integrals over rectangles. However, the function in the inner integral $x \mapsto f(x, y)$ changes as the value of y changes, so we need to pass this (changing) environment to the inner function. The outer function is the function $y \mapsto \int_c^d f(x, y) \, dy$. All these functions as well as the function $(x, y) \mapsto f(x, y)$ need to be represented in the same way.

   Given a function integrate1d that implements integration over an interval using
   (a) pointer passing,
   (b) reverse communication, or
   (c) classes
   to represent the environment of the function, write a function integrate2d that computes the two-dimensional integral.
   [**Hint:** For the pointer passing approach, our original function would look like this:

```
double (*f)(void *params, double x, double y);
```

and the one-dimensional integration routine would be:

```
double integrate1d(double (*f)(void *, double,double),
   void *params,
      double a, double b, double tolerance);
```

The environment of the inner function $x \mapsto f(x, y)$ must contain y as well as f and its environment. So we create a structure that contains this information:

```
struct inner {
   double (*f)(void *,double,double);
   void *f_params;
   double y;
};
```

which we use like this:

```
double inner(struct inner *in, double x)
{
   return (*in->f)(in->params,x,in->y);
}
```

Then to compute the integral $\int_c^d f(x, y)\,dx$ we execute code such as:

```
struct inner my_in;
my_in.f = f;
my_in.params = params;
my_in.y = y;
return integrate1d(inner,&my_in,c,d);
```

Now what is the environment of the function $y \mapsto \int_c^d f(x, y)\,dx$? This environment includes f and its environment, but also c and d, and the error tolerance for the inner integral. So let us have another structure that contains these things:

```
struct outer {
   double (*f)(void *, double, double);
   void    *params;
   double c, d, eps;
};
```

The outer function can then be written in the form

```
double outer(struct outer *out, double y)
{
   struct inner in;
   in.f = out->f;
   in.params = out->params;
   in.y = y;
   return integrate1d(inner,&in,out->c,out->d,
      out->eps);
}
```

Then the outer integral $\int_a^b \left(\int_c^d f(x, y)\, dx \right) dy$ can be computed with this code:

```
double integrate2d(double (*f)(void *, double,double),
    void *params, double a, double b,
    double c, double d, double eps)
{
    struct outer my_out;
    my_out.c = c;
    my_out.d = d;
    my_out.eps = eps;
    my_out.f = f;
    my_out.params = params;
    return integrate1d(outer,&my_out,a,b,eps);
}
```

The overhead is some "glue" code that links the functions through the two structures containing the environments for the one-dimensional functions.]

5. Repeat the previous exercise using classes in an object-oriented language to compute a double integral $\int_a^b \int_c^d f(x, y)\, dy\, dx$ as a repeated one-dimensional integral.

6. In October 1960 the US Strategic Air Command was put on high alert because their systems had identified a massive nuclear missile strike from the Soviet Union. After some time it was realized that it was a mis-identification of radar reflections off the moon [56].

   (Similar mistaken identifications had occurred before, including alerts triggered by a flock of geese.)

   (a) What kind of testing can you think of that would identify this problem before the identification software was put in service?

   (b) Can you think of other possible events or objects that could be mis-identified as a threat?

   (c) What do examples like this imply for how software is designed? In particular, how would you deal with wrong or undesirable behavior in critical real-time software?

7. The developers of LAPACK (see Section 12.9) have decided to continue the development of the library only in Fortran 77. For other languages they will continue providing *interfaces* to the Fortran 77 library in languages such as Fortran 95, C, C++, and Java. Critically evaluate this strategy for a large scientific software package that is publicly funded, such as LAPACK. How would you handle cross-language portability problems? As these programming languages (except Fortran 77) develop, what changes would be needed or desirable for the interfaces?

8. Can you give some examples of layering of scientific or numerical software?
   [**Hint:** Consider MATLAB and LAPACK and BLAS. Alternatively, have a look at PETSc.]

Part III

Efficiency in Time, Efficiency in Memory

11

Be algorithm aware

Be aware of algorithms that can be useful to you. There are many textbooks on algorithms and data structure. One of the more encyclopedic is the book by Cormen, Leiserson, Rivest, and Stein [23].

Scientific and engineering software almost always needs to be efficient in both time and memory. You should first consider optimizing at a high level, choosing data structures and algorithms that are inherently efficient. At a lower level, you should understand how computers work, and how to efficiently use modern computer architectures.

Choosing good algorithms and data structures is the foundation of designing efficient software. Without this, no amount of low-level tweaking of the code will make it run fast. This is especially true for large problems. By tuning your code you could gain an improvement of anything from, say, a factor of two to a factor of ten, in the speed of an algorithm. But moving from an algorithm that is $O(n^3)$ in time and $O(n^2)$ in memory to one that is $O(n^2)$ in time and $O(n)$ in memory can give you a much greater benefit, especially if $n \approx 10\,000$ or larger. Sometimes you can get approximate algorithms that are fast, but the speed will depend on how accurately you want the answer. Here you need to know the problem well in order to see how large an error can be tolerated.

11.1 Numerical algorithms

Since the development of electronic digital computers (and even well before then) there has been a great deal of development of numerical algorithms. Many are highly efficient, accurate, and robust. Apart from checking numerical analysis texts, you should have a look at advanced textbooks like *Matrix Computations* [46], and even the research literature. Other sources include *Collected Algorithms of the ACM* [38], which can provide many surprisingly effective algorithms. *Collected Algorithms* includes discrete algorithms as well as numerical algorithms, such as in-place transposition of non-square matrices, sparse matrix bandwidth reduction, and Euclid's algorithm. Most of the implementations are in Fortran.

You should be aware that broad techniques for constructing algorithms, such as divide and conquer, are often applicable to numerical algorithms. One of the best examples of this is the Fast Fourier Transform [22] for computing discrete Fourier transforms

$$y_k = \sum_{l=0}^{n-1} e^{2\pi ikl/n} x_l, \quad i = \sqrt{-1}$$

in $O(n \log n)$ time and $O(n)$ memory. If the input vector x_l is split into even-index (x_{2l}) and odd-index (x_{2l+1}) parts, we can compute the discrete Fourier transform of each part, and combine these to obtain the output (y_k).

Sometimes linear systems with special structure can have efficient solution methods. An example of this is the solution of symmetric Toeplitz equations (which arise in the context of signal processing, for example):

$$
\begin{bmatrix}
r_0 & r_1 & r_2 & \cdots & r_{n-1} \\
r_1 & r_0 & r_1 & \cdots & r_{n-2} \\
r_2 & r_1 & r_0 & \cdots & r_{n-3} \\
\vdots & \vdots & \vdots & \ddots & \vdots \\
r_{n-1} & r_{n-2} & r_{n-3} & \cdots & r_0
\end{bmatrix}
\begin{bmatrix}
x_0 \\
x_1 \\
x_2 \\
\cdots \\
x_{n-1}
\end{bmatrix}
=
\begin{bmatrix}
b_0 \\
b_1 \\
b_2 \\
\cdots \\
b_{n-1}
\end{bmatrix}.
$$

The Levenberg algorithm for solving Toeplitz systems of this type is described in [46]; it can solve this system in $O(n^2)$ time and $O(n)$ memory instead of the usual $O(n^3)$ time and $O(n^2)$ memory needed for LU factorization.

Some fast methods are not exact, but only approximate (even with exact real arithmetic). Examples of this include multipole methods [20, 47], which were first used to compute approximate sums of the form

$$\sum_{i=0}^{N-1} m_i m_j \frac{\mathbf{x}_i - \mathbf{x}_j}{\|\mathbf{x}_i - \mathbf{x}_j\|_2^3}, \quad j = 0, 1, \ldots, N-1.$$

With the multipole method, all N sums can be computed with an error bounded by ϵ in $O(N \log N \log(1/\epsilon))$ time. These algorithms work by first creating a hierarchy of clusters, and then approximating clusters by a multipole approximation.

Another idea that uses hierarchies is multigrid methods. These are methods for solving large linear (and occasionally, nonlinear) systems of equations, usually those arising from elliptic partial differential equations. These are iterative methods (and therefore only give approximate answers), but are among the fastest iterative methods available. Multigrid methods, when applied to equations from nice discretizations of nice elliptic partial differential equations, can solve systems of N

equations in N unknowns to an accuracy of ϵ in $O(N \log(1/\epsilon))$ time and $O(N)$ memory. We will discuss multigrid methods again in Chapter 10.

A final example of divide-and-conquer is a matrix multiplication algorithm called Strassen's algorithm. The remarkable fact about this algorithm is that it can compute the product of two $n \times n$ matrices in $O(n^{\alpha})$ time where α is less than three. Consider the block matrix product

$$\begin{bmatrix} A_{11} & A_{12} \\ A_{21} & A_{22} \end{bmatrix} \begin{bmatrix} B_{11} & B_{12} \\ B_{21} & B_{22} \end{bmatrix} = \begin{bmatrix} C_{11} & C_{12} \\ C_{21} & C_{22} \end{bmatrix}.$$

Strassen in 1969 [95] found a way to write the block matrices C_{ij} using seven block matrix multiplies instead of the usual eight, but with 18 block matrix additions instead of the usual four. If we perform the seven block multiplications recursively we get Strassen's algorithm. From this information we get a total of $O(n^{\log_2 7})$ floating point operations provided n is a power of two. Strassen's algorithm has not been widely adopted for two main reasons: (1) concern over some subtle questions of numerical stability, and (2) the matrices have to have $n > 660$ for Strassen's algorithm to beat the standard algorithm for matrix multiplication. It turns out that the second reason is only partly true: by stopping the recursion and applying the standard algorithm for small matrices the cutoff is reduced to $n \approx 18$. Still the complexity of implementing Strassen's algorithm has been a deterrent to widespread use. For more information regarding the accuracy of Strassen's algorithm see [14, 78].

Another general issue that commonly arises is the use of sparse matrices. Dense matrix arithmetic is straightforward to use and implement; however, if you have large problems, in all probability the matrices involved are sparse, or have some structure that does not require all n^2 entries to be separately stored. There are many sparse matrix packages available (unfortunately, most are mutually incompatible) and worth considering. But beware: many operations destroy sparsity. Inverses of sparse matrices are almost never sparse, and even products of sparse matrices are far less sparse than the original matrices. As always, don't try computing matrix inverses if all you want to do is to solve linear systems. Use the factored matrices instead.

11.2 Discrete algorithms

Discrete algorithms are the province of "classical" computer science. Nevertheless, they are very often key to efficient implementation of numerical algorithms. There are numerous textbooks on these "classical" algorithms, such as [23, 50, 66]. If you are new to the area, it is probably easiest to start with [50].

Amongst the most "classical" of these algorithms are sorting algorithms, especially quicksort and mergesort, which can sort N items in $O(N \log N)$ time.

Quicksort has the additional benefit that it needs no additional memory. But this is not the end of methods you should know about. Heaps (or priority queues) are a fast way of storing a collection where you want to repeatedly get the smallest of the collection.

Other algorithms that you should be aware of are quicksort-based algorithms for finding the kth-largest item out of N in just $O(N)$ time independently of N. An example of this is the problem of finding the median of N numbers; it can be done in $O(N)$ time without having to spend $O(N \log N)$ time sorting the list.

Sets can be represented in a number of ways (as an array of bits, as a list, or in a tree), but a partition (a collection of disjoint sets whose union is given) is probably most efficiently represented by a find–union data structure. A find–union data structure can quickly tell you if two elements belong to the same set of a partition, and can be efficiently modified to represent the result of replacing two sets in the partition by their union. This can be very efficient for various kinds of clustering algorithms. These data structures are also very important for sparse matrix factorizations.

Computational geometry is a more specialized area, but is of crucial importance for computer graphics and many kinds of simulations and for mesh generation for finite element methods. There are many kinds of problem and technique developed for computational geometry that can be useful. For example, did you know that there are algorithms for finding the two closest points out of a set of N points in the plane that take just $O(N \log N)$ time? Questions about convex sets and convex hulls lead to problems in linear programming. Most computational geometry tasks are about low-dimensional problems (no more than three dimensions, usually). There are $O(N)$ algorithms for linear programming in d dimensions for fixed d. (The hidden constant in the "O" grows something like $d!$ so their algorithms are not suitable for most large-scale linear programming problems.) Some good references for algorithms in computational geometry are [27, 68].

Many discrete algorithms do *not* have efficient algorithms. This is the subject of the theory of NP-completeness. Although this theory is described in most textbooks on algorithms, the standard reference is still Garey and Johnson's book [42]. This book not only describes the theory and its uses, it has an extensive list of problems that are known to be NP complete or NP hard. There are a number of open questions that have been resolved since their book, but the most important open problem, whether NP problems have polynomial time algorithms, remains unanswered.

What do you do if your problem is NP complete or NP hard? Since we cannot do the exact problem quickly, it is often quite acceptable to solve a problem approximately. Approximations and heuristics for NP complete or NP hard problems are a large and important research area, and many things are known – both positive and negative. To find out more, you can have a look at Garey and Johnson or the research literature. The *Journal of Algorithms* has had many papers on NP completeness and approximation algorithms in it. Some problems are (apparently) hard while not being NP-hard. For more information, see [50].

11.3 Numerical algorithm design techniques

There are a number of techniques for designing algorithms, numerical and otherwise. While there are too many to present here, we will present two that seem particularly useful for numerical problems. The first is design through recursion. This approach seems especially useful for many matrix computations. The second is for developing iterative methods by treating an approximation as if it was exact. This can be used for a great many nonlinear problems as well as matrix computations.

11.3.1 Design through recursion

Design through recursion reduces a larger problem to a smaller problem. Usually the reduction is to a problem that is smaller by one in some crucial quantity, although sometimes it can be to a problem that is much smaller (say, half the size). As long as there is a bottom limit that can be dealt with easily, this approach can result in effective algorithms. Here is an example.

Consider the problem of solving (for $\mathbf{z}$) the symmetric Toeplitz linear system

$$
\begin{bmatrix}
r_0 & r_1 & \cdots & r_n \\
r_1 & r_0 & \cdots & r_{n-1} \\
\vdots & \vdots & \ddots & \vdots \\
r_n & r_{n-1} & \cdots & r_0
\end{bmatrix}
\begin{bmatrix}
z_0 \\
z_1 \\
\vdots \\
z_n
\end{bmatrix}
=
\begin{bmatrix}
r_1 \\
r_2 \\
\vdots \\
r_{n+1}
\end{bmatrix}.
$$

This kind of system arises often in certain statistical estimation problems.

Let's write this as $R_n \mathbf{z}_n = \mathbf{r}_n$. Let $\check{\mathbf{r}}_n = [r_{n+1},\ r_n,\ \ldots,\ r_1]^\mathsf{T}$ be the reversed vector of $\mathbf{r}_n$. Then we can partition the linear system as:

$$
\begin{bmatrix}
R_{n-1} & \check{\mathbf{r}}_{n-1} \\
(\check{\mathbf{r}}_{n-1})^\mathsf{T} & r_0
\end{bmatrix}
\begin{bmatrix}
\mathbf{z}_n^* \\
z_n^*
\end{bmatrix}
=
\begin{bmatrix}
\mathbf{r}_{n-1} \\
r_{n+1}
\end{bmatrix}.
$$

That is, we have $R_{n-1}\mathbf{z}_n^* + \check{\mathbf{r}}_{n-1}z_n^* = \mathbf{r}_{n-1}$ and $(\check{\mathbf{r}}_{n-1})^\mathsf{T}\mathbf{z}_n^* + r_0 z_n^* = r_{n+1}$. Now let's assume that we know $\mathbf{z}_{n-1}$, where $R_{n-1}\mathbf{z}_{n-1} = \mathbf{r}_{n-1}$. Note that if we reverse all the components of $\mathbf{r}_{n-1}$ and $\mathbf{z}_{n-1}$ we have $R_{n-1}\check{\mathbf{z}}_{n-1} = \check{\mathbf{r}}_{n-1}$. Then we can put $\mathbf{z}_n^* = \mathbf{z}_{n-1} - z_n^*\check{\mathbf{z}}_{n-1}$. The only unknown here is z_n^*. But we can work that out from the second equation: $(\check{\mathbf{r}}_{n-1})^\mathsf{T}\mathbf{z}_n^* + r_0 z_n^* = r_{n+1}$. Substituting our formula for $\mathbf{z}_n^*$ we get

$$
(\check{\mathbf{r}}_{n-1})^\mathsf{T}(\mathbf{z}_{n-1} - z_n^*\check{\mathbf{z}}_{n-1}) + r_0 z_n^* = r_{n+1}.
$$

That is,

$$(r_0 - (\check{\mathbf{r}}_{n-1})^{\mathsf{T}} \check{\mathbf{z}}_{n-1}) z_n^* = r_{n+1} - (\check{\mathbf{r}}_{n-1})^{\mathsf{T}} \mathbf{z}_{n-1}.$$

This new formula gives us z_n^*; substituting it into $\mathbf{z}_n^* = \mathbf{z}_{n-1} - z_n^* \check{\mathbf{z}}_{n-1}$ gives us the other components of $\mathbf{z}_n$.

We need a starting point for the recursive algorithm. This is easy: if $n = 1$ our equation just becomes

$$r_0 z_0 = r_1, \qquad \text{so } z_0 = r_1/r_0.$$

The resulting algorithm takes just $O(n^2)$ operations instead of $O(n^3)$ for Gaussian Elimination or LU factorization. Also note that the resulting algorithm can be written using a for or do loop and no recursive function calls by computing $z_0 = \mathbf{z}_0$, $\mathbf{z}_1, \mathbf{z}_2$, etc., in order. This is an example of replacing ***tail-end recursion*** with a loop. For more information about tail-end recursion, see [23, p. 162].

11.3.2 Treat approximations as if they are exact

Newton's method is based on the approximation

$$f(x + p) \approx f(x) + f'(x)\, p \quad \text{for } p \text{ small.}$$

If we want to solve the equation $f(x + p) = 0$, then one approach is to treat the approximation $f(x + p) \approx f(x) + f'(x)\, p$ *as if it were exact*. That is, we set

$$f(x) + f'(x)\, p = 0.$$

This is an equation we can solve (for p):

$$p = -f(x)/f'(x).$$

Our new estimate of the solution is $x + p = x - f(x)/f'(x)$.

Of course, our original approximation was not exact, so $x + p$ is not expected to be the exact solution, but it should be much better than x. This leads us to the iterative method

$$x_{n+1} = x_n - f(x_n)/f'(x_n),$$

which is nothing other than Newton's method.

Another example comes from matrix computations. Suppose we wish to solve $A\mathbf{x}^* = \mathbf{b}$, but we only know an approximate inverse B. Suppose we have an approximate solution $\mathbf{x}$. Then $A(\mathbf{x}^* - \mathbf{x}) = \mathbf{b} - A\mathbf{x}$, so

$$\mathbf{x}^* = \mathbf{x} + A^{-1}(\mathbf{b} - A\mathbf{x})$$
$$\approx \mathbf{x} + B(\mathbf{b} - A\mathbf{x}).$$

Instead of treating this as an approximation to the exact solution, treat it as the exact value of an improved approximation:

$$\mathbf{x}_{n+1} = \mathbf{x}_n + B(\mathbf{b} - A\mathbf{x}_n).$$

As long as all the eigenvalues of $I - BA$ are smaller than one, we will get convergence of our method: $\mathbf{x}_n \to \mathbf{x}^*$ as $n \to \infty$. This iterative algorithm is called *iterative refinement*.

   Numerical analysis abounds with many other examples of this principle: numerical integration and differentiation formulas derived from the exact integral or derivative of a polynomial approximation:

- Richardson extrapolation of a series $x_1, x_2, \ldots \to x^*$ by assuming $x_{k+1} - x^* = \alpha(x_k - x^*)$;
- Heun's method for $dy/dt = f(y)$ with step size h, where $y_{n+1} = y_n + (h/2)[f(y_n) + f(y_{n+1})]$ is approximated by $y_{n+1} = y_n + (h/2)[f(y_n) + f(y_n + h\, f(y_n))]$;
- and multipole methods which (in their simplest form) approximate $\sum_i m_i(\mathbf{x} - \mathbf{x}_i)/\|\mathbf{x} - \mathbf{x}_i\|^3$ by $m^*(\mathbf{x} - \mathbf{x}^*)/\|\mathbf{x} - \mathbf{x}^*\|^3$ with $m^* = \sum_i m_i$ and $\mathbf{x}^* = (1/m^*)\sum_i m_i\mathbf{x}_i$.

12

Computer architecture and efficiency

If you really need your program to run as fast as possible, you need to understand modern computer hardware. The most crucial concept in all this is that of a *memory hierarchy*. You should also understand some things about *optimizing compilers*. Optimizing compilers know more about the target architecture(s) than most programmers, so we should write code that the compiler can make best use of. Keep simple, intelligible (unoptimized) code in comments for future reference since architectures and compilers change frequently.

12.1 Caches and memory hierarchies

Since the advent of computers, CPUs have been getting faster. Memories have been getting faster too, but not fast enough to keep up with the CPUs. As a result, CPUs are becoming starved of the data they need to compute with. The fastest memory in a CPU consists of the *registers*; operations act directly on the values in the registers. In effect, the registers can be accessed in one *clock cycle*. (This means that if you have a 1GHz computer, registers can usually be accessed in one nano-second, 1 ns.) However, it often takes from tens to hundreds of clock cycles to send a memory address to the memory chips, access the data within the memory chips, and return it to the CPU. This means that code like

```
for ( i = 0; i < n; i++ )
  sum = sum + a[i]*b[i];
```

will take from tens to hundreds of clock cycles each time through the loop.

To alleviate this problem, CPU designers have inserted one or more levels of *cache* memory between the registers and main memory. See Figure 12.1 for an illustration of a system with two levels of cache. An excellent reference on caches (and other aspects of memory hierarchies) is [72]. This book has a great deal of

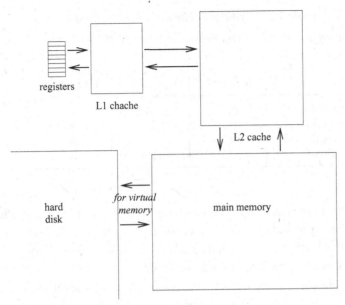

Figure 12.1. Memory hierarchy.

information on the design of caches and related systems, as well as information on how to program to make the best use of these facilities.[1]

The cache is on the same chip as the rest of the CPU so it is much faster to access. But there is limited space on a chip, so there are limits on how big the cache can be. Each cache is broken up into *cache lines*, which are short blocks of memory within each cache. Each cache line is a copy of a block of memory within main memory. In addition, there is a table in hardware that indicates which blocks of memory are in the cache.

Here is how a CPU with cache handles a request to read an address in main memory. First, it checks to see if the cache has a cache line containing the data from that address. If it does, it reads the data from the cache. This is called a *cache hit*. If the cache does not contain data from that address, then the block of memory is read from main memory into a cache line, and the data read from that cache line into a register. If necessary, a different cache line may need to be *evicted* (that is, removed) from the cache to make room for the new block of memory. A memory reference that is not in the cache is called a *cache miss*.

For a CPU with cache, writing to memory is a little more complicated, and there are two main choices: *write-through* and *write-back*. For a write-through cache, data is written to both the cache line and to main memory. For a write-back cache,

---

[1] Beware, however, not to copy the code examples verbatim without checking them. A number of the code examples suffer from off-by-one bugs.

Table 12.1. *Typical cache data for Pentium 4 CPUs*

Note that a single register is regarded as a "line" or "block". Also: $1K = 1024$ and $1M = 1024^2$.

	registers	L1 cache	L2 cache	main memory
Access speed (ns)	0.4	1.0	8.0	150
Total size (bytes)	64	8K	256K	512M
Block/line size (bytes)	8	64	64	—
# blocks/lines	8	128	4K	—

data is written to the cache line. The cache line has a special bit called the dirty bit, which is then set to indicate that the cache line is different from what is in main memory. If that cache line is needed for some other piece of memory, then the cache line has to be written back to main memory first.

For multiple caches, the CPU first looks in the lowest level cache. If there is a miss for this cache, it then looks to the next level cache, and so on. A cache miss on the first level which leads to a cache hit on the second level will result in the first level cache reading the cache line from the second level cache. This can be extended in a recursive fashion to include an arbitrary number of caches. Hardware limits and practicalities limit CPUs to no more than three cache levels at present. This will probably increase as time goes on, however.

Lower level caches tend to be faster and smaller, with smaller cache lines; the smallest "cache" is the set of registers. Some typical figures for Pentium 4 CPUs are in Table 12.1. The figures for "main memory" of course depend on the memory system used, not on the CPU. Since new versions of CPUs are being released all the time, not to mention their different clock speeds, the data presented in Table 12.1 can only be regarded as indicating the relative speeds of the different levels of memory.

12.2 A tour of the Pentium 4^{TM} architecture

This section is intended to give a quick overview of the architecture of the hardware in a Pentium 4 CPU. This overview will be very rough as there are many techniques used to accelerate microprocessors, and CPU designers have developed an extensive set of terms to describe how to achieve the goals of high-speed. These notes are based on the documentation provided by Intel [60, 61].

12.2.1 Historical aspects

The Intel Architecture (IA) started in 1978 with the 8088 and 8086 CPUs, and has continued with the development of the 80188/80186, 80286, i386, i486, Pentium and Xeon CPUs. With the i386 CPU, Intel introduced their 32-bit architecture – previous CPUs had only 16-bit addresses. With the i386, 4 GB of memory was directly addressable. Prior to that, a more complicated system of memory segments was used where each segment had (up to) 64 KB of memory, the maximum amount addressable with 16-bit addresses. With the 32-bit Intel Architecture (IA-32) a more uniform address system was available for Intel CPUs. Since the i386 CPU, more registers and facilities have been added, and low-level parallelism of an SIMD kind has been introduced. With the i486 CPU, what has been a floating point co-processor (the 8087) has been integrated into the CPU. Before the i486, if you did not buy the floating-point co-processor, then floating-point operations were done purely in software, which made them quite slow. From the initial version of the floating-point co-processor (for the 80186 CPU in 1986) IEEE floating-point arithmetic was implemented.

An important aspect of Intel's CPUs is the need for **backward compatibility**: that is, newer IA CPUs should be able to execute code written for older IA CPUs and give identical results.[2] This means (for example) that the registers in the original 8086 CPU must be present in the latest Pentium computer. Operations on 16-bit addresses must still work correctly on the current 32 bit CPUs (and on future 64-bit CPUs).

12.2.2 Basic architecture

The 32-bit Intel Architecture (IA-32) is a basic design for a CPU with eight general purpose 32-bit integer and pointer registers,[3] eight 80-bit floating-point registers, eight 64-bit MMX[4] and eight 128-bit XMM registers, six 16-bit segment registers, and various control and status registers. The floating-point registers store IEEE extended precision floating-point numbers, and all floating point operations on the floating-point registers are carried out in extended precision.

The set of instructions available in the machine code for an IA-32 CPU is extensive. An operation can act on data that can be specified in the instruction itself, in a register, in a fixed memory location (specified in the instruction), in a memory location specified by a register or registers, or in an I/O (input/output) port; outputs can be sent to registers, fixed memory locations, locations specified by a register or registers, or an I/O port. Memory operations can use the results of several registers with (for example) one register storing the base address of an array, and another storing the index or offset into the array. In addition there are more specialized machine instructions for acting on multiple data items in MMX and XMM registers.

---

[2] Excepting, of course, the infamous Pentium floating-point division bug!
[3] Four in the original 16-bit CPUs. The names of the 32 bit general-purpose registers are EAX, EBX, ECX, EDX, ESI, EDI, EBP, and ESP.
[4] MMX stands for MultiMedia eXtensions.

The IA-32 architecture is a Complex Instruction Set Computer (CISC), unlike many of the CPUs in non-Linux Unix systems, which are commonly Reduced Instruction Set Computers (RISCs). For a Pentium CPU, there are over 500 assembly language operation codes. This means that decoding IA-32 machine instructions is a fairly complex task. Different instructions will have different lengths, and must be interpreted in different ways depending on the kind of instruction, the number of operands (i.e., data items being operated on), and the way that the operands are specified. IA-32 CPUs do not attempt to decode and execute a single instruction each clock cycle. Instead instructions pass through a pipeline which can handle many instructions at once, but which takes many clock cycles to pass from the start of the pipeline to the end of the pipeline. Since we want to look at the more advanced high-performance features, we will focus on the recent Pentium 4's "Net-Burst microarchitecture" hardware features in the rest of this section. Much of this information comes from the description in the Intel Technology Journal issue that describes the Pentium 4 and its features and capabilities [53].

12.2.3 Caches and memory accesses

In addition to the registers, Pentium CPUs also have on-chip caches to improve performance and use high clock speeds. Note that the Pentium 4 contains some 42 million transistors, so there are plenty of opportunities to use extra hardware to improve performance.

There are multiple arithmetic and logic units for doing the actual computations. To gain performance, there are separate arithmetic and logic units (ALUs) for the simpler integer operations (shifts, adds, subtractions) that operate at twice the clock speed of the rest of the CPU, operating on 16 bits at a time, so 32-bit integer adds, shifts and subtractions can be done in $1\frac{1}{2}$ or 2 clock cycles. More complex integer operations (multiplications, divisions) are carried out by separate ALUs, which can take many clock cycles (14 clock cycles for integer multiply, 60 clock cycles for division). There are a total of four of the simpler integer ALUs, and one ALU for the more complex integer operations. The floating-point units can perform one extended or double-precision addition in a single clock cycle; one extended precision multiplication can be done in two clock cycles while a double-precision multiplication can be done in one clock cycle. Single precision operations can be done in half the time using the MMX/XMM registers. Floating-point division and square roots can be computed at a rate of two bits per clock cycle (so an extended precision division can take about 32 clock cycles, a double-precision division would take about 26 clock cycles, and a single-precision division would take about 12 clock cycles).

There are several different kinds of cache. There are two level-one (L1) caches: one for data and one for instructions. The instruction cache does not contain simple copies of the instructions to execute; rather it contains *traces* which are sequences of hardware instructions called μops ("micro-operations"). This cache is called the Trace Cache. The L1 data cache is more straightforward and does contain simple copies of data in memory. The L1 data cache is a write-through cache so that writes to the L1 cache are automatically copied into the level-two (L2) cache. The L2 cache is a large unified cache (usually 256 KB to 1 MB).

12.2.4 Decoding and execution

Machine instructions are read from memory and fed to the decoding pipeline. The output of this pipeline is a stream of direct hardware instructions called μops which are fed to the Trace Cache. The Trace Cache can hold about 12K of these μops. The execution engine of a Pentium CPU takes these μops, re-orders and schedules them, and then executes them. Note that the execution of the μops can happen *in a different order than the corresponding machine operations appeared in the program*. Up to three μops can be executed in parallel. In order to use this parallelism it is important to be able to re-order the μops and to check that the re-ordering will not result in incorrect results.

Since the execution of even a single μop is carried out by a pipeline, references to quantities whose computation has been initiated, but not completed, have to be delayed. If a particular quantity has been computed, but is waiting to be written to a register or to the L1 cache, then there is a hardware sub-system to use that quantity in further computation if that is possible. In spite of the hardware support for using computed values before they are written to registers or memory, code should be written to avoid loop carried dependencies such as

```
a[0] = 1.0;
for ( i = 1; i < N; i++ )
    a[i] = 0.5*a[i-1];
```

The problem is that a[i] depends on a[i-1] which was computed in the previous iteration of the loop, and so the computation of a[i] cannot begin until the computation of a[i-1] is complete. More advice about how to handle pipelines will be given in the section on loop unrolling.

A recurring issue that limits the performance of modern CPUs is how to handle conditional branches. Consider, for example, the above for loop. It is usually compiled into machine code that looks like this C code (noting that eax and ebx represent two of the general purpose registers, and fp0 represents one of the floating point registers):

```
ebx = a;      /* set ebx to address of a[0] */
eax = 1;      /* eax will hold the value of i */
*ebx = 1.0;   /* a[0] = 1.0; */
ebx++;        /* ebx now points to a[1] */
loop:
   if ( eax >= N ) goto end;
   fp0 = *ebx;
   fp0 = 0.5*fp0;
   ebx += sizeof(double);
   /* ebx now points to a[eax] */
   *ebx = fp0;
   eax++;
   goto loop;
end:
```

The problem is with

```
if ( eax >= N ) goto end;
```

If we know which way the branch goes, we can start executing the following code. What the hardware does is *guess* which way the branch will go before it has computed if eax >= N. By looking at past history, we can get a good idea. If N is large, then we will not do the goto, but instead continue to fp0 = *ebx many times before we finally exit the loop. Once this has happened a few times, the hardware (which keeps track of this) is able to guess that that is what will happen, at least most of the time. The first time a branch is seen, a simple rule is used: backwards branches are assumed taken but forward branches are not. Continuing to execute code with an assumption like this is called **speculative execution**. This technique has been part of microprocessor design for over a decade at the time of writing.

The guess of not doing the goto will eventually be wrong. Then there will be a considerable amount of "patching-up" that has to be done. Pipelines have to be cleared, and values restored to registers. (The pipeline that has to be cleared in the Pentium 4 contains 20 μops – quite a long pipeline.)

These characteristics of the Pentium 4 architecture should give some guidance for writing high-performance code.

• Avoid if statements inside short inner loops.
• It is better for short inner loops to execute for a moderate to large number of iterations. (One or two iterations may result in a lot of time spent clearing pipelines.)

- Avoid loop-carried dependencies in short inner loops. That is, avoid making the computation in the following iteration depend on the computation in the current iteration.

The following code has a loop-carried dependency.

```
for ( i = 1; i < n; i++ )
  a[i] = a[i-1] + 1;
```

Equivalent code that does not have a loop-carried dependency is:

```
for ( i = 1; i < n; i++ )
  a[i] = a[0] + i;
```

12.2.5 Register re-naming

Since there are only a limited number of registers available in the IA-32 architecture, many of them (like the EAX register) tend to be heavily used. This can create a problem with dealing with parallel execution: often there will be several operations "in flight" at one time that specify operations with the same register. Usually there is no logical dependence – registers are often used as temporary storage for computing address, or storing a result, and then loaded with some other value for doing an independent computation. To deal with this situation, the Pentium 4 uses *register renaming* along with a much larger register file (containing the equivalent of 128 registers in the Pentium 4) to handle the multiple but independent uses of the registers such as EAX. When there are multiple references to a single register by the instructions being processed, different registers in the register file are identified as corresponding to the different (and independent) uses of the EAX register.

12.2.6 SSE SIMD extensions

The Pentium 4 architecture includes a number of instructions that explicitly provide Single Instruction, Multiple Data parallelism using the MMX and XMM registers. A single XMM register with 128 bits can be loaded with two double-precision numbers or four single-precision numbers in packed form. A packed SIMD add of two double-precision or four single-precision floating-point numbers in two clock cycles and computing one product of two double-precision numbers or two products each of two single-precision numbers can each be computed in one clock cycle. These use the parallelism available in the floating-point unit of the Pentium 4. The 64 bit MMX registers can perform similar operations on integer (or pointer) data in parallel. This can lead to greater on-chip parallelism – up to 8 characters can be operated on simultaneously. This is particularly useful in digital signal processing where integer or fixed-point operations are being carried out and it is critical that the processing meets time constraints. However, the SSE floating point operations do *not* use extended precision arithmetic.

12.3 Virtual memory and paging

Caching is built into CPUs, but virtual memory is about using storage devices like hard disks (see Figure 12.1) to *increase* the amount of available memory. Although the terminology is different, the principles are the essentially the same.

If virtual memory is in use, blocks of memory (called *pages*) can be written to hard disk if they are not needed, and read back off disk when they are needed. In this way a hard disk is a reservoir of memory. With it you can carry out much larger computations than would otherwise be possible. However, there is a substantial cost: reading data from a hard disk or writing to a disk is *much* slower than reading or writing data to and from main memory.

Hard disks are divided into circular tracks, and each track is divided into segments which can hold anything from 128 bytes to 8 or 16 KB. Usually a segment corresponds to a *page* of virtual memory, which is analogous to a cache line for caches. When a memory address is accessed using virtual memory, a table is looked up to find the physical address. If the physical address is in main memory, then that address is accessed directly. If it is not in main memory, then the corresponding page of memory on the hard disk is read in to main memory and the table of virtual memory pages is updated (this is called a *page fault*). Often there is hardware support for the table of physical addresses in the form of a *table lookaside buffer* (TLB) which contains the physical addresses of the most recently accessed virtual addresses.

As with caches, efficient use of virtual memory involves keeping a close eye on memory locality: inner loops should avoid accessing widely spaced locations in memory, and should re-use blocks of memory, where possible. Inefficient codes can result in a page fault for (almost) every memory access, slowing the code down by a factor of ten thousand or more. Generating many page faults in rapid succession is called *thrashing*, and is the subject of the next section. The same effect can easily occur when using cache, although the effect reduces speed only by a factor of two to ten.

12.4 Thrashing

Consider the following piece of Fortran code for $y \leftarrow Ax + y$:

```
do i = 1, m
   do j = 1, n
      y(j) = y(j) + A(i,j)*x(j)
   enddo
enddo
```

This uses the minimum number of floating point operations, and is simple, direct code, and yet it is inefficient if A is $m \times n$ and m and n are large. Why?

After each time we go though inner loop, we increment j. Since Fortran uses column major order, the memory address of A(i,j+1) differs from A(i,j) by m floating-point numbers. If we are using single-precision real numbers, this amounts to $4m$ bytes. This means that if $m \geq 64/4 = 16$, we need to read in a new L1 cache line every time we go through the inner loop, at least on the first time through the outer loop. Since there are only 128 L1 cache lines, we will need to start re-reading the L1 cache lines after $128/n$ times through the outer loop. If n is 128 or more, this means that for *every* time we go through the inner loop we have to read a cache line to do a multiply and an add. The time to do a multiply and add is typically a few clock cycles on modern CPUs, so most of the time will be spent filling the L1 cache, not on doing floating-point operations.

This is **thrashing**. Thrashing can occur at any level of a memory hierarchy. Whichever level of the memory hierarchy we consider, the principles of how to avoid thrashing are basically the same. These principles are discussed in the next section.

12.5 Designing for memory hierarchies

The main principle for designing software for memory hierarchies is *locality*. There are two kinds of locality to consider: *temporal locality* (which is about the executable code) and *spatial locality* (which is about the data).

For good *temporal locality*, the code being executed should not jump around too much. Ideally, most of the actual computation should be spent in small, tight loops. Most times that a jump or branch to a far-away address occurs, cache lines need to be filled with the new instructions to be executed. Consider, for example, the difference between

```
double x[N], y[N], z[N];
...
for ( i = 0; i < N; i++ )
  z[i] = x[i] + y[i];
```

and

```
double d_add(double a, double b)
{  return a + b;  }
...
double x[N], y[N], z[N];
...
for ( i = 0; i < N; i++ )
  z[i] = d_add(x[i],y[i]);
```

There are several sources of inefficiency in the second example.

- Function calls usually involve setting up (and later tearing down) a stack frame.
- The function call usually involves branching to somewhere far away in memory.
- Variables often have to be saved from registers to memory or copied from memory to registers.

No-one would consciously write code like the second example (calling a routine to add a pair of numbers), but similar things can occur easily in object-oriented languages unless you take care to *inline* small routines.

Other programming constructs like if-then-else statements also tend to reduce temporal locality, but not as much. The conditions and the code to execute in situations like this should be kept small. If the code for the whole loop can be kept in a part of the cache, the loop will often run much faster as memory will not need to be accessed for the instructions to execute. For example, it is better to write a matrix–vector multiply in the obvious way

```
for ( i = 0; i < m; i++ )
  for ( j = 0; j < n; j++ )
    y[i] = y[i] + a[i][j]*x[j];
```

than to try to make it faster by avoiding zeros in the inner loop:

```
for ( i = 0; i < m; i++ )
  for ( j = 0; j < n; j++ )
  {
    if ( a[i][j] != 0.0 )
      y[i] = y[i] + a[i][j]*x[j];
  }
```

Not only is time lost in the comparison with zero, but the compiler will find it harder to optimize the second example, and temporal locality is reduced.

The main rule-of-thumb you should bear in mind for temporal locality is:

keep the inner loops short and tight wherever possible.

Spatial locality is about how the data is accessed in memory. Ideally, memory accesses should stay close together most of the time. Because C uses row-major order, the matrix multiplication example above will access (in order) y[0], a[0][0], x[0], y[0], y[1], a[0][1], x[1], y[1], y[2], a[0][2], x[2], y[2], ... We are accessing three arrays; the entries in the x array that we access are x[0], x[1], ...; the entries in the y array that we access are y[0], y[1], ...; the entries in the a array that we access are a[0][0], a[0][1], a[0][2],.... In all three arrays, we are accessing sequential memory locations. This results in good spatial locality.

If we used Fortran, which uses column-major order, with the code

```
do i = 1, m
  do j = 1, n
    y(i) = y(i) + a(i,j)*x(j)
  enddo
enddo
```

then we would have poor spatial locality because a(1,1), a(1,2), a(1,3), ... are separated by (at least) m floating point numbers. Each time we accessed the matrix we would have to read in a new cache line, and probably evict a cache line containing the part of the x and y arrays that we need.

In this example, the Fortran code should be written with the loops reversed: the loop on i should be the inside loop and the loop on j should be the outside loop:

```
do j = 1, n
  do i = 1, m
    y(i) = y(i) + a(i,j)*x(j)
  enddo
enddo
```

Whether an algorithm is "cache friendly" is not always obvious. What about binary search? If we are searching for widely spaced items, then, apart from the initial test against the middle entry of the list, we are unlikely to be making the same tests in successive searches. This would be cache unfriendly. But if the searches are for close items, then most of the tests in successive binary searches would be the same. Most of the list entries used in one binary search will be re-used in the following search.

Matrix transposition is simple to define and program, but it is distinctly cache-unfriendly:

```
for ( i = 0; i < m; i++ )
  for ( j = 0; j < n; j++ )
    B[j][i] = A[i][j];
```

No matter how you order the loops (or if you use Fortran instead of C), each time through the inner loop will result in a cache miss (unless both A and B can reside together in cache). Cache-friendly algorithms for transposition are typically blocked. Transposition can also be done using so-called "cache-oblivious" algorithms; see Section 12.10.

12.6 Dynamic data structures and memory hierarchies

Dynamic data structures, such as linked lists and trees, are commonly used in advanced algorithms. However, if we create and destroy the nodes for these data structures using the standard memory allocation and de-allocation routines or commands, we lose all control over memory locality, plus we have the expense of managing the memory heap. For example, in an array, consecutive entries are stored consecutively, while there is no guarantee that this is true for linked lists. In fact, heavily modified linked lists usually have consecutive entries that are widely scattered. Also, modifying linked lists usually involves memory allocation and deallocation.

How can we create dynamic data structures and still keep some memory locality for efficient use of memory hierarchies? Here are some ideas that you can use to help.

- One piece of advice given in [72] is to copy the data structure. The original process of creating the data structure may have been very complicated. Then performing a deep copy of the data structure will usually result in most nodes being allocated sequentially in memory.
- Another approach is to regain control of the memory allocation and de-allocation. For example, it is possible to allocate memory out of an explicit array for small dynamic data structures. That way the allocated memory for the data structure is all contained in the array – if the array is not large, then the data structure will not be too spread out in memory. The size of the array should be limited by what can fit in the L2 cache, for example. Code for performing this kind of memory allocation is given in Section 14.6.

12.7 Pipelining and loop unrolling

Often it is too expensive for a CPU to execute an instruction in one clock cycle. One alternative is to create a *pipeline* in hardware, which is a sequence of independent units which together accomplish a certain task, such as a floating-point operation. IBM's RS/6000 series of CPUs (the forerunner to the PowerPC CPUs) had a fused floating-point multiply–add (FMA) operation which could compute $a \times b + c$ using three pipelined units. Each unit could carry out its operation in one clock cycle, so computing $a \times b + c$ could be done in three clock cycles. However, because each unit was independent of the others, it could carry out one multiply–add each clock cycle – as long as the pipeline was full. This has an important effect on how to write code to get the most out of this CPU. Consider carrying out a dot product:

```
sum = 0.0;
for ( i = 0; i < n; i++ )
  sum = sum + a[i]*b[i];
```

Each addition to sum must be carried out before the next can begin. So the CPU must wait for the pipeline to clear before starting a new multiply–add. The RS/6000 had independent integer arithmetic units, so the loop operations could be done simultaneously with the floating point operations. So this code (if compiled with the optimization switches set) could compute a direct product of two n-vectors in $3n$ clock cycles.

If we re-wrote the code using **loop unrolling**, we could reduce the time for a multiply–add to nearly one clock cycle, increasing the speed by a factor of nearly three:

```
/* do inner product in blocks of length 4 */
sum0 = sum1 = sum2 = sum3 = 0.0;
for ( i = 0; i < n; i += 4 )
{
   sum0 = sum0 + a[i  ]*b[i  ];
   sum1 = sum1 + a[i+1]*b[i+1];
   sum2 = sum2 + a[i+2]*b[i+2];
   sum3 = sum3 + a[i+3]*b[i+3];
}
sum = sum0 + sum1 + sum2 + sum3;
/* take care of fractional block:
     4*(n/4) = 4*floor(n/4) */
for ( i = 4*(n/4); i < n; i++ )
   sum = sum + a[i]*b[i];
```

Note that, in the first loop, the statement incrementing sum0 is independent of the statement incrementing sum1, the statement incrementing sum2 and the statement incrementing sum3. This independence means that there is no need to wait for the pipeline to clear before starting a new multiply–add. Also, as there are four increments carried out, by the time that the statement

```
   sum3 = sum3 + a[i+3]*b[i+3];
```

is started, the statement

```
   sum0 = sum0 + a[i  ]*b[i  ];
```

has finished. So when the first loop starts the next iteration, we can begin updating sum0 without waiting for the pipeline to clear.

The second loop

```
   for ( i = 4*(n/4); i < n; i++ )
      sum = sum + a[i]*b[i];
```

ensures that the final few entries of a and b are included in the dot product. While this short loop suffers from the problems of the original code for computing the dot product, it adds only a small amount of overhead.

Astute readers may note that we did not need to unroll the loop into four sums, but only three. Why should we unroll the loop into four sums? One reason is that the division $n4 = n/4$ usually amounts to shifting bits while $n3 = n/3$ is a true division operation, and can be remarkably expensive.

On a Pentium 4 a division takes 23–30 clock cycles for integers or single-precision floating point numbers and 38–40 for double-precision, while multiplication takes 7 or 8 clock cycles in full precision [25, Appendix C].

A similar pipelining problem occurs for the Pentium 4, which has about 20 stages in its pipeline. Four fused multiply–adds take sufficient time for the pipeline to clear, so this loop unrolled code should work well on a Pentium 4 as well as the RS/6000. How much loop unrolling is needed depends on the details of the architecture, and the effectiveness of the compiler's optimization. Careful experiments are the best way to determine optimal loop unrolling.

12.8 Basic Linear Algebra Software (BLAS)

The Basic Linear Algebra Software (BLAS) routines are a collection of routines for performing standard operations in numerical linear algebra: forming inner products, matrix–vector and matrix–matrix multiplication, solving triangular systems of equations, and so on, for matrices and vectors stored as dense arrays. These are available for arrays of single-precision floating point numbers, double-precision floating point numbers, and both single and double-precision complex numbers. Since the BLAS routines were originally written in Fortran, they assume that the arrays are laid out in memory as they are in Fortran. BLAS routines are divided into three different levels.

- BLAS–1: These routines do not have nested loops, and include inner products routines and "axpy" operations: $\mathbf{y} \leftarrow a\mathbf{x} + \mathbf{y}$. These were first described in [69]. BLAS-1 routines use $O(n)$ operations for n-dimensional vectors.
- BLAS–2: These routines involve doubly nested loops, and include matrix–vector products, matrix–transposed-vector products, and solving upper or lower triangular linear systems. These were first described in [30]. BLAS-2 routines use $O(n^2)$ operations for $n \times n$ matrices.
- BLAS–3: These routines involve triply-nested loops, and include matrix–matrix, matrix–transposed-matrix multiplies, and solving $LX = B$ and $UX = B$ for a matrix X where L is a lower triangular matrix and U is an upper triangular matrix. These were first described in [29]. BLAS-3 operations use $O(n^3)$ operations for $n \times n$ matrices.

Because of this standardization, many computer manufacturers have implemented these routines using all the tricks their hardware and compilers provide. This has made the BLAS routines a basis for efficient algorithms involving dense matrices and vectors. BLAS-3 routines have been especially important. We will see why in Subsection 12.8.2.

12.8.1 BLAS in detail

The BLAS assumes a flat column-major layout of array entries in memory. Since we often wish to apply BLAS operations to sections or *slices* of arrays, there are a number of additional parameters used to identify a particular part of an array.

Vectors are passed by passing the starting address, the dimension of the vector (that is, the number of entries), and also the *stride*. The stride is the distance between consecutive entries of the vector in the array. Usually the stride is one, but if we are trying to operate on a particular row (or column) of a matrix, we can use the stride to specify this. From the point of view of memory accesses, it is best to have the stride equal to one, or at least something small. On the other hand it is better to have a large stride for a vector than to transpose a matrix.

Matrices are two-dimensional arrays in a column-oriented layout. The physical number of rows of the array is called the *leading dimension* of the array, or *LDA*. Then $A(i, j)$, the entry of A in row i and column j, is located at the address of the start of A plus $(i - 1 + LDA \times (j - 1))$ times the size of the items stored in the array. In Fortran, a double-precision array passed like this would be declared

```
subroutine xxx(..., A, LDA, ...)
   integer LDA
   real(kind=0d0) A(LDA,*)
```

The BLAS has a systematic naming scheme. The names of most routines begin with a letter indicating the type of vectors and/or matrices that are being operated on: "s" for single-precision real, "d" for double-precision real, "c" for single-precision complex and "z" for double-precision complex arrays. There is also the possibility (provided it is supported by local hardware and/or software) for extended precision versions where the routine names start with "es", "ed", "ec", and "ez".

The matrix type on which the operation is applied also appears in the BLAS naming scheme:

Matrix type	Standard storage		Banded storage		Packed storage	
General (G)	GE	General	GB	General band		
Symmetric (S)	SY	Symmetric	SB	Symm. band	SP	Symm. packed
Hermitian (H)	HE	Hermitian	HB	Herm. band	HP	Herm. packed
Triangular (T)	TR	Triangular	TB	Triang. band	TP	Triang. packed

For all but the general matrix or general banded matrix formats, the data for the matrix could be stored in the upper or the lower triangles of the matrix. For example, a symmetric matrix A needs only a_{ij} for $i \leq j$ to be stored; this is storage of the upper triangular part of A. Alternatively, A could be stored as a_{ij} for $i \geq j$; this is storage of the lower triangular part of the matrix. The remainder of the matrix could be used for other purposes (for the SY, HE, and TR formats), or the remainder would be eliminated for the packed formats (SP, HP, and TP formats). Whether the upper or lower triangular parts of the matrix is stored is indicated by the UPLO argument: this is a string argument and is either "Lower triangular" or "Upper triangular". The string argument can be shortened to the initial letter – "L" or "U" respectively – and are case insensitive. This is true of all the following string arguments for BLAS routines.

Since it is frequently required to compute $A^{T}x$ or $\overline{A}^{T}x$ and undesirable to explicitly transpose or conjugate A, there is an additional parameter to indicate whether to apply the operation to or with A, its transpose A^{T}, or its Hermitian (or conjugate) transpose $A^{H} = \overline{A}^{T}$. The last case only makes sense for complex matrices. The choice of operations is determined by the TRANS argument, which is another string argument with the values "No transpose" ($op(A) = A$), "Transpose" ($op(A) = A^{T}$), and "Conjugate transpose" ($op(A) = A^{H}$).

For triangular matrices (the TR, TB, or TP formats), it can be important to know if the diagonal of the array is truly the diagonal of the matrix, or (as is often the case) the diagonal of the matrix consists of ones and is therefore not stored. This information is passed in the DIAG argument, which can have the values "Non-unit triangular" or "Unit triangular".

Symmetric and Hermitian matrices are stored in the upper or lower triangle of a matrix. If we chose to store a symmetric matrix A as the upper triangle of the array A(n,n), then A(i,j) would a valid reference to a_{ij} only if $i \leq j$. If $i > j$ we would have to access $a_{ij} = a_{ji}$ in A(j,i). For a Hermitian matrix, we could do the same thing, except that if $i > j$ we would need to remember that $a_{ij} = \overline{a_{ji}}$ which is the conjugate of A(j,i).

The packed format removes the unused space when a symmetric or Hermitian matrix is stored. For example, in the packed upper triangular storage format, the matrix entries are laid out in memory like this:

$$a_{11}, \; a_{12}, \; a_{22}, \; a_{13}, \; a_{23}, \; a_{33}, \; a_{14}, \ldots$$

The code to access a particular entry is obviously more complex in this case.

Banded matrices need an additional parameter, namely the bandwidth (K); a general banded matrix has two bandwidth parameters: a lower (KL) and an upper (KU). The upper bandwidth (KU) is the number of non-zero diagonals in the banded

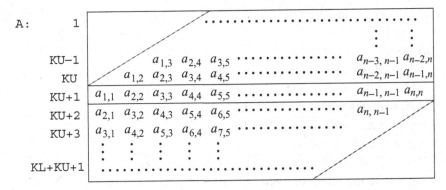

Figure 12.2. LAPACK banded matrix storage.

matrix *strictly above* the diagonal. Similarly KL is the number of non-zero diagonals *strictly below* the diagonal. General banded matrices are stored so that the jth column of the Fortran array is the jth column of the banded matrix; however, only the KL + KU + 1 entries in the band of each column are actually stored. With this approach there is some wasted memory in the first and last KL + KU columns of the array, but this is usually small compared to the amount of memory needed for the non-zero entries unless the bandwidth starts becoming a significant fraction of n. Only the upper triangular or lower triangular part of symmetric or Hermitian banded matrices is stored so that KL = 0 (and K = KU), or KU = 0 (and K = KL), depending on which part is stored.

The a_{ij} entry of a banded matrix A is stored in A(1+KU+i − j, j). Figure 12.2 illustrates the LAPACK banded matrix storage format.

The BLAS-1 routines are

```
subroutine xSWAP(N,         X, INCX, Y, INCY)
    x ↔ y
subroutine xSCAL(N, ALPHA, X, INCX)
    x ← αx
subroutine xCOPY(N,         X, INCX, Y, INCY)
    y ← x
subroutine xAXPY(N, ALPHA, X, INCX, Y, INCY)
    y ← αx + y
function    xDOT (N,         X, INCX, Y, INCY)
    xᵀy    real version
function    xDOTU(N,         X, INCX, Y, INCY)
    xᵀy    complex only
function    xDOTC(N,         X, INCX, Y, INCY)
    xᴴy    complex only
```

```
function    xNRM2 (N,          X,  INCX)
    ||x||₂
```
$\|x\|_2$
```
function    xASUM (N,          X,  INCX)
```
$\sum_i (|\mathrm{Re}\,(x_i)| + |\mathrm{Im}\,(x_i)|)$
```
function    IxAMAX (N,         X,  INCX)
```
$\mathrm{argmax}_i\,(|\mathrm{Re}\,(x_i)| + |\mathrm{Im}\,(x_i)|)$
```
subroutine  xROTG (A, B, C, S)
    generate plane rotation
subroutine  xROTMG (D1, D2, A, B, PARAM)
    generate modified rotation
subroutine  xROT  (N, X, INCX, Y, INCY, C, S)
    apply plane rotation
subroutine  xROTM (N, X, INCX, Y, INCY, PARAM)
    apply modified rotation.
```

The prefix "x" represents the component types: "s" for single-precisioncision real, "d" for double-precision real, "c" for single-precisioncision complex, and "z" for double-precision complex.

Many of these routines are clearly in the nature of utility routines: xSWAP, xCOPY, xSCAL, IxAMAX; however, xDOT, xNRM2 and xAXPY are clearly of relevance to linear algebra; the xROT routines are for generating and applying Givens' rotation, which is the basis for a number of algorithms related to least-squares problems and to computing eigenvalues and eigenvectors.

There are limited opportunities for improving the performance of BLAS-1 routines. The dot product routines xDOT can be improved by loop unrolling, especially in architectures with long pipelines. The xNRM2 routines can be improved over "naive" implementations to avoid overflow or underflow: the entries are scaled by a power of two so that the largest entry has magnitude between (say) one and two.

The BLAS-2 routines really only implement four operations: MV for a matrix–vector product ($y \leftarrow \alpha Ax + \beta y$), SV for solving a triangular system of equations ($x \leftarrow A^{-1}x$), R for a rank-1 update ($A \leftarrow A + \alpha xy^{\mathrm{T}}$), and R2 for symmetric rank-2 updates ($A \leftarrow A + \alpha xy^{\mathrm{T}} + y(\alpha x)^{\mathrm{T}}$). The matrix–vector multiply (MV) and the solve (SV) routines can be used with the banded matrix routines, but the rank-1 (R) and rank-2 (R2) update routines cannot, as rank-1 and rank-2 updates usually do not result in banded matrices. The rank-1 updates for symmetric and Hermitian matrices are restricted in the kind of update that can be carried out since the result must be of the same type (symmetric or Hermitian as appropriate).

We use the prefix "x" as for BLAS-1 routines to indicate the component type, and follow it with the prefix "yz" ("yz" can be GE, GB, SY, SB, SP, HE, HB, HP, TR, TB, or TP). We can compactly represent all the BLAS-2 operations below:

```
xyzMV(UPLOᵃ, TRANSᵇ, DIAGᶜ, Mᵈ, N, KLᵉ, KUᶠ,
    ALPHAᵍ, A, LDAʰ, X, INCX, BETAᵍ, Yᵍ, INCYᵍ)
```
$$y \leftarrow \alpha \, op(A) \, x + \beta \, y \quad \text{(matrix–vector multiply)}$$
```
xTzSV(UPLO, TRANS, DIAG, N, Kᵉ, A, LDAʰ, X, INCX)
```
$$x \leftarrow op(A)^{-1} x \quad \text{(triangular solve)}$$
```
xyzR(UPLOᵃ, Mᵈ, N, ALPHA, X, INCX, Yᵇ,
      INCYᵇ, A, LDAʰ)
```
$$A \leftarrow \alpha \, x \, y^H + A \quad \text{(rank-1 update}^k\text{)}$$
```
xyzR2(UPLO, N, ALPHA, X, INCX, Y, INCY, LDAʰ)
```
$$A \leftarrow \alpha \, x \, y^H + y(\alpha \, x)^H \quad \text{(rank-2 update}^l\text{)}.$$

Notes:

[a] Not used for the general matrix operations ($y = G$).

[b] Not used for the symmetric matrix types ($y = S$ or H); $op(A) = A$ in the MV routines, $y = x$ in the R routines.

[c] Used only for the triangular matrix types ($y = T$).

[d] Used only for the general matrix types ($y = G$).

[e] Used only for the banded matrix formats ($z = B$).

[f] Used only for the general banded matrix format ($yz = GB$).

[g] Not used for the triangular matrix types ($y = T$); in this case $\alpha = 1$ and $\beta = 0$.

[h] Not used for the packed formats ($z = P$).

[k] In the case of general complex matrices there are two routines: GERU which computes $A \leftarrow A + \alpha x y^T$ and GERC which computes $A \leftarrow A + \alpha x y^H$. These routines do not apply to triangular matrices.

[l] These routines only apply to the symmetric formats ($y = S$ or H).

For BLAS-3 the central operations are the matrix-multiply (MM) operations, but the other operations are rank-k (RK) and rank-$2k$ (R2) updates and solve-matrix (SM) operations. All of the BLAS-3 operations are for matrices in the standard storage format, not for either the banded or packed formats. The matrix-multiply (MM) operations compute $C \leftarrow \alpha \, op(A) \, op(B) + \beta \, C$ where $op(A)$ is A, A^T, or A^H according to the associated TRANS argument for the GEneral matrix type. For the SYmmetric and HErmitian matrix types the MM routines compute $C \leftarrow \alpha AB + \beta C$ or $C \leftarrow \alpha BA + \beta C$ according to the SIDE argument, which can be "Left" or "Right". Note that it is the A matrix that is symmetric or Hermitian as the prefix "yz" indicates.

The rank-k update routines compute $C \leftarrow \alpha A \, op(A) + \beta C$ or $C \leftarrow \alpha \, op(A) \, A + \beta C$ for symmetric or Hermitian C according to the TRANS argument. Note that $op(A)$ is A^T or A^H according to whether C is symmetric or Hermitian. Here the A matrix is $n \times k$ (TRANS is "No transpose") or $k \times n$ (TRANS is "Transpose" or "Conjugate transpose") where C is $n \times n$.

The rank-2k update routines compute $C \leftarrow \alpha A\, op(B) + \bar{\alpha} B\, op(A) + \beta C$ or $C \leftarrow \alpha\, op(A)\, B + \bar{\alpha}\, op(B)\, A + \beta C$ according to the TRANS argument. Again $op(A)$ is A^T or A^H according to whether C is symmetric or Hermitian. Here the A and B matrices are $n \times k$ (TRANS is "No transpose") or $k \times n$ (TRANS is "Transpose" or "Conjugate transpose") where C is $n \times n$.

Finally, there is the BLAS-3 triangular solve routine (SM). This computes $B \leftarrow \alpha\, op(A^{-1})\, B$ or $B \leftarrow \alpha\, B\, op(A^{-1})$ according to SIDE argument. Note that $op(A) = A$, A^T or A^H according to the TRANS argument. Note that A must be the triangular matrix.

The routines can be summarized as follows.

```
xGEMM(TRANSA,TRANSB, M,N,K, ALPHA,
     A,LDA, B,LDB, BETA, C, LDC)
     C ← α op(A) op(B) + βC, C is m × n
xSYMM(SIDE,UPLO, M,N, ALPHA,
     A, LDA, B,LDB, BETA, C,LDC)
     C ← αAB + βC or
     C ← αBA + βC, C is m × n, Aᵀ = A
xHEMM(SIDE,UPLO, M,N,K, ALPHA,
     A,LDA, B,LDB, BETA, C,LDC)
     C ← αAB + C or
     C ← αBA + βC, C is m × n, Aᴴ = A
xyzRKᵃ(UPLO,TRANS, N,K, ALPHA,
     A,LDA, BETA, C,LDC)
     C ← α A op(A) + βC or C ← α op(A) A + βC,
     C is n × n, A is n × k or k × n
xyzR2Kᵃ(UPLO,TRANS, N,K, ALPHA,
     A,LDA, B,LDB, BETA, C,LDC)
     C ← α A op(B) + ᾱ B op(A) + βC or
     C ← α op(A) B + ᾱ op(B) A + βC
     C  is n × n, A,B are n × k or k × n
xTRMM(SIDE,UPLO,TRANSA,DIAG, M,N, ALPHA,
     A,LDA, B,LDB)
     B ← α op(A) B or B ← α B op(A), B is m × n
xTRSM(SIDE,UPLO,TRANSA,DIAG, M,N, ALPHA,
     A,LDA, B,LDB)
     B ← α op(A⁻¹) B or B ← α B op(A⁻¹), B is m × n.
```

Notes:

[a] $op(A) = A^\mathrm{T}$ if yz = SY (symmetric case), and $op(A) = A^\mathrm{H}$ if yz = HE (Hermitian case).

12.8.2 Why BLAS is a good foundation

In modern computer architectures we have seen that memory access times are starting to dominate computation times. From this perspective we will look at typical BLAS routines to compare the number of floating-point operations with the number of memory accesses.

- BLAS-1: "axpy" routines compute $y \leftarrow \alpha x + y$. That is, $y_i \leftarrow \alpha x_i + y_i$ for all i. If x and y are n-vectors, then this has $2n$ floating point operations and $3n$ memory accesses. The ratio of memory accesses to floating point operations is $(3n)/(2n) = 3/2$.
- BLAS-2: Matrix–vector multiply routines compute $y \leftarrow Ax + y$. That is, $y_i \leftarrow \sum_j a_{ij} x_j + y_i$ for all i. If x and y are n-vectors, then this has $2n^2 + n$ floating point operations and $n^2 + 3n$ memory accesses. For large n the ratio of memory accesses to floating-point operations is $\approx (n^2)/(2n^2) = 1/2$. This is a lower ratio than for BLAS-1, but not particularly small.
- BLAS-3: Matrix–matrix multiply routines compute $C \leftarrow AB + C$. That is, for all matrices $n \times n$, $c_{ij} \leftarrow \sum_k a_{ik} b_{kj} + c_{ij}$. This has $3n^2$ memory accesses (in principle; implementations could easily have more) and $2n^3$ floating point operations. The ratio of memory accesses to floating point operations is then (in principle) $(3n^2)/(2n^3) = 3/(2n)$. If n is large, then this is small.

Thus BLAS-3 routines have the potential to get very close to the theoretical peak performance of the CPU. To realize this potential we have to use *blocked algorithms*, and to use the cache to hold blocks of the matrices in BLAS-3 algorithms. This is described in more detail in Section 12.9.

The BLAS have been the foundation of the algorithms developed in LAPACK, and BLAS-3 routines are particularly important for the efficiency of LAPACK routines. To make effective use of the BLAS-3 routines, the algorithms in LAPACK must also be blocked algorithms. For example, the standard LU factorization algorithm (with or without pivoting) must be modified to factorize a small block on the diagonal of the matrix; then the remainder of the matrix to the left and right of the diagonal block are modified, and the factorization continues with the next block on the diagonal. The optimal size of the block depends on the size of the cache.

12.8.3 BLAS, ATLAS, and other issues

One of the difficulties with the current state of affairs regarding the BLAS is the difficulty in keeping implementations in step with CPUs. CPU manufacturers like Intel are producing a range of CPUs with different characteristics (clock speed, cache size, pipelines, arithmetic units, etc.). Ideally each change should result in a different implementation of the BLAS. Given that it takes a substantial number of programmer–months to develop BLAS-3 routines, the continual modification of the BLAS routines has tended to fall behind except where there has been particular demand. One response to this has been the development of ATLAS (*Automatic Tuning of Linear Algebra Software*) [105] to automatically produce implementations of BLAS routines. ATLAS works by running a series of timing experiments using standard techniques for improving performance (loop unrolling, blocking, etc.) to determine optimal parameters and structures.

Another issue that has received some scrutiny is the matter of handling C-style pointer-to-pointer representations of matrices, rather than assuming a Fortran-style layout in memory. In the absence of a C-BLAS standard that uses pointers to pointers, one approach is to use an object-oriented language such as C++ to provide a more C-like interface to arrays using a Fortran-style layout in memory. There is also a C interface to the original BLAS that respects the row-oriented nature of C's matrices, but works with a pointer to `floats` or `doubles` (that is, *not* with a pointer to an array of pointers to arrays of `floats` or `doubles`) [8].

Other solutions (such as cache-oblivious algorithms and data structures) may result in complicated memory layouts and require access functions to update individual entries.

It should be kept in mind that the BLAS were introduced as computational kernels for the construction of direct LU- and Cholesky-based linear solvers and for solving eigenvalue/eigenvector problems for dense or banded matrices. They do *not* contain all the kernels needed for numerical computations. Specifically missing are kernels for iterative solvers, sparse direct solvers, and most PDE solvers. Work has proceeded on "sparse BLAS" kernels [33] (current information available through [8]) to remedy some of these deficiencies, as well as high-performance software for iterative methods such as multigrid methods [101] and Krylov subspace methods [7, 6] for the iterative solution of linear systems and eigenvalue/vector problems.

12.9 LAPACK

LAPACK [5] (*Linear Algebra PACKage*) is a package of linear algebra routines. It is based on BLAS, and uses all three levels of BLAS routines to achieve performance. Since the BLAS-3 routines give the best performance, the designers of LAPACK preferred to use BLAS-3 routines over BLAS-2 or BLAS-1 routines. If we have a look at the pseudo-code for a common operation, such as LU factorization for solving a linear system, we will see that there are apparently no opportunities to use BLAS-3 or matrix–matrix operations.

```
LUfactorization(A, pivot)   /* A is m × n */
  for k ← 1,...,min(m,n) − 1
    /* find row to pivot */
    p ← arg max_{i≥k+1} |a_{ik}|
    if a_{pj} = 0 then return /* singular matrix */
    swap a_{kj} ↔ a_{pj},  j = 1,...,n
    pivot[k] ← p
    /* do row operations */
    for i ← k+1,...,m
      a_{ik} ← a_{ik}/a_{kk} /* compute multiplier */
      for j ← k+1,...,n
        a_{ij} ← a_{ij} − a_{ik}a_{kj}
      end for j
    end for i
  end for k
end LUfactorization
```

There are opportunities for using BLAS-1 and BLAS-2 operations here. The BLAS-1 routine IxAMAX can be used to compute $p \leftarrow \arg\max_{i \geq k+1} |a_{ik}|$; the routine xSWAP can be used to perform "swap $a_{kj} \leftrightarrow a_{pj}, j = 1, \ldots, n$". The multipliers a_{ik} for $i > k$ can be computed in one application of xSCAL for scaling column k below the diagonal by $1/a_{kk}$. Finally, the doubly-nested loop over i and j actually computes a rank-1 update on the sub-matrix $[a_{ij} \mid i, j = k + 1, \ldots, n]$. This can be performed by one call of the BLAS-2 routine xGER.

This can be seen in the LAPACK routine SGETF2; an abbreviated and slightly modified version of the Fortran 90 source file from LAPACK version 3E follows. Note that the 3E version of LAPACK is in Fortran 90 and uses Fortran 90 features, rather than being written purely in Fortran 77.

```
#include "lapacknames.inc"
SUBROUTINE SGETF2( M, N, A, LDA, IPIV, INFO )
  USE LA_CONSTANTS
  USE LA_AUXILIARY, ONLY: XERBLA
  USE LA_BLAS1, ONLY: LA_IAMAX, LA_SCAL, LA_SWAP
  USE LA_BLAS2, ONLY: LA_GER
  !     .. Arguments ..
  INTEGER           INFO, LDA, M, N
  INTEGER           IPIV( * )
  REAL(WP)          A( LDA, * )
  INTEGER           J, JP    ! Local Variables
```

```
INTRINSIC              MAX, MIN ! Intrinsic Functions
INFO = 0
...
IF ( M == 0 .OR. N == 0 ) RETURN
DO J = 1, MIN(M,N)
   JP = J - 1 + LA_IAMAX( M-J+1, A(J,J), 1 )
   IPIV(J) = JP
   IF ( A(JP,J) /= ZERO ) THEN
      IF ( JP /= J ) &
      CALL LA_SWAP( N, A(J,1), LDA, A(JP,1), LDA )
      IF ( J < M ) &
      CALL LA_SCAL( M-J, ONE/A(J,J), A(J+1,J), 1 )
   ELSE IF( INFO == 0 ) THEN
      INFO = J
   END IF
   IF ( J < MIN(M,N) ) THEN
      CALL LA_GER( M-J, N-J, -ONE, A(J+1,J), 1, &
      A(J,J+1), LDA, A( J+1, J+1 ), LDA )
   END IF
END DO
RETURN
END SUBROUTINE SGETF2
```

In LAPACK 3E there is no need to have separate single-precisioncision and double-precision routines as this information is encoded in the REAL(WP) declaration; WP is a KIND parameter which is defined in the LA_CONSTANTS module. The LA_BLAS1 and LA_BLAS2 are modules which define interfaces to the BLAS-1 and BLAS-2 routines. The module LA_BLAS1, for example, defines an interface LA_SCAL which it selects from SSCAL (for single-precisioncision) and DSCAL (for double-precision) according to WP. LAPACK 3E for single-precision or double-precision can be generated automatically by compiling with the appropriate value of WP in the LA_CONSTANTS module. (This is an example of the *once and only once!* principle of p. 177 in action. The precision need be specified in only one place.)

Some argument tests have been removed in this abbreviated code; in its place is an ellipsis (...) after "INFO = 0".

The code for SGETF2 clearly shows the usefulness of the BLAS, but only levels 1 and 2. To use BLAS-3 we need to use blocked algorithms. The basic idea is to partition the matrix A into

$$A = \begin{bmatrix} A_{11} & A_{12} \\ A_{21} & A_{22} \end{bmatrix},$$

and we begin by computing the LU factorization (with row-pivoting) of the first block column:

$$P_1 \begin{bmatrix} A_{11} \\ A_{21} \end{bmatrix} = \begin{bmatrix} L_{11} \\ L_{21} \end{bmatrix} U_{11},$$

where L_{11} is lower triangular, U_{11} is upper triangular, and P_1 is a permutation matrix. Notice that we are making use of the fact that we can compute LU factorizations of *rectangular* matrices. This initial factorization is done using the *unblocked* algorithm in SGETF2. Now adding the second block column back in gives us

$$P_1 \begin{bmatrix} A_{11} & A_{12} \\ A_{21} & A_{22} \end{bmatrix} = \begin{bmatrix} L_{11}U_{11} & A'_{12} \\ L_{21}U_{11} & A'_{22} \end{bmatrix} = \begin{bmatrix} L_{11} & 0 \\ L_{21} & I \end{bmatrix} \begin{bmatrix} U_{11} & L_{11}^{-1}A'_{12} \\ 0 & A'_{22} - L_{21}L_{11}^{-1}A'_{12} \end{bmatrix},$$

where

$$\begin{bmatrix} A'_{11} & A'_{12} \\ A'_{21} & A'_{22} \end{bmatrix} = P_1 \begin{bmatrix} A_{11} & A_{12} \\ A_{21} & A_{22} \end{bmatrix}.$$

Note that $A'_{22} - L_{21}L_{11}^{-1}A'_{12} = A'_{22} - L_{21}U_{11}U_{11}^{-1}L_{11}^{-1}A'_{12} = A'_{22} - A'_{21}(A'_{11})^{-1}A'_{12}$ is the **Schur complement matrix** [55] to A'_{11} in P_1A. We can set $U_{12} = L_{11}^{-1}A'_{12}$. Note that these two steps $U_{12} \leftarrow L_{11}^{-1}A_{12}$ and computing the Schur complement $A'_{22} - L_{21}L_{11}^{-1}A'_{12} = A'_{22} - L_{21}U_{12}$ can be done using BLAS-3 operations.

We can then carry out the LU factorization of the Schur complement:

$$P_2(A'_{22} - L_{21}U_{12}) = L_{22}U_{22}.$$

This LU factorization can be done recursively using the blocked algorithm. Since this is **tail-end recursion**, it can be implemented using loops.

We still need to combine the two permutations into one. Here is what we have so far:

$$P_1 \begin{bmatrix} A_{11} & A_{12} \\ A_{21} & A_{22} \end{bmatrix} = \begin{bmatrix} A'_{11} & A'_{12} \\ A'_{21} & A'_{22} \end{bmatrix}$$

$$= \begin{bmatrix} L_{11} & 0 \\ L_{21} & I \end{bmatrix} \begin{bmatrix} U_{11} & U_{12} \\ 0 & A'_{22} - L_{21}U_{12} \end{bmatrix}$$

$$= \begin{bmatrix} L_{11} & 0 \\ L_{21} & I \end{bmatrix} \begin{bmatrix} I & \\ & P_2^{-1} \end{bmatrix} \begin{bmatrix} U_{11} & U_{12} \\ 0 & L_{22}U_{22} \end{bmatrix}$$

$$= \begin{bmatrix} I & \\ & P_2^{-1} \end{bmatrix} \begin{bmatrix} L_{11} & 0 \\ P_2L_{21} & I \end{bmatrix} \begin{bmatrix} U_{11} & U_{12} \\ 0 & L_{22}U_{22} \end{bmatrix}.$$

So

$$\begin{bmatrix} I & \\ & P_2 \end{bmatrix} P_1 A = \begin{bmatrix} L_{11} & 0 \\ P_2L_{21} & L_{22} \end{bmatrix} \begin{bmatrix} U_{11} & U_{12} \\ 0 & U_{22} \end{bmatrix}.$$

So after we have computed L_{22} and U_{22} we need to apply the permutation to L_{21} and to combine the two permutations.

LAPACK represents permutation matrices by integer arrays; however, these integer arrays are not direct representations of the corresponding permutation. Instead, a permutation is represented by an integer array P like this: `for` $k \leftarrow 1, 2, \ldots, n$, swap k with `P(k)`.

In what follows, a lightly edited version of the LAPACK 3E (Fortran 90) version of `SGETRF` will be used. The modified version uses the `DO/END DO` constructs and the free format features of Fortran 90. Here is how `SGETRF` works: first the header for the routine:

```
#include "lapacknames.inc"
SUBROUTINE SGETRF( M, N, A, LDA, IPIV, INFO )
  USE LA_CONSTANTS
  USE LA_AUXILIARY, ONLY: ILAENV, XERBLA, LA_LASWP
  USE LA_BLAS3, ONLY: LA_GEMM, LA_TRSM
  USE LA_XGETF2
```

The array A is M × N with leading dimension LDA. `IPIV` contains the pivot array. `INFO` is an output; on exit it contains zero to indicate success, negative values to indicate invalid inputs, and positive values to indicate failure of the routine. The input data goes through some "sanity checking". Then there is the main body of the routine:

```
  ...
!      Determine the block size for this environment.
NB = ILAENV( 1, SPREFIX // 'GETRF', ' ', M, N, -1, -1 )
IF( NB <= 1 .OR. NB >= MIN(M,N) ) THEN
    !          Use unblocked code.
   CALL LA_GETF2( M, N, A, LDA, IPIV, INFO )
ELSE
    !          Use blocked code.
   ...
END IF
RETURN
```

This computes the block size NB first. If the matrix is smaller than the block size we use the unblocked routine `SGETF2` (which has been renamed to `LA_GETF2`). But usually we use the blocked code. This code implements the algorithm described above:

```
DO J = 1, MIN(M,N), NB
  JB = MIN(MIN(M,N)-J+1, NB)
  !              Factor diagonal and subdiagonal blocks
  !              and test for exact singularity.
  CALL LA_GETF2( M-J+1, JB, A(J,J), LDA, IPIV(J), IINFO )
  !              Adjust INFO and the pivot indices.
  IF( INFO == 0 .AND. IINFO > 0 ) &
        INFO = IINFO + J - 1
  DO I = J, MIN(M,J+JB-1)
      IPIV(I) = J - 1 + IPIV(I)
  END DO
  !              Apply interchanges to columns 1:J-1.
  CALL LA_LASWP( J-1, A(1,1), LDA, J, J+JB-1, IPIV(1), 1 )
  !
  IF( J+JB <= N ) THEN
      !          Apply interchanges to columns J+JB:N.
      CALL LA_LASWP( N-J-JB+1, A(1,J+JB), LDA, J, J+JB-1,
          IPIV(1), 1 )
      !          Compute block row of U.
      CALL LA_TRSM( 'Left', 'Lower', 'No transpose', 'Unit', &
          JB, N-J-JB+1, ONE, A(J,J), LDA, A(J,J+JB), LDA )
      IF( J+JB <= M ) THEN
          !    Update trailing submatrix.
          CALL LA_GEMM( 'No transpose', 'No transpose', &
              M-J-JB+1, N-J-JB+1, JB, -ONE, &
              A(J+JB,J), LDA, A(J,J+JB), LDA, &
              ONE, A(J+JB,J+JB), LDA )
      END IF
  END IF
END DO
```

At each stage through the loop, the algorithm factorizes the sub-matrix $[a_{ij} \mid i, j \geq J]$, and J increases by the block size NB with each iteration. Note that we use the unblocked routine SGETF2 to do this factorization. The INFO and IPIV arguments have to be increased by $J - 1$ because SGETF2 assumes that the indexes start at 1. The pivot swaps have to be applied to columns 1 through $J - 1$ of A using LA_SWAP. If $J + JB \leq N$ then we have to recursively factorize the sub-matrix consisting of columns $J + JB$ through M and rows $J + JB$ through N. To do that we first apply the row swaps to the sub-matrix. We then use the BLAS-3 triangular solve routine to compute $U_{12} \leftarrow L_{11}^{-1} A'_{12}$, and then the BLAS-3 matrix-multiply routine to compute $A'_{22} - L_{21}U_{12}$. By using blocked algorithms like this, LAPACK is able to use BLAS-3 routines and obtain near maximum performance on most computer architectures.

12.10 Cache-oblivious algorithms and data structures

Since cache sizes are constantly changing, one approach to getting high performance is to use algorithms and data structures which give near optimum performance no matter what size of cache is available. These algorithms and data structures should also perform well with deep memory hierarchies.

The term cache-oblivious data structures was first used by Prokop [88], and later described in [39]. A more recent description of the behavior of cache-oblivious algorithms in practice was given by Olsen & Skov [83]. Good surveys of cache-oblivious algorithms include one by Demaine [28] and Elmroth, Gustavson, Jonsson and Kågström [35]. One of the most straightforward cache-oblivious algorithms is a divide-and-conquer matrix multiplication algorithm. If we wish to multiply two large $n \times n$ matrices A and B we use the formula

$$\begin{bmatrix} A_{11} & A_{12} \\ A_{21} & A_{22} \end{bmatrix} \begin{bmatrix} B_{11} & B_{12} \\ B_{21} & B_{22} \end{bmatrix} = \begin{bmatrix} A_{11}B_{11} + A_{12}B_{21} & A_{11}B_{12} + A_{12}B_{22} \\ A_{21}B_{11} + A_{22}B_{21} & A_{21}B_{12} + A_{22}B_{22} \end{bmatrix}.$$

Suppose n is a power of 2. The block matrices A_{11}, A_{12} etc. are all $n/2 \times n/2$. Applying the block matrix formula recursively to computing $A_{11}B_{11}$ etc. gives a cache-oblivious algorithm. An algorithm like this can be accelerated by using a cache-oblivious data structure for storing the matrices. Instead of storing the matrices in either row-major or column-major order, we can store the matrices in a way that makes this algorithm particularly convenient: to store A we first store A_{11}, then A_{12}, followed by A_{21} and A_{22}. Each block sub-matrix should be (recursively) stored in the same fashion. Here is an example of an 8×8 matrix showing the order in which the entries are stored in this data structure:

$$\begin{bmatrix} 1 & 2 & 5 & 6 & 17 & 18 & 21 & 22 \\ 3 & 4 & 7 & 8 & 19 & 20 & 23 & 24 \\ 9 & 10 & 13 & 14 & 25 & 26 & 29 & 30 \\ 11 & 12 & 15 & 16 & 27 & 28 & 31 & 32 \\ 33 & 34 & 37 & 38 & 49 & 50 & 53 & 54 \\ 35 & 36 & 39 & 40 & 51 & 52 & 55 & 56 \\ 41 & 42 & 45 & 46 & 57 & 58 & 61 & 62 \\ 43 & 44 & 47 & 48 & 59 & 60 & 63 & 64 \end{bmatrix}$$

Many other data structures which can be regarded as "cache oblivious" have been developed. There is reason to believe that these techniques are almost ready for general use. Several issues have delayed their acceptance:

- computing the address of a specific entry is much more complex than for standard layouts of matrices;
- natural algorithms for dealing with these data structures are recursive, which causes difficulties for optimizing compilers – for one thing, recursive routines cannot be "inlined";
- the natural base cases for the recursion are 1×1 or 2×2 block matrices, which are too small to be efficiently handled by modern deeply pipelined CPUs.

Getting the best performance out of cache-oblivious algorithms takes some careful implementation [35, 83]. The biggest overhead is perhaps the use of recursion for the smallest matrices. One way of avoiding this is to stop the recursion, and to lay out the blocks in memory the standard way, when the blocks are "small enough". For example, if the blocks can fit in the L1 cache they are probably "small enough". This is not purely "cache oblivious", but it is close enough. For high performance applications it is probably necessary to convert matrices stored in the standard way into a cache-oblivious format near the beginning of the main computations, and convert back to a standard format at the end of the computations.

12.11 Indexing vs. pointers for dynamic data structures

If you are using linked lists or trees or other dynamic data structures, there is usually a problem with keeping memory locality. If we use a conventional approach for (say) linked lists, then we would have a structure in C like this:

```
struct link {
    void        *data;
    struct link *next;
};
```

and to get a new link we would use `malloc`. However, `malloc` and `new` and related functions and operators which allocate memory from a heap in general do not pass pointers to nearby blocks of memory on successive calls. This means that traversing a linked list can mean jumping around in memory and losing any memory locality. This is even truer if, in between allocating links in a linked list, your code is allocating memory for completely different purposes.

There are several different ways of improving memory locality for dynamic data structures like this.

- Write your own memory allocation and de-allocation routines for linked lists, which use one or more memory pools from which to allocate the links.
- Instead of using a pointer field for `next`, allocate a single array to contain the entire linked list and make next an integer index into the array.

Writing your own memory allocation and de-allocation routines is more flexible, and relies on the fact that all the link objects are allocated from one or a small number of pools of memory. If the pools fit in cache, then traversing the list repeatedly will probably not result in many cache misses.

Allocating an array of objects and using array indexes in place of pointers can achieve the same effect even more efficiently. However, even more of the burden of writing allocation code is put on the programmer. But, if there are no de-allocations to do, this should not be overwhelming.

These techniques are useful only if efficiency is of the utmost importance. As noted above, profile your code to see where time is being spent before optimizing.

13

Global vs. local optimization

13.1 Picking algorithms vs. keyhole optimization

Optimizing the performance of software requires working with at least two different points of view. One is the global view where the questions are about how to structure the overall architecture of the system. Another view is how the individual routines are written, and even how each line of code is written. All of these views are important. Selecting good algorithms is as important as selecting good hardware and implementing algorithms efficiently.

When the term "optimization" is used in computing, it is often taken to mean something like picking compiler options or "writing tight code" that uses the least number of clock cycles or operations. This is clearly important in writing fast, effective software, but it is only a part of the process, which begins early in the design stage.

Usually the first part of the design stage is the design of the central data structures and databases that will be used. These should be chosen so that there are well-known efficient algorithms for handling these data structures, preferably with readily available implementations that perform correctly, reliably and efficiently. Then the algorithms to carry out the main tasks need to be selected. An important guide to selecting them is their asymptotic complexity or estimate of the time needed. However, this is not the only guide; see the last section of this chapter for more information about how to refine this information and to make sure that the asymptotic estimates are relevant in practice. The last part is the detailed design process where the algorithms are implemented, and this should be done with an eye on efficiency to ensure that the whole system works well. On the whole, optimizing compilers can do a great deal of the detailed "optimization" that programmers used to spend considerable time on. Where possible, use the optimization that compilers can provide as it is much less error prone than doing the equivalent task "by hand".

187

Note that it is usually not important to make every routine optimal. Often only a small fraction of the code in a large system has a significant impact on efficiency. This is sometimes expressed by the slogan that

95% of the time is spent in 5% of the code.

The values 95% and 5% should not be taken literally for every large software project. But we have seen similar figures for the systems we have worked on. Often, in many pieces of large-scale scientific software, most of the time is spent in linear algebra: solving systems of linear equations.

Profilers are useful tools for identifying where most of the time is being spent in a program. See the chapter on tools for more information on them and how to use them to identify the parts of the code that could have a substantial impact on the performance of the overall system. Use a profiling tool to find bottlenecks. If there is a bottleneck in your code, have a close look at it. Ask yourself: could better algorithms be used? Could it be implemented more efficiently? Should a higher level of compiler optimization be used? Should the data structures be re-designed? Repeat the process until the system is performing as expected.

13.2 What optimizing compilers do

Optimizing compilers carry out their work on several different levels to improve the quality of code, mainly to reduce execution time, although they can also be used to reduce memory requirements. There have been many advances in optimizing compilers, and they use a number of techniques to improve performance. These transformations are best left to compilers so that your code remains clear and portable.

• *Keyhole optimization.* This is the simplest kind of optimization, and it is carried out on the assembly language or machine code output of the compiler: it scans the output for a pre-selected set of patterns of instructions, which are then replaced by more efficient instructions. For example, multiplying an integer by two can be replaced by shifting the bits of the integer to the left by one; adding zero to a register can be replaced by a no-operation (and removed entirely). There are a great many limits on the operation of keyhole optimizers since they have to be careful not to violate implicit assumptions and dependencies that are used by the code. For example, subtracting one number from another in most CPUs does not just carry out an arithmetic operation – it usually sets bits in the condition code to indicate, for example, if the result is positive, negative, or zero. Sometimes that is the sole purpose of the subtraction: to perform a comparison between two numbers to see which is the larger. A naive keyhole optimizer that removed the subtraction because no use was made of the difference is likely to produce incorrect code.

- *Common sub-expression elimination.* The same sub-expression occurring two or more times is often an opportunity for optimization, provided the value of the sub-expression cannot be modified between their occurrences. The value of the sub-expression can then be computed once, and the value re-used without re-computing it. The reader may notice that this only makes sense if the programmer is writing the same piece of code repeatedly. Why would a programmer leave the same sub-expression many times over in the same piece of code? The answer is that many do for clarity, or because they use macros to navigate data structures. Code inlining (discussed below) can also be a common source of repeated sub-expressions.

- *Code hoisting.* Another example of common sub-expression elimination is to remove quantities that are independent of the loop index. Thus the sub-expression is "hoisted" outside the loop and computed once before the loop, and the value is used inside the loop. Consider, for example, the Meschach MAT data structure for storing matrices: MAT *A; the entries in the matrix are stored in a field of the MAT structure (double **me, for matrix entries). Summing all the entries of a matrix A could then be done using code like this:

```
int i, j;
double sum = 0.0;
for ( i = 0; i < m; i++ )
    for ( j = 0; j < n; j++ )
        sum += A->me[i][j];
```

In the inner loop on j there is a common sub-expression: A->me[i]. This is the pointer to the start of the ith row. This can be pre-computed outside the loop on j, but inside the loop on i. The expression A->me[i] inside the loop on i also has a common sub-expression: A->me, which can be computed outside the loop on i. Code hoisting in effect results in the code

```
int i, j;
double sum = 0.0, **A_me, *A_me_i;
A_me = A->me;
for ( i = 0; i < m; i++ )
{
    A_me_i = A_me[i];
    for ( j = 0; j < n; j++ )
        sum += A_me_i[j];
}
```

Now we see that inside the inner loop, apart from the floating-point operations, there are only a simple memory address computation and a memory access. In the original code there were two memory address computations and three memory accesses in each pass through the inner loop.

- *Dead code elimination.* Dead code is code that can never be executed. Again, it sounds strange that this would ever happen. But it does: debugging code, for example, is often preceded by "if (debug)" conditions. If debug is a constant whose value is known at compile time, and the value if false, then the debugging code is dead code and the compiler can remove it. It can also occur in code inlining and templates in C++, where general code might handle situations that never occur in certain uses.

- *Code inlining.* Inlining is the process of substituting the text of a routine into another (possibly changing variable names in the process) to create code equivalent to the function call. This almost certainly requires additional memory for the inlined code, but has the potential to reduce the execution time. The time needed for a function call is definitely eliminated; but greater savings are possible by combining inlining with other optimization techniques.

- *Register allocation.* Register allocation for variables is a vital, if low-level, optimization that compilers must carry out. It is desirable to keep frequently used variables and computed values in registers for fast access. But if there are more values that are frequently accessed than registers to hold them, there can be some difficult decisions to make regarding which values to keep in registers and which to keep in memory. These issues are particularly acute in CPUs with a small number of registers, such as Intel CPUs. However, recent Intel CPUs aggressively use register renaming to overcome this limitation so that the hardware performs as if there were a very large number of registers.

- *Strength reduction.* Sometimes a sequence of multiplications can be replaced by a sequence of additions, which allows us to replace a more expensive operation (integer multiplication) with a faster one (integer addition). This is particularly useful for very low-level operations such as computing memory addresses. For example, consider the code

```
double a[N];
int i;
for ( i = 0; i < N; i++ )
    a[i] = i;
```

The memory address of a[i] is the address of a plus 8 times i. Instead of doing this computation on each pass through the loop, we can keep a pointer to a[i] which is initialized to a before the loop and incremented by 8 (one double) in each pass through the loop. The optimized code would look like this:

```
double a[N], *a_i;
int i;
a_i = a;
for ( i = 0; i < N; i++ )
{
    *a_i = i;
    a_i++;   /* increments by 1 double */
}
```

One aspect of optimizing compilers that will undoubtedly improve in the future is **interprocedural optimization**. These optimizations involve code in one or more routines. The need for separate compilation means that compilers cannot "see" beyond a single compilation unit – typically a file – to determine what optimizations can or should be carried out.

While there have been considerable advances in compiler optimization technology, they all involve some form of pattern matching. Optimizing compilers are fundamentally local optimizers: they can improve on local patterns and operations, but they do not understand the global issues and they cannot derive optimal algorithms for you.

13.3 Helping the compiler along

While optimizing compilers are able to do a great many things, there are many things that they cannot do. How things get done is ultimately in the hands of the programmer. While some things that a programmer can do have limited effect (such as using the `register` keyword in C/C++), there are many others that can be crucial for performance. This is particularly true for memory locality.

Other keywords such as `const` are very useful for optimizing compilers to produce efficient code. This is particularly true when used in combination with the `restrict` keyword from the C99 standard.[1] The `const` keyword means that the indicated variable cannot be assigned to. This is particularly important for pointers and arrays: to pass an array so that it cannot be changed by a routine, we use the `const` keyword like this in the declaration of the routine:

```
void my_routine(double const *my_array, ...)
```

or

```
void my_routine(double const my_array[], ...)
```

However, the `const` keyword cannot prevent changes due to *aliasing*. That is, the same memory location can be referred to through different pointers. Consider the example routine below:

```
void aliased_func(double const *px, double *py)
{
    double temp;
    temp = *px;
    *py = 3.0;
    temp = *px;
}
```

---

[1] The GNU C++ compiler supports the `_restrict_` keyword which has the same effect in C++.

If this routine is called with px == py, then the memory location *px is aliased; it can be accessed both as *px and as *py. This has an effect on optimization of the code: since the compiler cannot be sure that px and py are different, it has to assume that assigning to *py can change the value of *px. So the compiler cannot save the value of *px obtained for the first assignment to temp for the second assignment.

The restrict keyword in the C99 standard for C is a way of telling a compiler to *assume that aliasing does not occur* for a particular variable. That is, if a variable is declared restrict, the compiler assumes that changes to other variables cannot affect that variable. Whether aliasing does or does not occur is the responsibility of the programmer.

Using restrict for all pointer variables is essentially equivalent to what happens with Fortran, as Fortran compilers can assume that aliasing does not occur, whether or not it actually does. What happens if aliasing occurs but is assumed not to? The standards documents say that it is undefined. In practice it depends on the compiler, and perhaps how much optimization is requested – the more optimization, the more likely that unexpected things will happen. Sometimes it will be harmless, but sometimes it can break the program.

In Fortran 90 we can use the intent(in), intent(out), and intent(inout) declarations to inform the compiler about how arguments are used. Note that intent(in) in Fortran 90 works like const in C/C++, but intent(out) has no equivalent in C/C++. An intent(out) argument must be assigned a value before use and before the routine returns.

Normally optimizing compilers can only work on local information – they can optimize a routine, but they usually cannot use any information about where the routine is called. This can be partly overcome by *inlining* routines. In C/C++ this is done with the inline keyword. Where an inlined function is called, the text of the inlined function is copied to where it is called, possibly with variable names changed to avoid name clashes. This is particularly important in C++ where the goals of security and information hiding result in lots of small access and updating functions – these are natural candidates for inlining. Inlining combined with template programming (discussed in Section 8.6.4) provides a powerful mechanism for creating efficient programs in a fully object-oriented framework.

13.4 Practicalities and asymptotic complexity

The most common measure of the performance of algorithms is the asymptotic bound on the time (or number of operations) needed to complete the algorithm with an input of a given length. Asymptotic notation is convenient and concise, and widely used.

Mathematically, we say that a function $f(n)$ is $O(g(n))$ (pronounced "order of g of n") as n goes to infinity if there are numbers N and C where

$$|f(n)| \leq C\, g(n) \qquad \text{for all } n \geq N.$$

Because C can act as a scale factor between, say, operations and time in seconds it doesn't matter which of these is measured – they have the same asymptotic behavior. This also means that differences in compilers, access speeds, and units of measurement are irrelevant. Thus, for example, we can readily show that bubble sort is $O(n^2)$ and that the average case time for quicksort is $O(n \log n)$. Usually these kinds of asymptotic estimates give good indications of what performs better in practice, at least for large input sizes. But sometimes following only the asymptotic behavior gives a poor guide for algorithm selection. For example, the value of C could be very large – 10^6 or 10^{12} or more for example. But unless the algorithm is enormously complicated, the constant C is usually not large.

Consider, for example, Strassen's algorithm for matrix multiplication. This is asymptotically $O(n^{\log_2 7})$ with $\log_2 7 \approx 2.807$, while the conventional algorithm is $O(n^3)$. Clearly Strassen's algorithm is asymptotically faster. However, n has to be quite large before it beats the conventional algorithm. To see where this "break-even" point is, we need to know the constants involved. For the conventional algorithm, the number of floating point operations is $\approx 2n^3$, while for Strassen's algorithm, if n is a power of 2 then the number of floating point operations is $\approx 7n^{\log_2 7}$. These two estimates are equal when $n = (7/2)^{1/(3-\log_2 7)} \approx 667.11$. So the matrices would have to be at least 667×667 for Strassen's algorithm to have fewer floating point operations. If n is not a power of 2, we could use the simple strategy of padding the A and B matrices by zeros to become $2^k \times 2^k$ with $k = \lceil \log_2 n \rceil$, then in the worst case n would be roughly doubled. Comparing the worst case (n is doubled) $7(2n)^{\log_2 7}$ and $2n^3$ we find these are equal when $n = (7 \times 2^{\log_2 7 - 1})^{1/(3-\log_2 7)} \approx 1.626 \times 10^7$. Dense $n \times n$ double-precision matrices with $n \approx 1.6 \times 10^7$ need about $2\,000\,000$ Gigabytes of memory! Clearly this approach to using Strassen's algorithm is impracticable.

Fortunately there are ways of reducing the constant in Strassen's algorithm by using a recursive hybrid of Strassen's algorithm with the conventional algorithm: when the matrices are smaller than a certain threshold t use the conventional matrix-multiply algorithm, and otherwise use Strassen's formulas recursively. In this way it can be ensured that the algorithm never uses more floating point operations than the conventional algorithm, and the hidden constant in the $O(n^{\log_2 7})$ is substantially smaller. In fact, the cutoff point for this hybrid algorithm to use fewer floating point operations is $n \approx 18$.

Another issue that can arise in some asymptotic measures of the performance of algorithms is hidden parameters. Consider, for example, linear programming in

d unknowns with n linear inequality constraints: this is the task of minimizing a linear cost function of $x_1, x_2, \ldots, x_d$ subject to a collection of linear inequality constraints:

$$c(x) = c_1 x_1 + c_2 x_2 + \cdots + c_d x_d \qquad \text{subject to}$$
$$b_i \geq a_{i1} x_1 + a_{i2} x_2 + \cdots + a_{id} x_d, \qquad i = 1, \ldots, n,$$
$$x_j \geq 0, \qquad j = 1, \ldots, d.$$

There are randomized algorithms for this problem which have $O(n)$ complexity for fixed d [27]. This makes them excellent algorithms for one, two, or three unknowns. However, the hidden constant in the $O(n)$ estimate is a function of d – in fact, the average number of floating point operations needed grows like $C\, d!\, n$ for a modest constant C. This behavior is very nice in n but very bad in d since $d!$ grows so fast ($d = 10$ gives $d! \approx 3.63 \times 10^6$). If d is 5 or more, more conventional algorithms such as the simplex method or an interior point method should be used [82].

Another trap in blindly using asymptotics is the matter of slowly growing functions such as $\log n$. Since $\log n$ grows much slower than n, $O(n \log n)$ algorithms (e.g., quicksort) are usually much faster than $O(n^2)$ algorithms (e.g., bubble sort). However, we should be more careful with functions like $n \log^d n$ if d starts becoming larger than about 2 or 3. An example comes from computational geometry for a task involving range queries of d-dimensional data [27]. The complexity of the algorithm is $O(n \log_2^d n)$ compared with $O(n^2)$ for a naive algorithm. The ratio $n \log_2^d n / n^2$ goes to zero as n goes to infinity for any d, but it may become large for modest n. In fact, the ratio has a maximum value of $(d/2)^d$ at $n = 2^d$. If $d = 10$ this gives a worst-case ratio of $5^{10} \approx 9.76 \times 10^6$ at $n = 2^{10} = 1024$. This would be worth taking into account before implementing a complex algorithm like this for d as large as 10.

To summarize, while asymptotic estimates of performance are very valuable, don't start using or relying on an asymptotically faster algorithm until you have investigated the hidden constants in the "big O" formulas, and checked that it makes sense for the parameters you have in mind. Replacing a factor of n in the asymptotic formula with $\log n$ or $\log^2 n$ can result in substantial speed improvements even for a more complex algorithm. But removing a factor of $\log n$ might or might not be useful. More slowly growing functions like $\log \log n$ should usually regarded as approximately constant. When you have an opportunity to compare algorithms with similar asymptotic estimates for time, dig deeper to see what the hidden constants are. And remember, even if an algorithm uses fewer floating point operations, there are many other effects which can make it run slower.

14

Grabbing memory when you need it

14.1 Dynamic memory allocation

In the middle of a routine you realize that you need some scratch space n floating point numbers long, and n is a complicated function of the inputs to the routine. What do you do? Do you add another scratch space argument to your routine along with its length as an argument and check that it is big enough (stopping the program immediately if it is not)? Often a better idea is to allocate the memory needed. In Fortran 90 this is done using the `allocate` command; in C you use the `malloc` function; in C++ and Java the `new` operator will do this task; in Pascal the allocation is done by the `new` operator, but the syntax is different from C++ or Java. These can be used to dynamically allocate memory. All of these commands return, or set, a pointer to the allocated block of memory.

The allocated block of memory is taken from a global list of available memory which is ultimately controlled by the operating system. This block of memory remains allocated until it is no longer accessible (if garbage collection is used), explicitly de-allocated, or the program terminates. So dynamically allocated memory can be used to hold return values or returned data structures. Dynamically allocated memory can be passed to other routines, and treated like memory that has been statically allocated, or allocated on a stack in most respects.

The data structure that controls the allocation and de-allocation of memory is called a ***memory heap***. A memory heap may contain a pair of linked lists of pointers to blocks of memory. One linked list contains pointers to the allocated blocks of memory (the allocated list), while the other linked list contains pointers to the unallocated (or *free*) blocks or memory (the free list); see Figure 14.1. Many implementations only have one linked list for the free memory blocks for efficiency, but incorrectly de-allocating a block of memory that was not dynamically allocated from the memory heap cannot be prevented. These bugs typically result in program termination in an apparently unrelated part of the program. More careful

195

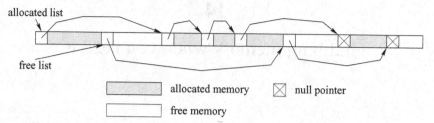

Figure 14.1. Memory heap structure. Note that some systems do not have an "allocated list".

memory heaps can do a great deal of checking to catch these and other bugs, but are considerably slower.

In C, where the allocation is done by a function call rather than an operator built into the language, there needs to be a special way of passing information about the type of the object(s) being allocated. The reserved word for this purpose is `sizeof`, and to allocate an array of n double-precision floating point numbers in C we use:

```
xp = (double *)malloc(n*sizeof(double));
```

In C++, the `new[]` operator is used:

```
double *xp = new double[n];
```

In any language there has to be a way to deal with the possibility that dynamic memory allocation fails. If it fails in C, the `malloc` routine returns `NULL`; in C++ and Java the `new` operator throws an exception; in Fortran 90 if the `allocate` statement is used with an optional status variable, the status variable is non-zero if there has been an error:

```
real, allocatable :: x(:)
integer :: allocstat, n
allocate( x(n), STAT=allocstat )
IF ( allocstat /= 0 ) ...    ! error
```

You should always ensure that the program cannot "fall through" the allocation step without the allocation occurring. So in C, the value returned from `malloc` should always be checked:

```
xp = (double *)malloc(n*sizeof(double));
if ( xp == NULL ) ... /* error */
```

This issue is not as important in C++ since the default behavior of `new` is to throw an exception, which will prevent this kind of "fall through" from happening.

Table 14.1. *Allocation and deallocation commands*

Language	Allocation	Deallocation
C	malloc/calloc	free
C++	new	delete
Fortran	allocate	deallocate
Java	new	—

Beware of relying on a NULL return or a thrown exception if you are close to running out of memory. In the authors' experience, operating systems do not always behave in a crisp way, returning a good pointer or NULL, or throwing an error. Sometimes programs crash anyway, or "freeze". One cause of strange behavior is virtual memory: an allocated block of memory might not fit in main memory, and so might require swapping memory onto and off of disk. If things are very tight with other processes starting and stopping, this might lead to ***thrashing*** (see Section 12.4): a great deal of swapping memory on and off disk, making the system extremely slow – even "frozen". Another possibility is that, since stacks can grow and shrink unpredictably, there can be a sudden overflow due to a stack needing an extra page of virtual memory. This can cause immediate program termination.

14.2 Giving it back

Being able to grab memory as it is needed is a wonderful convenience, and can greatly simplify the calls to routines that use scratch memory. However, if the memory is not returned to the heap, and fresh memory allocated from the heap instead, eventually the heap will run out of blocks of memory to allocate. Then the memory allocator has no option but to force a program error. Systems with garbage collection will return inaccessible memory to the heap, which makes running out of free memory a very unlikely event. Garbage collection is very convenient, but it comes at a cost. Most programming languages which are designed with efficiency in mind do not have it. These languages include C, Fortran 90, and C++. Java, C#, and Lisp do have garbage collection. More on how to program efficiently in a garbage collected language is discussed in the next section.

Allocation and deallocation commands are listed in Table for C, C++, Fortran and Java.

There are a number of rules you should follow in de-allocating memory.

1. *Prevent access to de-allocated memory.* This can be done by setting the pointer to null after de-allocating. In C set the pointer to NULL; in C++ set the pointer to zero; in Fortran 90/95 use nullify(x) for pointers. The only way that access to that

de-allocated memory can occur is if the pointer was copied before de-allocating, creating a "dangling pointer". Access to the de-allocated memory can result in catastrophic failure as the contents of the memory block may be changed either by the memory heap routines, or by another piece of code that has allocated that block.

2. *De-allocate memory in the reverse order it was allocated.* This makes sure that any dependencies between the allocated memory will not result in "dangling pointers". So if one allocated data structure has a pointer to another allocated data structure, the second should be de-allocated first.

3. *For a temporary memory block, de-allocate the block before leaving the routine.* If the de-allocation is not done before the routine ends, access to the memory is lost. While this does not lead directly to catastrophic failure, it does mean that that memory block becomes unusable. Later calls to the routine will result in more memory being allocated. If this is repeated often enough, this **memory leak** can exhaust the entire supply of allocatable memory and *that* can be catastrophic.

De-allocating NULL pointers in C can lead to program termination in some implementations. Also, de-allocating a pointer twice can cause problems in C and C++. Memory bugs can be difficult to track down and fix. For more information on how to do this, see Chapter 15.

14.3 Garbage collection

Garbage collection in computing is as convenient and helpful as it is in real-life. Some languages build it in, such as Lisp, Java, and C#. Memory leaks are (almost) a thing of the past!

But there is a cost. To understand that cost, you should have some awareness of how garbage collection is carried out. Generally there are three main approaches to garbage collection.

- *Mark-and-sweep.* This is perhaps the most common. When memory runs out, then the garbage collector is brought into action to reclaim what memory is available. It is assumed that the garbage collector has access to all pointer (or reference) variables in the system, and can navigate all the data structures in the system. From these starting points, it finds all the accessible memory, marking it as it finds it as referenced. Everything else is available to be reclaimed, which is added to the free list.
- *Reference counting.* Each object allocated contains a reference count of the number of references to it. Whenever a reference to an object is passed to a routine or assigned to a variable, the object's count is incremented; whenever a routine exits, the reference count of each local object is decremented. Whenever the reference count becomes zero, the object is garbage and is destroyed and the memory returned to the memory heap. Whenever an object is destroyed, the reference count of all objects it refers to are decremented.
- *Copy collection.* Memory is divided into two partitions. When one partition becomes full, the garbage collection system, starting from all the pointers in the system, navigates all the accessible data structures, copying the data structures into the second partition. As

it does this it updates all pointers in the data structures that it finds. Like the mark and sweep approach, this assumes that the garbage collection system has access to all pointer variables and can navigate all the data structures. One advantage of this method is that it compacts memory; that is, after garbage collection, all the free memory is contiguous.

The mark-and-sweep and copy collection approaches result in a program stopping all activity but garbage collection until this is finished. Users of the emacs editor (which uses a version of Lisp) may notice it doing this sometimes. Various techniques have been used to reduce this cost of garbage collection, which have resulted in significant advances. However, the principle of "don't create garbage unless you have to" applies. That is, instead of creating objects that are soon destroyed, re-cycle already created objects.

The reference counting approach results in more computation in normal operations, but the program will not stop for long while garbage collection is being carried out. Reference counting does not require knowledge of all the variables in the system, and can be implemented in C++, for example.

14.4 Life with garbage collection

Garbage collection means never having to explicitly give memory back. The system with garbage collection will do it for you! Memory leaks practically cease to exist.

Garbage collection is an intrinsic part of some programming languages, such as Lisp. Lisp became important enough that special hardware was developed for running Lisp code (which is normally interpreted). This effort culminated in the MIT Lisp Machine. With systems like this, a considerable amount of experience was gained with the effects of garbage collection, particularly for the mark-and-sweep approach to garbage collection.

A particular problem with the mark-and-sweep is that while garbage collection is happening across most of main memory, the computer cannot do anything else. And if the amount of main memory is large, this can take a long time. One lesson learned was that

to minimize the amount of time spent in garbage collection, minimize the amount of garbage produced.

In practice this means that objects allocated should be re-used. This is particularly important if you have many small objects – the time spent allocating and de-allocating small objects can become much larger than the time spent doing computations with these small objects.

Consider, for example, the Jama [11, 10] package in Java for dense matrix operations. A typical use of Jama would be to solve a small system of linear equations, which can be done like this (with checking for a small residual):

```
double[][] array = {{1.,2.,3},{4.,5.,6.},
  {7.,8.,10.}};
Matrix A = new Matrix(array);
Matrix b = Matrix.random(3,1);
Matrix x = A.solve(b);
Matrix residual = A.times(x).minus(b);
double rnorm = residual.normInf();
```

This is an excellent use of many of the object-oriented facilities of Java. However, if the matrix A is small, and this code is repeated many times, there are hidden creations and destructions of `Matrix` objects. Take a look at the line

```
Matrix residual = A.times(x).minus(b);
```

This computes $Ax - b$. But note that it does this first by computing Ax and storing the result in a newly created `Matrix` object; then b is subtracted from this `Matrix` to give the `residual` object. The `Matrix` holding the product Ax is thrown away. If the code is part of a loop, then `residual` is thrown away with each subsequent iteration before being replaced by the new result of `A.times(x).minus(b)`. In this case, there can be a great deal of memory allocation and de-allocation.

If the matrix A is $n \times n$ with large n, then these concerns are not as important: the time spent performing `A.solve(b)` (which involves a matrix factorization) will far exceed the time spent in allocating and de-allocating memory.

But if you want maximum performance, then you should be able to re-use memory. The designers of Jama could have accommodated this by including functions where the user passed a `Matrix` to hold the result as well:

```
class Matrix ... {
  ...
  Matrix minus(Matrix B, Matrix out)
  ...
  Matrix minus(Matrix B)
  {
    Matrix out = new
      Matrix(B.getRowDimension(),
             B.getColumnDimension());
    return minus(B,out);
  }
  ...
}
```

There is an additional function call if we use A.times(x) with this modified version of Jama, but the cost of this will be insignificant compared to the cost of creating the output Matrix, which must be done anyway with this way of using times. And if you want the fast version, you will need to think about where to put the output, but the code will execute faster: A.times(x,residual). We can put this into a loop which can execute many times without creating much garbage.

```
Matrix A, b, x, residual;
...
b = new Matrix(A.getRowDimension(), 1);
x = new Matrix(A.getColumnDimension(), 1);
residual = new Matrix(A.getRowDimension(), 1);
double rnorm;
for ( int i = 0; i < 100000; i++ )
{
  // Set up A matrix
  ...
  // Now set up right-hand side
  ...
  // Solve linear system and compute residual
  A.solve(b,x);            // output in x
  A.times(x,residual);     // output in residual
  residual.minusEquals(b);
  rnorm = residual.normInf();
  // Do something with the results
  ...
}
```

Since we are re-using memory, we are avoiding the additional cost of allocating and de-allocating memory. It also means that the code is accessing the same piece of memory each time the code is executed.

This is an example of providing more than one interface to an algorithm. Furthermore, the additional interface comes at very little programming cost, since implementing the easy-to-use interface minus(Matrix b) does not require any knowledge about the internal structure of minus(Matrix b, Matrix out).

Finally, in garbage collected systems it is a good idea to nullify references and pointers to data structures that are no longer needed. This signals that these structures are ready for garbage collection.

14.5 Conservative garbage collection

Conservative garbage collectors can provide garbage collection services for languages that do not have it built in, such as C and C++.

Conservative garbage collectors typically use a mark–sweep algorithm with a conservative method for determining what objects are "live" and what is "garbage". By conservative we mean that it will mark some things as being live which should be marked as garbage. This is crucial, since any de-allocation of a live object would likely crash the program.

Conservative garbage collectors scan the stack and the global data area for anything that could be a pointer into an allocated memory block. When one is found, then that allocated block is similarly scanned for possible pointers to allocated memory blocks, and the process repeated recursively. Any allocated memory block found this way is potentially live, and kept. Any memory block that is not found this way is considered garbage and de-allocated.

The most commonly used conservative garbage collector is the Boehm–Demers–Weiser garbage collector, which can be used as a replacement for `malloc` or `new` in C/C++. There are a number of papers on this topic; one of the more recent at the time of writing is [9]. The garbage collector and user documentation can be found on Hans Boehm's site `http://www.hpl.hp.com/personal/Hans_Boehm/gc/`. Conservative garbage collectors can also be used with conventional programs that do their own de-allocation, for finding memory leaks.

Typically the Boehm–Demers–Weiser garbage collector can reclaim all but a few percent of the "garbage". However, it is possible for this and other conservative garbage collectors to perform badly by *not* freeing most of the garbage. For example, if a significant fraction of the address space is taken up by allocated memory then these garbage collectors will not perform as well: a "random" entry in memory is likely to point to some block of allocated memory. This can happen on 32-bit machines if you have a gigabyte or several hundred megabytes of memory allocated. On 64-bit machines, you would need to allocate hundreds of petabytes (1 petabyte is approximately 10^{15} bytes) before this effect would start to occur.

It is also possible to fool conservative garbage collectors by storing pointer information in a way that makes it impossible to tell that a block of allocated memory is potentially alive. For example, consider the (bad) C++ code:

```
int *p = new int[10];
// bottom 16 bits of p
long l1 = 0x0000FFFF & reinterpret_cast<long>(p);
// top 16 bits of p
long l2 = 0xFFFF0000 & reinterpret_cast<long>(p);
```

```
p = 0;
// Allocated memory could be considered garbage here,
// but we can reconstruct p:
p = reinterpret_cast<int *>(l1 | l2);
```

But disguising pointers like this is dangerous, non-portable and should be avoided. (Note the use of `reinterpret_cast`.) Leave pointers as pointers and conservative garbage collectors can do their job.

14.6 Doing it yourself

Designing your own general memory allocation and de-allocation system takes some effort. Usually this is not worthwhile, but if certain conditions hold, you can write simple and fast allocators (and de-allocators). Things are simplest for fixed-size objects with no de-allocation. In this case, all that is needed is an array and counter. If you need to include de-allocation then you need to have pointers as well. Both of these situations can be handled with allocation (and de-allocation) algorithms that cost $O(1)$ time and memory per allocation (or de-allocation).

C++ programmers should note that creating memory allocation operations for particular data types should be done via `allocator` template classes [96, pp. 567–578].

14.6.1 Fixed-size objects and no de-allocation

This is the simplest case, and where "doing it yourself" is the most profitable. At its simplest it amounts to allocating items out of an array and keeping an index of the next item available for allocation. When we come to the end of the array, we normally have to stop.

Here is an example in C++. The objects are stored in an array, but we also need to know the length of this array and how many elements have already been allocated. This can be done using a pointer and two integers:

```
T    *array;   // allocate from this array
int  length;   // length of array
int  start;    // index of next item to allocate
```

Note that T is the type of the objects to allocate; this can be made part of a template in C++ to make it useful for allocating whatever objects you wish.

Creating the memory heap is easy: allocate the array and set the size of the array, setting the starting point for allocation at the start of the array (index zero):

```
MemHeap1(int max_size)
{
  array = new T[max_size];
  if ( array != 0 )
    length = max_size;
  else // error!
    length = 0;
  start = NULL;
}
```

Now allocation can be done very easily:

```
T *allocate()
{
  if ( start >= length )
    throw bad_alloc();
  else
    {
      // initialize to default value
      array[start] = 0;
      return &(array[start++]);
    }
}
```

Note that there is very little memory overhead in this: just two integers for the entire set of objects available for allocation. However, if we come to the end of the array there is not much we can do. We cannot, for example, re-allocate the `array`, as then the pointers returned by `allocate` would all become invalid.

14.6.2 *Fixed-size objects with de-allocation*

Allowing de-allocation as well for fixed-size objects means that we need more bookkeeping. The simplest strategy is to keep the memory heap for the objects concerned as a linked list. De-allocating a memory block then becomes a simple matter of making the block the head of the list. Coming to the end of the list means that a new large block of memory must be obtained from the underlying allocator (`malloc` or `new`). This should be done in C++ by creating an `allocator`. There are some complications in C++ because at some point there must be a conversion of "raw memory" into objects (which require that the constructor for its class is called). An example of how to do this in C++ can be found in [96, pp. 570–573].

14.7 Memory tips

Since memory allocation and de-allocation can take up a great deal of time, or result in memory leaks which can crash a program, it is worthwhile to be aware of some techniques which can help you use dynamic memory allocation efficiently and safely. Here, two techniques are described which we have found helpful.

14.7.1 High-water mark technique

A situation that is not uncommon is that a vector used for intermediate calculations has a size that will need to change unpredictably as the computation progresses. How can we handle this situation?

Allocating the largest conceivable vector is very likely wasteful of memory. Allocating and re-allocating the vector with every new size could take considerable time. An alternative is the **high-water mark** technique: keep a separate field or variable which holds the *physical* size of the vector, and another which holds the *logical* size of the vector (that is, how much we actually need to use). If the physical size is as large or larger than the logical size requested, then we simply change the logical size. If the physical size is smaller than the logical size requested, then we must increase the physical size. Typically with the high-water mark technique, the physical size is increased to the requested logical size.

This technique is used in Meschach; it is implemented in the vector and matrix resize functions. The vector data structure contains information about how much memory has been allocated along with the current size of the vector:

```
/* vector definition */
typedef          struct          {
   unsigned int          dim, max_dim;
   Real          *ve;
} VEC;
```

Here is part of the Meschach vector resize function `v_resize()`:

```
/* v_resize -- returns the vector x with dim new_dim
   -- x is set to the zero vector */
VEC          *v_resize(VEC *x, int new_dim)
{
   . . .
   if ( new_dim > x->max_dim )
     {
        . . .
        /* reallocate for new_dim Real's */
```

```
        x->ve = RENEW(x->ve,new_dim,Real);
        if ( ! x->ve )
            /* if allocation fails... */
            error(E_MEM,"v_resize");
        x->max_dim = new_dim;
    }
    ...
    /* now set new dimension */
    x->dim = new_dim;

    return x;
}
```

If we have a rough (but not always correct) estimate of the likely maximum size
of the vector that we need, then we can first size the vector to this estimate, and
then re-size it to the desired logical sizes as needed. If you are using the C++·STL,
use `reserve()` for the initial sizing. Since the physical size never gets smaller,
we know that we have covered most of the logical size requests and so we will not
need many memory allocation or de-allocation calls. But if our estimate is wrong,
the code will still operate correctly and increase the available physical memory on
the few cases this is needed.

In Meschach, the high-water mark technique is used inside functions, so that
intermediate vectors keep their memory between function calls, like this:

```
#include         "matrix.h"


VEC *my_function(VEC *x, VEC *out)
{
    static VEC *temp = NULL;   /* holds intermediate results */

    if ( ! x )
        error(E_NULL,"my_function");
    temp = v_resize(temp,x->dim);
    /* do computations... */
    return out = v_copy(temp,out);
}
```

It is important that the intermediate vector `temp` be declared `static`, so that
it retains its values and the memory between function calls. This approach is *not*
applicable for re-entrant or threadsafe code, which is an important issue in shared
libraries – then `static` variables must be avoided wherever possible.

The weakest point of this approach is that once the vector is no longer needed, it still might have a great deal of memory in it – resizing the vector will not make that memory available for other computations. The simplest way to deal with this situation is to de-allocate the entire vector. This is not possible for static local variables. Meschach provides some alternative ways of dealing with this situation involving registering these `static` temporaries.

14.7.2 *Amortized doubling*

The high-water mark technique can handle many irregular size requests, but it does not efficiently handle one common situation: what if we are adding one entry to the end of a vector? This would mean that we would probably need to increase the size of the vector each time through the loop – one allocation and vector copy with each iteration. This can be expensive.

One way to avoid this is to keep the physical and logical sizes separate, as for the high-water mark, but instead we approximately *double* the physical size each time we get a request for a small increase in the physical size. (We could set the physical size to max($2 \times$ current physical size, requested logical size), for example.) If this initial size of the vector is s_0 and the maximum size requested is s_{max}, we will not need more than $\log_2 \lceil s_{max}/s_0 \rceil$ memory allocation calls. Since this technique does not know the actual amount of memory needed, it may allocate up to twice as much memory as is actually used. However, this is often acceptable.

Assuming we are preserving the previous entries with each increase in size, we will have to copy values from the old array to the new array. However, the number of copies is no more than $2n$, where n is the number of entries in the final array.

This technique is used in Meschach's sparse matrix code when inserting entries into a sparse matrix: the size of a sparse row is doubled when more memory is needed for a row. That way the usual operations (incrementally adding entries to a row) can be handled efficiently.

15

Memory bugs and leaks

Memory problems are harder to debug because where the bug seems to be can be very far from where it actually is. There are several kinds of memory problems that you should be especially aware of:

- forgetting to allocate memory;
- reading or writing to memory outside the allowed regions;
- dangling pointers which result in improper accesses to memory;
- access being lost to useful pieces of memory, resulting in a memory leak.

15.1 Beware: unallocated memory!

The simplest mistake with memory is to forget to initialize a pointer variable:

```
double *p;
/* ... */
for ( i = 0; i < n; i++ )
  p[i] = 0.0;
```

In many languages and systems, uninitialized variables simply take on the value left on the stack. If it is an uninitialized pointer, then accessing it will usually result in a segmentation violation. Attempting to de-allocate memory associated with an uninitialized pointer can cause a program to terminate unexpectedly far from the creation of the pointer.

Use of uninitialized variables can be quickly identified by most compilers. Check your compiler for options that will force it to check for this error, which can cause other kinds of problems as well.

15.2 Beware: overwriting memory!

This is a particularly common bug in C and Fortran. In languages where the compiler or the run-time system knows the sizes of arrays (such as Java and Pascal), most of these errors can be prevented. Often Fortran compilers have switches that enable checking array bounds where the array bounds are known. Writing to memory outside the permitted limits often results in the program crashing, *but often not where the bug is*. Here is an example in C:

```
double *array1, *array2;
int    i, length;
/* some code goes here */
length = 10;
array1 = (double *)malloc(length*sizeof(double));
/* more code goes here */
array2 = (double *)malloc(length*sizeof(double));
/* bug is here: should have "i < length" */
for ( i = 0; i <= length; i++ )
  array1[i] = exp(-(double)(i));
/* even more code goes here */
printf("array1[3] = %g\n", array1[3]);
/* program could crash here */
free(array2);
```

The bug is that the valid indexes for `array1` are 0, 1, ..., length−1. The final time through the `for` loop results in a piece of memory outside the array being written to. (This is an example of an "off-by-one" bug.) If `array1` was obtained using a memory allocator, as in this example, then there is usually some extra header information used by the memory allocator there. As a result, when one of the memory allocation or de-allocation routines is called afterwards, it is likely (but not certain) that the program will crash there. Even if the allocation or de-allocation routines do not crash, the memory heap is in a bad state and something bad is likely to happen later on.

Probably the most common error in numerical programming is going beyond the bounds of arrays. This can be eliminated in languages like Java and Pascal which have array bounds checking built in. If you use access routines to control access to vector entries in C++, this problem can be controlled there as well. Many Fortran compilers also offer array bounds checking as a compile-time option. This is worth using.

But array bounds checking simply means that you know when you have gone beyond the array. Then you need to fix the bug that caused it.

Whatever language you program in, it is almost always best to program defensively to prevent over-running array bounds. This is particularly true for input routines where you do not know the size of the input – strings are a particular problem here. Routines that read or produce a string of unknown (maximum) size should be avoided. One such function is `gets` in C for inputting a string from a file or input device. This function should not be used. Instead, you should use `fgets` where you can specify the longest string you will read in. For example, consider the code:

```
char line1[11], line2[11];
printf("Input string: ");
gets(line2);
printf("line1: %s\n", line1);
printf("line2: %s\n", line2);
```

Here is an example of what can happen with it:

```
Input string: This is a very long string.
line1: ong string.
line2: This is a very long string.
```

The trouble is that there is no limit to the length of the string read in. Although 80 characters plus the terminating null character might seem enough, long strings can be read in which result in overwriting memory far beyond the limits of the `line` array. In fact, this is a favorite attack of hackers who can input a special string that is (perhaps) megabytes long to reach a particular point in (say) a Web server program and alter that program to do something else (usually to take over the program and gain access to the system running it).

When reading in strings, always use a means of controlling the length of the string read in. This can be done in C using `fgets`, or putting a count on the "`%s`" format string:

```
  fgets(line,80,stdin);
  /* or... */
  scanf("%80s",line);
```

The `fgets` call is the most recommended.

15.3 Beware: dangling pointers!

A *dangling pointer* is a pointer to a piece of memory that was once allocated, but is now de-allocated. Dangling pointers can happen in most programming languages, including Fortran 90. Here is a simple example of how this can happen in C++:

```
double *p1, *p2;
int    n = 10;
p1 = new double[n]; // allocate array
```

```
p2 = p1;            // p2 points to array
delete[] p1;        // p2 now ``dangles''
p2[3] = 5.7;        // Ooopppsss!!!
```

Use of p2 after p1 is deleted will (likely) result in a program error or a program crash. Avoid copying pointers unless the copy is being used for a short, temporary operation.

While most programmers will avoid dangling pointers in simple situations like this, avoiding them in general can be a major design issue. One of the ways in which problems arise is when a ***shallow copy*** is made of a data structure when a ***deep copy*** is really needed. Consider a vector data structure

```
type :: myvec
   integer :: length, max_len
   real, kind(0d0), pointer :: array(:)
end type myvec
```

and we write a *shallow copy* routine:

```
subroutine shallowcopy(x,y)
   type(myvec), intent(in) :: x
   type(myvec), intent(inout) :: y

   y%array  => x%array   ! pointer assignment
   y%length =  x%length
   y%max_len = x%max_len
end subroutine shallowcopy
```

If we try to use this, then changing the copy will also change the original:

```
type(myvec) :: x, y

call createvec(10,x)
call createvec(10,y)

do i = 1, x%length
   x%array(i) = i*i
end do
call shallowcopy(x,y)
y%array(4) = 5.0d0
! Now x%array(4) is 5, instead of 4*4
```

Furthermore, if we decide to delete the copy, we are inadvertently destroying the block of memory that the original needs:

```
call deallocvec(y)
! Now x%array is a dangling pointer
```

What we really need is a deep copy routine that copies the array entries into a safe and separate block of memory:

```
subroutine deepcopy(x,y)
   type(myvec), intent(in) :: x
   type(myvec), intent(inout) :: y
   integer :: i

   if ( allocated(y%array) ) then
      deallocate(y%array)
   end if
   allocate(y%array(x%length))
   y%length = x%length
   y%max_len = y%length
   do i = 1, x%length
      y%array(i) = x%array(i)
   end do
end subroutine deepcopy
```

Then updating the copy will not change the original, and destroying the copy will not result in dangling pointers.

There is another way in which dangling pointers can arise without using `malloc` or new. That is if you violate the rule

never return a pointer to a local variable!

Here is a simple example:

```
double *add_3d_vectors1(double a[3], double b[3])
{
   double sum[3];
   sum[0] = a[0] + b[0];
   sum[1] = a[1] + b[1];
   sum[2] = a[2] + b[2];
   return sum;     /* DON'T DO THIS!!! */
}
```

Why is this a problem? Well, local variables are allocated *on the stack*. The stack is a data structure used by the system to keep local variables, return addresses for when routines finish, and some related data and memory. It is constantly changing as calls are made and functions return. As soon as you return from the routine, none of its local variables should be referenced. That memory will soon be over-written with other data.

How should you write the add_3d_vectors1 routine? The best approach is probably to pass an array for the result.

```
double *add_3d_vectors2(double a[3], double b[3],
                        double sum[3])
{
   sum[0] = a[0] + b[0];
   sum[1] = a[1] + b[1];
   sum[2] = a[2] + b[2];
   return sum;
}
```

Note that in C/C++ it is common to return the output argument, as it can be ignored by the calling routine if convenient.

An alternative is to allocate the memory needed (which will be in the memory heap) when the function is called. It could be implemented like this:

```
double *add_3d_vectors3(double a[3], double b[3])
{
   double *sum;
   sum = (double *)malloc(3*sizeof(double));
   if ( sum == NULL )
     return NULL;
   sum[0] = a[0] + b[0];
   sum[1] = a[1] + b[1];
   sum[2] = a[2] + b[2];
   return sum;
}
```

This is correct, but it tends to lack efficiency, since we have to call malloc on every call to add_3d_vectors3. If add_3d_vectors3 is called a lot then this will be a serious slow-down of your code. A compromise is this: pass a pointer for the output (sum), and if sum is NULL, then allocate it.

```
double *add_3d_vectors4(double a[3], double b[3],
                        double *sum)
{
  if ( sum == NULL )
  {
    sum = (double *)malloc(3*sizeof(double));
    if ( sum == NULL )
      return NULL;
  }
  sum[0] = a[0] + b[0];
  sum[1] = a[2] + b[1];
  sum[2] = a[2] + b[2];
  return sum;
}
```

This way, you have a routine which allocates the memory only when it is necessary. But there is still a warning you should heed. Local variables can have any value – whatever junk is left on the stack when the function is called. Therefore you should *always* initialize variables before use, especially pointers.

Even this new routine is vulnerable to memory leaks, which we look at next.

15.4 Beware: memory leaks!

Suppose we have written the last version of add_3d_vectors, and we are feeling proud of being able to get it to handle the memory allocation problems. So we use it in a program for three-dimensional graphics, for example:

```
double *sum, list[1000000][3];
int    i;

sum = list[0];
for ( i = 1; i < 1000000; i++ )
{
  sum = add_3d_vectors4(list[i],sum,NULL);
  if ( sum == NULL )
    /* no more memory */
    exit(0); /* failure! */
}
/* success! */
```

If you do this loop many times, you will find that you will run out of memory. If the problem is small enough, everything will work fine and give correct values. But on the large problems you will run out of memory. Why?

Because every call to add_3d_vectors4 will allocate the memory needed for the array, and then be thrown away so that access to that array is lost. The memory is lost to the program. Without *garbage collection*, the loss of memory will become more serious and eventually will cause the program to stop or crash.

If we do not have garbage collection, then we need a way to avoid losing memory. One way of doing this is to *re-use* the memory we have allocated. Here is one way to do that:

```
double sum[3], list[1000000][3];
int    i;

/* create sum <- list[0] + list[1] */
add_3d_vectors4(list[0],list[1],sum);
for ( i = 2; i < 1000000; i++ )
{
   add_3d_vectors4(list[i],sum,sum);
}
/* success! */
```

Memory leaks are not bugs *per se* – they do not result in incorrect results. But they do reduce the amount of memory available and they can make your program crash or fail where it should succeed. Memory leaks occur when the pointer to a piece of allocated memory is overwritten, so that access to that allocated memory is lost.

One of the more frustrating things about memory leaks is that there is no point in the program where anything is obviously wrong. One of the best tools you can use to track down memory leaks is to instrument your code so that you can find out where and for what memory has been allocated. One approach is used in the dmalloc debugging malloc library, which keeps the file name and line number where the memory was allocated. This will be a help, but not a panacea for memory leaks.

Free and commercial tools for checking memory leaks are available, and include valgrind (described in the next section) and the conservative garbage collectors described in Section 14.5.

15.5 Debugging tools

One class of debugging tools is debugging memory allocators. These record considerable additional information, and often also lay down a bit pattern in the unallocated blocks so that unauthorized writes to unallocated memory can be detected.

Examples of this style of debugging memory allocator are `dbmalloc` by Conor Cahill [19] and `dmalloc` by Gray Watson [104]. These are purely software tools that provide "drop in" replacements for `malloc` etc. The simplest way to use them is to include them at link time as libraries before the standard library:

```
cc -o program program.o file1.o ... -ldmalloc
```

Check their documentation for the correct command line to use. To get the most out of these libraries, you should also use the include files and the additional functions provided with these libraries. These additional functions can help with memory leaks and checking for self-consistency of the heap. The latter is important as it can be used to identify where memory is being improperly overwritten.

A more hardware-based system is Electric Fence by Bruce Perens [85]. This is also a drop-in replacement for `malloc` and `new`. However, the way it works is a little different from the way that `dmalloc` and `dbmalloc` work: it places an inaccessible virtual memory page just before and just after each memory allocation. *Any* access that runs outside the properly allocated area will result in the program terminating. A quick look with a debugger will show you the offending instruction. Note that Electric Fence will stop the program at an improper *read* instruction, something the software-only approach cannot. Since Electric Fence relies on this hardware feature, there can sometimes be limits on its usability. Also, since virtual memory pages are often much larger than the objects allocated, the executable size can become huge with Electric Fence, as can the `core` file that is dumped on an error.

There is also the `checkergcc` compiler for C which builds in memory access checks. This is part of the GNU project and is available via `www.gnu.org`. A program compiled with `checkergcc` will emit warnings when illegal writes are made, and memory leaks can be also be identified.

For Linux systems running on Intel x86 CPUs, a powerful memory debugging system is Valgrind. Valgrind is actually a framework for a number of tools for investigating memory problems, memory accessing and caching behavior, amongst others. Amongst the tools that are available in Valgrind is `memcheck`. This can detect a large number of problems, including not only what can be caught by debugging memory allocators, but also use of uninitialized memory. `Memcheck` can also identify memory leaks and inappropriate reading or writing of the stack (which can occur when pointers to local variables are returned). `Memcheck` can also detect mismatches between how memory is allocated and how it is de-allocated in C/C++ systems: in particular it can detect when memory allocated with `new` (from C++) is de-allocated with `free` (from C) or `delete[]` (from C++).

Part IV

Tools

Part IV

1916

16

Sources of scientific software

The development of the Internet has contributed to the development of public libraries of scientific software. Some of this development has occurred through the efforts of individuals, through Internet collaborations (as with the development of Linux), and through government supported software development by academics and others (as with the development of LAPACK). There is a wide range of other software packages for scientific computing, many now written in C/C++, although Fortran and other languages are used for parts of many of these systems: PETSc (which supports the use of MPI for parallel computation), IML++ (an iterative methods library in C++), SparseLib++ (for handling sparse matrices in C++), and PLTMG (for solving partial differential equations).

In parallel with this, there has also been a tremendous development of commercial numerical software. Beginning in 1970 the Numerical Algorithms Group (NAG), based in the UK, developed libraries which have been sold commercially as the NAG libraries since 1976; the Harwell library was also developed in the UK; the IMSL libraries were developed commercially in the US. Another set of numerical libraries, called SLATEC, was developed by the Sandia and Los Alamos US National Laboratories and the US Air Force. These are available through `netlib` (see the next section). Perhaps the most spectacular example of commercial numerical software is the development of MATLAB. Initially a collection of Fortran 77 routines based on the early LINPACK and EISPACK libraries for dense matrix computations with a text interface, MATLAB has evolved into a full-featured interactive programming language with special support for numerical computation and scientific visualization. Niche numerical software has also been highly successful commercially – CPLEX has sustained a presence in the marketplace because of its highly regarded software for linear programming (minimizing or maximizing linear functions subject to linear inequality constraints). There are also a number of other successful commercial packages for optimization, including, for example, MINOS, SNOPT, KNITRO, and LOQO.

219

Note that most of these packages originated in academic environments, but once established, most became widespread as commercial software.

In this chapter we will focus on freely available software for numerical computation. These are the most widely available, and, in many areas, the most important software.

16.1 Netlib

Netlib is perhaps the best collection of freely available numerical software in one place, and has software for a wide variety of different computational tasks: solving differential equations (ODEPACK and PLTMG), Fourier transforms (FFTPACK and FISHPACK), eigenvalue/eigenvector computations (ARPACK), sparse matrix operations (SPARSE and ITPACK), continuation methods (HOMPACK), numerical integration (QUADPACK) and of course BLAS and LAPACK for dense matrix computations. In addition to the actual routines, there is also documentation. Most of the software is in Fortran 77, but there are also significant contributions in C (e.g., Meschach, and Kahan's paranoia program for testing floating point arithmetic).

Netlib is now far from being the only collection of freely available numerical software, and much can be found with a suitable search by Google. But it is a good starting point.

16.2 BLAS

BLAS (*Basic Linear Algebra Subroutines*) is the foundation of many other matrix and vector algorithms. LAPACK is based on BLAS, which provides the low-level operations – matrix–vector multiplication, scalar multiplication and addition of vectors and matrices, solution of triangular systems of equations, and matrix–matrix multiplication.

The basic idea of the BLAS is that each CPU has its own optimal implementation of the low-level routines. The implementations of BLAS are often constructed painstakingly by optimizing and hand-tuning standard implementations of the routines so as to make best use of the available hardware. Traditionally this has been done by the manufacturer of the CPU, and sold to purchasers of the hardware. However, the rapid evolution of hardware and software has made this approach very expensive. Instead of modifying the routines for each new version of the hardware, automatic tuning through systems such as ATLAS [105] has become common. Even so, BLAS libraries optimized for standard architectures and CPUs can be found on the Web. For example, a library of Pentium 4 optimized BLAS is available publicly through Kazishige Goto's Web page http://www.cs.utexas.edu/users/kgoto/signup-first.html

along with optimized BLAS for a range of other architectures. Plain (unoptimized) versions of BLAS are available as Fortran 77 source, along with C interfaces, through `netlib`. Netlib also provides a number of links to optimized BLAS libraries available through a number of CPU vendors.

16.3 LAPACK

LAPACK is arguably the best dense matrix software currently available, at least as a general purpose library. While it suffers somewhat from the problems typical of Fortran 77-based software (e.g., no dynamic memory allocation or de-allocation, error handling is carried out by checking return codes or `iflag` variables, and no support for input/output), LAPACK carries out the core tasks of matrix computations efficiently and about as accurately as can be achieved. The efficiency of LAPACK was achieved mainly through the reliance on BLAS, which is discussed below. LAPACK covers most dense matrix computations – solution of linear systems of various kinds, eigenvalue/eigenvector tasks, condition number estimation, and updating matrix factorizations. If you want only to carry out dense matrix operations, you should consider looking here first.

16.4 GAMS

GAMS [12] stands for *Guide to Available Mathematical Software*, and provides a search facility for finding mathematical software. This service is supported by the National Institute of Standards and Technology (NIST). GAMS has a taxonomy of kinds of mathematical software: at the coarsest level it is divided into the areas of arithmetic and error analysis, elementary and special functions, linear algebra, interpolation, optimization, differentiation and integration, solution of ordinary and partial differential equations, integral equations, transforms, convolutions, approximation, statistics and probability, simulation, data handling, computational geometry, and software tools.

The software indexed by GAMS includes software in `netlib` and also some commercial libraries, such as IMSL and NAG.

16.5 Other sources

Mathematical software, like that for other purposes, has been developing very rapidly. As a result it is very hard for any one person or group to track all the developments in the area. So often the way to get the most current mathematical software is to use a Web search engine like Google or AltaVista or . . . (insert your favorite search engine here).

As always with online resources, you should check carefully for the background to the software and clues as to its quality. Look for the group or individual behind it. What sort of background do they have? Do they have experience with scientific software? Is the software based on some standard software (such as BLAS and/or LAPACK)? How extensive is the software? Does it really cover your needs? Is it extensible? Have all aspects of the software (accuracy, robustness, ease of use, flexibility, efficiency in time and memory) been well developed? Are there licencing or other legal restrictions on its use?

There are many, many matrix libraries available through the Web. Many of them are simply object-oriented interfaces to BLAS/LAPACK, or provide the basic non-numerical operations plus matrix–vector addition and multiplication. Others are fully-blown implementations of a wide range of matrix data structures and operations. The great variety is partly because matrix libraries are something almost everyone in numerical computing needs, partly because of the different languages used, and partly because of different aspects that are emphasized. *Blitz++*, for example, provides template classes and aggressive inlining in order to provide high performance. Other libraries provide expression templates to avoid the creation (and destruction) of temporary objects. The *GNU Scientific Library* (GSL) is written in ANSI C, and so does not use templates. However, it covers a great many areas including matrices and vectors, and operations such as LU and QR factorization and singular value decompositions. GSL is a threadsafe library, which can be important in real-time applications. On the other hand, GSL was not designed for either lots of very small (two- or three-dimensional) vectors, or for very large systems.

In some areas commercial solvers predominate. This is the case in continuous optimization, for example. For linear programming, for example, the most-used software is CPLEX, although there is a popular free package called `lp_solve`. CPLEX is noted for its speed and robustness, which is why many are willing to pay substantial amounts for it. On the other hand, `lp_solve` can handle moderately large problems, and may be sufficient for most users.

These days there are many sources for software. If you take care to evaluate the quality of software, you can usually find software that can be adapted to your needs. As always: test before you use.

17

Unix tools

The Unix operating system was developed at the outset by programmers who wanted to make their life easier. As a result the Unix operating system has a collection of tools for programming that other operating systems adopted or adapted.

While *Graphical User Interfaces* (GUIs) are extremely useful, they can be a hindrance to automating tasks. Consider, for example, the task of deleting every object code file in a directory or one of its sub-directories. In a GUI system, you would need to go into each sub-directory, highlight the files you wanted to remove, and then send them to the "Recycle Bin" or "Trashcan". By contrast, Unix provides a command called `find`, which is for more than just finding files, and can accomplish the job like this:

```
find . -name \*.o -exec rm {} \;
```

That is, starting from the current directory (`.`), find all files with a name ending in `.o` and then execute the command `rm` with that file. That is: delete all the ".o" files in this directory and its sub-directories.

Unix also emphasized the role of text. So many Unix tools were developed for handling text files, such as `grep` (short for Get Regular Expression and Print), `sed` (short for Stream EDitor), and `awk` (after the initials of its designers). A tool that combines the abilities of these tools is `perl` [90]. As noted in *The Pragmatic Programmer* [58], much of a programmer's work life is spent working with (writing, editing, modifying, and transforming) text. So these tools should be in most programmers' toolboxes. We will also look at tools for building programs from source code, managing revisions, and profiling.

17.1 Automated builds: make

The purpose of `make` is to ease the compilation of small to medium sized projects. Instead of having to remember all the source files, compiler options, and libraries,

223

this information is stored in a `makefile`. When the `makefile` is properly set up,

```
make myprogram
```

will re-compile all the source file(s) that have changed since the `myprogram` was last built, using all the appropriate compiler options, libraries, and other settings needed.

Unless the only source is `myprogram.c`, and no special compiler options or libraries are needed, you will need to write a file called `makefile` (or `Makefile`). Here is an example of what a `makefile` looks like:

```
myprogram: myprogram.o routine1.o
        cc -o myprogram myprogram.o routine1.o
myprogram.o: myprogram.c myheader.h
```

The first line says that to create `myprogram` the object files `myprogram.o` and `routine1.o` are needed, that is, `myprogram` *depends* on `myprogram.o` and `routine1.o`; the second line says how this done. Note that the first character of the second line is a *tab*. Using eight spaces instead of a tab will not work, only a tab will do. The third line says that `myprogram.o` depends on `myprogram.c` and `myheader.h`. It will use the default rule to do that, which we discuss next.

The `make` program knows some default rules about how to create certain files. For example, object code files (`.o` files) can be created from C source files (`.c` files) by using the C compiler with the `-c` compiler option. The name of the C compiler command is a macro with a pre-set value (`cc` on most Unix machines). But if you want to change it to something else, or include certain compiler options, you can do this too:

```
# Use the GNU C compiler
CC = gcc
# standard rule:
.c.o:
        $(CC) -c $(CFLAGS) $<
```

The rule for creating `.c.o` files is really a rule for creating `.o` files from `.c` files; the `.c` file that is being processed is represented by the mysterious symbol `$<`. Often, `make` will apply a sequence of implicit rules to, for example, check out a source file from an RCS file (see below), convert it to a C file via a transformation, and then compile the C file to create an object code file. And it will do this without any outside guidance, just using the implicit rules.

You can add rules for other kinds of files. In fact, the pattern syntax used in the GNU version (called gmake) [76] allows for more complicated ways in which file names are related:

```
%.o: %.c
            $(CC) -c $(CFLAGS) $< -o $@
```

The $@ symbol represents the file being created. You can add rules for converting PostScript files to PDF files, or LaTeX files to DVI files, or creating documentation files from source files, for example. If you use the older ".c.o" style of creating implicit rules, you will need to add the new suffixes to the system like this:

```
# Adding LaTeX, DVI, PostScript and PDF files
.SUFFIXES: .tex .dvi .ps .pdf
.tex.dvi: # Do latex twice to resolve references
        latex $<
        latex $<
.dvi.ps:
        dvips $< -o $@
.tex.pdf:
        pdflatex $<
        pdflatex $<
```

Readers who have compiled a large program downloaded from the Internet on Unix have probably seen a large number of makefiles in the files downloaded. Often these are organized in a hierarchical way with a number of directories, so that the makefile in the top directory will tell make to run make recursively in a number of sub-directories.

Very often makefiles also have pseudo-targets. These do not describe a particular file to create, but rather something to do. Pseudo-targets are often just symbolic names for a collection of real or pseudo-targets; examples include all (to create all target files associated with the makefile) and install (to install the main executable files, libraries, and resource files, in standard directories). For example, in a makefile for creating the executable files mainprog, supportprog and a shared library mylib.sl. we might define the pseudo-targets all, install and archive:

```
SOURCES = mainprog.cpp supportprog.cpp \
    package1.cpp package2.cpp package3.cpp \
    package1.h package2.h package3.h
EXECUTABLES = mainprog supportprog
SHAREDLIBS  = mylib.sl
```

```
all: $(EXECUTABLES) $(SHAREDLIBS)
install: all
        cp $(EXECUTABLES) $(EXECDIR)
        cp $(SHAREDLIBS) $(SHAREDLIBDIR)
archive: $(SOURCES)
        tar cf archive.tar $(SOURCES)
        gzip archive.tar
```

Note the use of symbolic names; any changes to the structure of the system (such as using a new package) can be accommodated with a minimal number of changes to this file.

As the authors of make noted in their initial descriptions of the program, make was not intended to be a complete tool for building extremely large systems. More sophisticated tools may be needed, but make is a powerful and useful way of controlling and automating the building of programs. Use it even for small projects. Then you don't have to worry about what compiler options you should use. They will be built in to the makefile you write for the project.

Some tools create makefiles: some of these are the configuration scripts generated by autoconf, a tool for automatically configuring build programs, that determines the compilers and libraries available on a given Unix system. An issue that arises in many large systems is automatically finding the directories, as different Unix systems (including different flavors of Linux) can have different directory structures. A part of the solution is to standardize on a particular directory structure for a system. Examples of this are the TEX and LATEX systems, and the X-windows system, which have standardized directory structures for where executable files, source files, macros, and other resources should be placed.

17.2 Revision control: RCS, CVS, Subversion and Bitkeeper

RCS, CVS, Subversion and Bitkeeper are examples of *revision* or *version control systems*. These maintain not only the current version of a file, but also keep all the previous versions in a compact form. In fact, most revision control systems allows the user to have several current versions (e.g., source code for different operating systems). RCS (*Revision Control System*) is perhaps easier to get started with, but CVS (*Concurrent Version System*), Subversion, and Bitkeeper seems to have better support for large software development projects. Earlier revision control software in Unix includes SCCS (*Source Code Control System*) which was more complex to use than RCS.

RCS and CVS [103] were designed for keeping versions of text files. The more recent systems like Subversion [74] and Bitkeeper [24] can handle binary files (including, for example, Microsoft Word files and images). Subversion is an open source system and so is freely available. Bitkeeper is a commercial package.

All revision control systems store the differences between the different versions. If you want to get an old version, the revision control software will start with the original or current version and work forwards or backwards respectively, incorporating the changes between the different versions to get the version you want. (SCCS starts with the original file and then works forward, while RCS starts with the current file and then works backwards. CVS is built on top of RCS, so it works backwards as well.) This way it can efficiently handle the usual situation: small numbers of changes between successive revisions.

All version control systems have a repository where all the information about the files under its control are kept. Once the repository is initialized (if necessary), new files can be added to the repository. Once a file is in the repository it can be *checked out* for editing. After changes are made, the file can be *checked in* or *committed* to the repository so that the current version of the file becomes a new revision of the file with its own revision number or identifier. For revision control systems that support group access, if several people are working on the same file(s), changes by different people can be *merged* unless there is a conflict (e.g., the same line is modified by more than one person). In that case, there must be some manual intervention to decide how the conflict should be resolved. Checking changes should be done with each significant completed change. If you have a regular (e.g., nightly) build of your system, files should generally be checked out and checked back in between builds.

With each revision, the user is asked to enter some message about the reason for the change. Later, a log file can be generated for each source file, indicating when and why the file was modified. However, this is not enough for some purposes, such as tracking bug fixes – that would need a separate data-base to identify a bug report, list when a bug fix was made, who by, and to which files, and the outcome of the bug fix. While RCS and CVS can track what happens to a particular file, it is not so good at finding out *which* files were changed for a particular reason. This deficiency is remedied in more recent version control systems. Subversion and Bitkeeper, for example, have the concept of a *change set* which is exactly for this purpose.

Since the older revision control software was designed for text files, they can be used for any source language where the source can be treated as a collection of text files. This can include just about any programming language, and other sorts of files such as documentation in LaTeX, and even figures in PostScript. RCS can't handle non-text data formats such as Microsoft Word files, RTF (*Rich Text Format*), or PDF (*Portable Document Format*) files. CVS has limited capabilities for handling non-text data. However, the newer version control systems such as Subversion and Bitkeeper can easily handle non-text formats, and indeed almost any kind of file.

Most revision control systems are based on other software that identifies differences between text files. In fact, SCCS and RCS were built using the Unix `diff` command, which can generate a set of differences between text files. However, `diff` and related commands work on lines as their basic unit of text. So, any change to a line (even just adding a space) results in a completely new line as far as SCCS is concerned, so re-formatting a source file may result in the new file being regarded as a completely new, unrelated file. While all revision control systems can handle this, it is inefficient.

17.3 Profiling: prof and gprof

Since we are interested in evaluating the performance of our algorithms, tools that time the various parts of an algorithm (called ***profiling tools***) are very useful. They can often surprise us about where most of the time is being spent, and point out the inefficiencies that we had forgotten, or never even considered!

The main profiling tools in Unix systems are `prof` and `gprof`. Of these, `prof` is the simplest, and `gprof` gives a much more complete picture of where and why time is spent in the different routines. To use either of these routines requires that when we compile the program, routines, and libraries we use some compiler options that generate the information that `prof` and `gprof` need. For most Unix compilers these options are "`-p`" for `prof` and "`-pg`" for `gprof`. Sometimes, vendors who supply libraries also supply libraries that have been compiled with these options so that more complete profiles of programs using the libraries can be generated.

Once the program has been compiled, the program can be run as normal (although input and output should be streamlined and reduced so that input/output does not dominate the timings). When the program completes normally, it generates an output file for the profiling program (`mon.out` for `prof` and `gmon.out` for `gprof`). The `prof` and `gprof` commands take the data put by these output files and displays them. The `prof` command produces a "flat" output showing simply how much time is spent (as well as `prof` can determine it) in each routine, and how many times each routine is called. The `gprof` command shows this, and also shows the number of times every routine is called from each routine that calls it; `gprof` also shows the amount of time each routine spends "in the service" of each calling routine. This can make it much easier to track where and why the program is spending its time. If considerable time is spent in library functions, it may be necessary to link the program with a library compiled with the `-p` (for `prof`) or `-pg` (for `gprof`) switches in order to see how much, and for what purpose, time is being spent in different parts of the library functions.

Here is an example of the "flat" output for repeatedly running the trapezoidal method to approximate $\int_0^1 x^2 \cos(x)\, dx$ (100 000 times):

```
  %     cumulative  self              self    total
 time    seconds   seconds    calls us/call us/call name
60.34     0.17      0.17    100000   1.75    2.55 trapezoidal
27.59     0.26      0.08 10100000    0.01    0.01 x_sqr_cosx
12.07     0.29      0.04                          main
```

The "call graph" output shows all the ways in which each function is called. In this case it's pretty simple: main calls trapezoidal which calls x_sqr_cosx.

```
index % time    self  children      called      name
                                                <spontaneous>
[1]    100.0    0.04    0.26                     main [1]
                0.17    0.08  100000/100000         trapezoidal [2]
-----------------------------------------------------
                0.17    0.08  100000/100000     main [1]
[2]     87.9    0.17    0.08  100000               trapezoidal [2]
                0.08    0.00 10100000/10100000     x_sqr_cosx [3]
-----------------------------------------------------
                0.08    0.00 10100000/10100000 trapezoidal [2]
[3]     27.6    0.08    0.00 10100000             x_sqr_cosx [3]
```

By following item [1] (main), we see that 0.04 seconds are spent in main itself, while 0.26 seconds are spent in trapezoidal (when called from main) and the routines that it calls. Looking at the line below [1], we see that only 0.17 seconds are spent in trapezoidal itself (when called from main) and 0.08 seconds in x_sqr_cosx. So about half the time is spent applying the trapezoidal rule, about half in evaluating the function $f(x) = x^2 \cos(x)$, with a small amount of overhead in the main routine.

When using prof or gprof with languages other than C, be warned that a certain amount of *name mangling* will occur as it does with other tools such as debuggers. For example, in object-oriented languages such as C++, the class or type name helps to distinguish the variables and functions, especially for overloaded functions. Thus this information must be included in the symbol information used by the linker. Similarly, in Fortran 90/95 modules separate name spaces, so module names must be incorporated into the symbol information used by the linker. Chapter 18 gives an example of how to use gprof for Fortran 90/95, and Chapter 19 gives an example using C++ with templates.

17.4 Text manipulation: grep, sed, awk, etc.

Text manipulation is a daily task for most programmers. If we are not writing, reading, searching or modifying text, we are thinking about it. Since we as programmers should try to automate whatever processes we can, we should be aware of the tools available for manipulating text. Unix has provided most of the best tools for handling text, and we will concentrate on the most popular of these: grep, sed, awk, and m4. The tasks carried out by these programs can often be done better in perl [90] or python [73]. Perl is a scripting language reminiscent of the Unix shells, but much, much more powerful. Python tries from the outset to be a fully-featured programming language, but with lots of support for text processing.

Of these commands, the most commonly used is grep (*get regular expression and print*): this will search one or more files for a given **regular expression**. A regular expression is a pattern of characters that we can build up recursively as follows: A regular expression is:

- a character string (which represents itself)
- a set of characters [*set-of-chars*] (which represents any of the characters in *set-of-chars*)
- a period "." (which represents any character except possibly the newline character)
- a caret "^" (which represents the start of a line or a string)
- a dollar sign "$" (which represents the end of a line or a string)
- a parenthesized regular expression \(r\) (which is the same as r)
- a sequence of regular expressions $r_1 r_2 \cdots r_m$ (representing concatenations of the strings represented by r_1, r_2, etc.)
- a regular expression followed by a symbol indicating multiplicity: $r*$ represents zero or more repititions of r, $r+$ represents one or more repititions, $r?$ represents zero or one repitition.

The characters that have special meanings ". ^ $ [ ] * ? \" can be included as regular characters as long as they are preceded by the escape character "\". Thus \$ represents an actual dollar symbol, and \\ an actual backslash character.

So, we can match regular expressions like this: the regular expression "abc\..*def" will match the strings "abc.Xdef" or "abc. def" or "abc. this is !!wow!! a long string def" and also "abc.def". (The ". *" can match the empty string.) If you wanted to find all include files in a C file, you can use this command:

```
grep '^#[    ]*include[    ]*[^    ]*' file.c
```

The [   ] part of the regular expression includes a space and a tab.

If we want to find all Fortran 90 files containing a certain identifier (like geom) we can use something like this:

```
grep -i 'g *e *o *m' *.f90
```

The -i option is to tell grep to ignore the case of the letters (so it will match upper case or lower case letters), and the "*" parts of the regular expression tell grep to ignore spaces (since Fortran allows spaces inserted in the middle of identifiers).

In addition to grep, Unix also has egrep which stands for *Extended GREP*. The egrep command also allows alternative patterns to be matched. These alternative strings are listed in parentheses like this: (pattern1|pattern2|...). For example, if you want a pattern to find all C and C++ source files in a directory, you could use the pattern .*\.(c|h|C|cc|cpp|cxx) (note that \. matches a period).

Other Unix commands use regular expressions, such as sed (*Stream EDitor*). This will take a collection of editing commands and an input file, and produce an output file (or on-screen) which is the result of applying those editing commands to the input file. The editing commands that sed has available include adding lines of input, deleting lines of input, substituting patterns found, changing lines, reading input from other files, and translating characters.

For example, to change strings from being bracketed by double quotes (") to being bracketed by <...>, we can use the following sed command:

```
sed -e 's/"\(.*\)"/<\1>/' file > output
```

The actual command for sed follows -e on the command line. The s command in sed is the substitute command. The regular expression inside the first pair of slashes ("\(.*\)") is the pattern to be substituted, and it is substituted by the string between the second and third slashed (<\1>). The \1 represents the first bracketed regular expression in the pattern, which in this case is .*. The "\(.*\)" regular expression matches any string contained in double quotes (including the quotes), so the .* regular expression in it matches the quoted string. This is then substituted into \1 in the output string.

Awk is a program for setting up and using small text-files as data bases. The data bases commonly consist of lines of strings or numbers separated by spaces. The strings and numbers in a line are fields of that line. (Other characters can be used as field separators, such as the colons (:) used in password files.) Awk programs have variables and functions, just like other programming languages. But the basic way awk operates is to read a line, and if a specified pattern matches the input, the associated operation is executed (which is often a print statement). For more information about sed and awk, see [31].

The m4 program is a macro preprocessor. It works somewhat like the C/C++ preprocessor, but with more sophisticated features, such as recursive macros, and arithmetic. This can make it a very useful tool in a number of areas. For example, loop unrolling can be an error prone process when done by hand. However, a recursive m4 `forloop` command can make it simple: running m4 on the file

```
define('unroll','define('var',$1)dnl
define('tempvar',$1_$3)dnl
for ( tempvar = 0; tempvar+$3 < $2; tempvar += $3 )
{
forloop('j',0,decr($3),'  pushdef($1,'tempvar'+'j')$4;
  popdef($1)')
}
undefine('$1')dnl
for ( var = tempvar; var < $2; var++ )
  $4;')dnl end definition of unroll macro
unroll('i','n',4,'sum[i] = a[i]+b[i]')dnl
```

will generate

```
for ( i_4 = 0; i_4+4 < n; i_4 += 4 )
{
    sum[i_4+0] = a[i_4+0]+b[i_4+0];
    sum[i_4+1] = a[i_4+1]+b[i_4+1];
    sum[i_4+2] = a[i_4+2]+b[i_4+2];
    sum[i_4+3] = a[i_4+3]+b[i_4+3];

}
for ( i = i_4; i < n; i++ )
    sum[i] = a[i]+b[i];
```

This kind of automatic generation of code for loop unrolling is impossible using the C/C++ macro preprocessor. Writing m4 macros can be tricky; it is said to be addictive as well.... But properly used, this is a powerful tool for dealing with text.

17.5 Other tools

Other tools worth mentioning that are available with Unix (including Linux and Mac OS X) include

- `lex` or `flex`. These perform lexical analysis, which is usually a preliminary stage for the syntactical analysis that a compiler carries out. They can be used independently or with `yacc` or `bison`. Lex was the original Unix program; `flex` is a near-equivalent program from the GNU project of the Free Software Foundation.

- yacc or bison. Yacc (*Yet Another Compiler-Compiler*) is a syntax-directed compiler generator. This is a convenient way to construct mini-languages for representing input data, or for parsing various kinds of data files, as well as for constructing compilers for programming languages. The bison program is a completely free version of this program which is part of the GNU project.
- find. Find is not only a search engine, it can automate many tasks, especially on files scattered across several directories. Combined with grep it can search for patterns inside files. Combined with sed, it can transform source code across an entire directory tree.
- diff and merge. Diff finds the differences between two text files on a line-by-line basis. This can be a powerful tool to see how a file has changed. However, for diff, lines either match exactly or not at all. This means that some trivial changes (like the difference between the end-of-line characters for Unix, Microsoft, and Macintosh) can render diff useless unless they are converted to a common format. Merge is a three-file command that compares an original file to two new versions, and creates an output that combines both the changes for the new versions. Diff and merge were the basis of the original RCS revision control system. Revision control systems typically provide equivalent operations for files in their repositories.
- gzip and tar. Unix has a long line of compression tools, starting with compress. Others include pack, zip, gzip and bzip2, although zip originated under the Microsoft operating systems. These are lossless compression programs – that is, they do not lose any information, and the original input can be completely reconstructed. On the other hand, tar (*Tape ARchive*) combines selected files into one. Most of the Unix tools for compression are solely for compression, while zip both combines and compresses sets of files. For storing or sending large sets of files both zip and tar/gzip are excellent tools.

This list is by no means complete, and more tools are being developed, modified, and updated all the time.

17.6 What about Microsoft Windows?

With the advent of Macintosh's OS X, virtually all of the operating systems in widespread use are a version of either Microsoft Windows or Unix. This means that almost all computer users will have access to Unix tools or will be working under Microsoft Windows. Since Microsoft Windows is targeted at non-programmers, effective tools for programmers do not come with standard distributions of the operating system. This means that programmers working under Microsoft Windows need to take steps to obtain compilers and other programming tools. These may include tools for development in the .NET framework created by Microsoft, such as Visual Studio .NET.

We will look at three ways of doing this. One is through Integrated Development Environments. The second is through free sets of Unix tools that run under Microsoft Windows. The third is through individual tools re-written for the Microsoft Windows environment.

17.6.1 *Interactive Development Environments*

Interactive Development Environments (IDEs) are environments that provide facilities for editing source code, compiling and linking files, defining the way to build the executable, and running executable code. Like most Graphical User Interfaces, IDEs are low-threshold systems – it is easy to get started and put together simple programs. But if you want to structure your programs differently from what the IDE expects, it is likely to be much harder.

In many respects, IDEs are replacements for the operating system. They provide access to compilers, and linkers, along with editors, building tools (like make), and usually provide access to debuggers and profiling tools. These are essentially standard components in Unix operating systems. IDEs are definitely useful in certain situations, such as GUI builders. But as general purpose tools, operating systems with good toolsets are nearly as easy to use, and provide much more flexibility.

17.6.2 *Unix toolsets for Windows*

One approach to supporting programmers in a Microsoft Windows environment is to provide collections of Unix tools in a Windows-compatible form. The degree to which the collections are self-contained differs between the different toolsets. At one extreme, Linux can be used as an alternative operating system in one partition of a hard disk, and Microsoft Windows can run in another partition; done properly the Linux system can "see" the Microsoft Windows files, although the reverse is not always possible. At the other extreme, separate programs that can run under Microsoft Windows can be used; this is the main approach of MinGW (*Minimalist Gnu for Windows*, available from `http://www.mingw.org`). In between is Cygwin, which includes a Linux emulation program, and provides its own command interface. Cygwin takes over a sub-tree of the directory structure. All the usual Unix tools are available in Cygwin, and in addition, there is a version of X-windows. Programs written with Cygwin can use Unix facilities; the resulting programs are usually run under Cygwin as they use the Linux emulation that Cygwin provides. It is possible to compile programs under Cygwin for Windows, although it is a more complex process. Cygwin is available from `http://www.cygwin.com`.

The most popular C/C++ compilers for Linux (`gcc` and `gpp`) are also available for Windows systems along with most of the tools for Unix described above. These compilers and tools have been ported by a number of people, including DJ Delorie who wrote djgpp, a Windows version of gcc/gpp.

17.6.3 Stand-alone tools

Some tools are useful enough on their own to be worth turning into stand-alone tools under Microsoft Windows and/or Mac OS X. Examples include WinZip (shareware), which is GUI version of a command line version of zip. Component Software developed a version of RCS which is integrated into Microsoft Windows, and has a GUI interface. There are also GUI versions of other revision control systems for both Unix and Microsoft Windows, including CVS and Subversion. Numerous other Unix tools have GUI interfaces and run under Microsoft Windows.

Part of the attraction of this conversion of Unix tools is to set up GUIs for command line tools. And GUIs often do make life easier. By way of analogy, paintings can capture qualities and textures that are hard to put into words, but literature can describe relationships on a level that pictures cannot represent. The world would be poorer without either one of them. At heart, this is about a choice of interfaces: often we are best off with more than one interface.

Part V

Design Examples

18

Cubic spline function library

In this chapter, we will consider the details of designing a cubic spline library. The examples given here use Fortran 90, but are based on the interface and data structure developed earlier in C in Sections 7.5 and 8.1.

Here is the Fortran version of the data structure:

```
type :: spline
    ! length is current length
    ! max_len is allocated length of arrays
    integer length, max_len
    ! For spline function f
    ! f(xlist(i)) = ylist(i), Mlist(i) = f''(xlist(i))
    real(kind=wp), pointer :: &
        xlist(:), ylist(:), Mlist(:)
end type spline
```

Note that the xlist, ylist, and Mlist components have the allocatable attribute, and so must be allocated before use. However, since they have the pointer but not pointer attribute, this means that the components will *not* be de-allocated when the data structure goes out of scope.[1]

The spline library is made into a Fortran 90 module that provides the data structure(s) needed together with the operations and tests. Here is an outline of the module:

```
module splines
    ! sets working precision (wp)
    use set_precision, only: wp
    ! use tridiagonal solvers
```

---

[1] Fortran 2003 allows allocatable components of data structures. This is already available in many compilers (such as g95 and Intel's ifort) at the time of writing.

```
  use tridiag
  implicit none

  ! spline data structure
  ...
contains
  ! Spline functions
  ...
  ! Spline tests
  ...
end module splines
```

Several things are worth noting about this outline for a module:

- Working precision (single, double, or extended precision) is set by the module set_precision. This module is used by splines and must be used by all other modules and routines that work with it. As long as all declarations of floating point variables and functions use real(wp), they will be using the same precision. If additional precision is desired for certain computations, the module could also define an "ep" parameter as being the parameter for a suitable "extended precision" floating point arithmetic.
- The module itself contains no variables, only type and parameter declarations. Any variables declared would essentially be global to the module, which we wish to avoid. Also, having a single "spline object" is very limiting.
- We use implicit none to ensure that all undeclared variables are caught. In fact, this caught a logical error. A mis-spelled variable is a new variable, and implicit typing will not alert the programmer when this happens. Implicit none can also be set via compiler switches.
- The software is layered, with the splines module built on top of the tridiag module. Since both are modules, calling routines can be checked to ensure that numbers and types of arguments are correct without needing to create separate interface blocks.
- Test routines are included in the module. Testing routines should be created along with the rest of the module. Test programs can simply call the test routines and are only a few lines long. (In Java, classes can have a main method, which is a good place to put testing routines. But this feature is not available in current dialects of Fortran.)

Remember, the data structure is part of the *implementation*, and not really part of the functionality of the library. So it could be changed if a better way was found. With this approach we could change this module, as long as the interfaces to the routines are kept the same, without changing any routine that used or called the routines in this module. We would still have to recompile the routines that used this module.

Errors in scientific software may occur for a number of different reasons: division by zero, memory allocation failure, or an input error, for example. Furthermore, if one routine calls another, and the called routine has an error, then almost always the calling routine must indicate that an error has occured. In long calling chains then, an error deep in the chain will propagate all the way to the top.

Error handling in Fortran has little support (even in Fortran 2003). So we adopt two different ways of handling errors: either the routine called returns a `logical` value with `.true.` returned for success, `.false.` for failure, or the routine called sets an integer argument `iflag`. If a routine normally returns something, or if more detailed information is desired about the error status, then an `iflag` argument is used. Otherwise we use the `logical` return value for indication of an error. In the following design example we use the following convention for `iflag`: if `iflag` is zero on exit, then the operation was successful; if `iflag` is negative on exit, then the operation had a fatal error; if `iflag` is positive on exit, then the operation's value(s) may be in doubt or inaccurate. While we might later assign more meaning for specific values of `iflag`, this convention will enable us to write simple code for handling most cases.

Here is a description of the interface as comments embedded in the module.

```
! spline_get(s,len) -- creates spline s of length len
!  -- returns .true. if successful, .false. if not
...
! spline_free(s) -- deallocates all memory associated
!   with s and resets length and max_len.
...
! spline_resize(s,new_len) -- resizes s to length new_len
!  -- re-allocates if necessary, possibly destroying
!     old values
...
! spline_set(s,x,y,len) -- sets xlist & ylist values in s
!        to x & y respectively
!  -- resizes s to ensure it has length = len
!  -- x must be ordered on entry: x(i+1) > x(i) for all i
!       but this is not checked by spline_set
...
! spline_print(s,output) -- prints representation of spline
!   on unit "output"
...
! spline_read(s,input) -- reads representation of spline
!   on unit "input" (reads output from spline_print)
...
! spline_eval(s,t,iflag) -- evaluates spline s at t:
     returns s(t)
```

```
!    -- extrapolates if t outside interval
!       [xlist(1),xlist(length)], but then sets iflag > 0
!    -- if fatal error (e.g., division by zero), set
!        iflag < 0
!    -- otherwise, set iflag == 0 on exit
...
! spline_peval(s,t,iflag) -- evaluates spline s at t:
!    returns s(t)
!    -- assumes spline is periodic
!    -- if fatal error, set iflag < 0
...
! spline_basic(s,mat,rhs,iflag) -- constructs basic linear
!    system for splines for computing Mlist
! This is common to spline_clamped, spline_natural,
! and spline_not_knot; sets iflag < 0 if fatal error
...
! spline_clamped(s,dy0,dy1,iflag) -- constructs clamped
!    spline f(.):
!       f(s%xlist(i)) = s%ylist(i), i = 1, ..., s%length
!       f'(s%xlist(1)) = dy0, f'(s%xlist(s%length)) = dy1
...
! spline_natural(s,iflag) -- constructs natural spline f(.):
!       f(s%xlist(i)) = s%ylist(i), i = 1, ..., s%length
!       f''(s%xlist(1)) = f''(s%xlist(s%length)) = 0
...
! spline_periodic(s,iflag) -- constructs periodic
!    spline f(.):
!       f(s%xlist(i)) = s%ylist(i), i = 1, ..., s%length
! Period of f is s%xlist(s%length)) - s%xlist(1)
...
```

Note that s is a type(spline), while iflag, len and new_len are integers; the other arguments are real(kind=wp) scalars or arrays.

18.1 Creation and destruction

The first task is to create-and-initialize the spline data structure. Since we want to have more than one spline function, this cannot be done at startup time: at startup we do not know how many spline functions will be needed. So we must have a function to create and initialize a spline data structure. Here is code to do this:

```
logical function spline_get(s,len)
   type(spline), intent(out) :: s
   integer, intent(in) :: len
   integer :: err
   s%length = 0
   s%max_len = 0
   allocate(s%xlist(len), s%ylist(len), s%Mlist(len), &
       STAT=err)
   if ( err /= 0 ) then
      deallocate(s%xlist, s%ylist, s%Mlist)
      spline_get = .false.
   else
      s%length = len
      s%max_len = len
      spline_get = .true.
   end if
end function spline_get
```

If we did not use the STAT=err option in the allocate statement, then execution would terminate if the allocation failed. The approach here allows the calling routine to decide what to do on failure.

Note that length and max_len are assigned *after* the allocation has succeeded, so allocation failure will not result in illegal accesses, although the data structure may still be in an inconsistent state (e.g., xlist allocated, but neither ylist nor Mlist allocated).

Since the allocated components xlist, ylist, and Mlist have the pointer rather than allocatable attribute, we need to explicitly de-allocate a type(spline) object before it goes out of scope. So we have included a function spline_free:

```
subroutine spline_free(s)
   type(spline) :: s
   deallocate(s%xlist, s%ylist, s%Mlist)
   s%length = 0
   s%max_len = 0
end subroutine spline_free
```

18.2 Output

The `spline_print` routine gives access to the internals of the data structure, which is very useful for debugging:

```
subroutine spline_print(s,output)
  type(spline) :: s
  integer i, output
  write (output,*) 'Spline:', s%length, &
       ', max length =', s%max_len
  write (output,*) 'xlist:'
  write (output,'(3G22.15)') (s%xlist(i), i = 1, s%length)
  write (output,*) 'ylist:'
  write (output,'(3G22.15)') (s%ylist(i), i = 1, s%length)
  write (output,*) 'Mlist:'
  write (output,'(3G22.15)') (s%Mlist(i), i = 1, s%length)
end subroutine spline_print
```

The output is human readable.

18.3 Evaluation

The first real numerical workhorse routine is the `spline_eval` routine. Evaluating a spline function once we have computed the M_i values is fairly straightforward: given an input t, we find the interval $[x_i, x_{i+1}]$ that contains t, and then apply the formula for the spline function.

What happens if t is outside the interval $[x_1, x_n]$? Officially there is no value defined. Such a policy could be enforced by raising an error if $t < x_1$ or $t > x_n$. However, this is probably not wise since roundoff error could mean that something that ought to be in the interval is not. Recall that even assigning $x = y$ does not guarantee that $y == x$ later, even if both are declared to be double-precision. So we should extend the function beyond the official interval $[x_1, x_n]$. Note, however, that there is no uniqueness to the extension. We would like it to have some properties of the cubic spline function that are important on $[x_1, x_n]$; it should probably be at least twice continuously differentiable. Since extrapolation cannot be expected to give accurate values for a spline interpolant far from $[x_1, x_n]$, we set `iflag` to +1 for extrapolation. This signals to the user that the value might not be trustworthy.

The simplest approach is if $t < x_1$ then we use the formula used for $[x_1, x_2]$, and if $t > x_n$ we use the formula used for $[x_{n-1}, x_n]$. Of course, once we go outside the interval $[x_1, x_n]$ we are really talking about *extrapolation*, not interpolation, and we do not expect that the errors will stay small as we go far from the interval

$[x_1, x_n]$. However, it will give us a twice-differentiable extension to the spline outside $[x_1, x_n]$.

18.3.1 Implementation of spline_eval()

Now we should consider how to implement the spline evaluation function.

There are two main parts to the function:

1. identify the interval $[x_i, x_{i+1}]$ containing the evaluation point t, or if $t < x_1$ or $t > x_n$;
2. evaluate the cubic polynomial given in Equation (9.1) on p. 125.

The first part should be carried out using a form of binary search. The second part is straightforward evaluation, although care should be taken to avoid excessive roundoff errors.

To implement the binary search, we will start with a loop invariant: xlist(lo) <= t <= xlist(hi), where lo and hi are indexes. After we tested and excluded the cases t < xlist(1) and t > xlist(length), we know that xlist(1) <= t <= xlist(length), which means we can set lo = 1 and hi = length. We stop when hi == lo or hi == lo+1, and we set i = lo. At each iteration we wish to roughly halve |hi-lo|. Note that using mid = (lo+hi)/2 does this, although we get mid == lo if hi == lo+1. But if hi >= lo+2, then mid $\geq$ (lo+lo+2)/2 == lo+1 using integer division, which rounds towards zero for non-negative arguments.

For the evaluation of the cubic expression for the interval $[x_i, x_{i+1}]$, it is usually worthwhile to use the differences $t - x_i$ and $x_{i+1} - t$. One reason for this is that these quantities are typically much smaller than t, x_i, or x_{i+1}. Subtracting first usually gives smaller roundoff errors – catastrophic cancellation is usually worse when quantities are amplified, say by squaring or cubing, before subtracting. In addition, we try to partially factor the expressions to improve efficiency and reduce roundoff errors.

The complete code is listed below:

```
function spline_eval(s,t,iflag) result(val)
   type(spline), intent(in) :: s
   integer, intent(out) :: iflag
   real(kind=wp) :: t, val, h, diff1, diff2
   integer i, lo, mid, hi

   if ( s%length == 1 ) then
      val = s%ylist(1)
      iflag = 1 ! extrapolation !
      return
```

```
   else if ( s%length == 0 ) then
      val = 0
      iflag = -1 ! no data !
      return
   end if

   ! binary search to find i: xlist(i) <= t <= xlist(i+1),
   ! or i = 1 if t < xlist(1),
   ! or i = length-1 if xlist(length) < t
   lo = 1
   hi = s%length
   if ( t < s%xlist(1) ) then
      i = 1
      iflag = 1 ! extrapolation !
   else if ( t > s%xlist(s%length) ) then
      i = s%length-1
      iflag = 1 ! extrapolation !
   else
      iflag = 0 ! normal case !
      ! binary search
      do while ( hi > lo + 1 )
         ! Loop invariant: xlist(lo) <= t <= xlist(hi)
         mid = (lo + hi)/2
         if ( t <= s%xlist(mid) ) then
            hi = mid
         else
            lo = mid
         end if
      end do
      i = lo
   end if

   ! Use interpolation formula on [xlist(i),xlist(i+1)]
   h = s%xlist(i+1) - s%xlist(i)
   if ( h == 0 ) then
      iflag = -1 ! fatal error !
      return
   end if
   diff1 = t - s%xlist(i)
   diff2 = s%xlist(i+1) - t
```

```
 val = diff1*(s%ylist(i+1)/h  -  s%Mlist(i+1)*h/6.0 &
       + diff1*diff1*s%Mlist(i+1)/(6.0*h)) &
       + diff2*(s%ylist(i )/h  -  s%Mlist(i  )*h/6.0 &
       + diff2*diff2*s%Mlist(i  )/(6.0*h))
end function spline_eval
```

Testing can be done using the specific examples given in Equations (9.2)–(9.4) on pages 127 to 127, using a number of different values of t. Plotting the spline function above for $t = 0$ to $t = 4$ can also provide a quick indication if the code is probably correct – such a plot can easily identify jumps in values and first derivatives, although it is unlikely to identify jumps in higher derivatives.

The place in the code where i has been determined is a good place to start debugging. By printing i out, it can be easy to identify if the problem is in computing i, or in the interpolation formula.

Sometimes, published formulas are incorrect. This can make debugging difficult since whoever debugs the code will spend a lot of time comparing the formula in the code with the published formula, swearing that the bug *can't* be there... But it has happened before and can happen again. So, in these cases, go through the derivation of the formula, or use a symbolic computation package (like Maple or Mathematica) to derive the formula yourself.

18.4 Spline construction

Constructing a spline is more involved than evaluating a spline. The basic material we need to construct a spline function are the knot points x_i, $i = 1, \ldots, n$ and the values to interpolate: y_i, $i = 1, \ldots, n$. In addition, you need to know what *kind* of spline to construct: whether it is a natural spline, a complete spline, a "not-a-knot" spline, or a periodic spline. To construct any of these, we have to solve a linear system. For all but periodic splines, this linear system is a tridiagonal system of equations. That is, it is a linear system of the form:

$$
\begin{bmatrix}
a_1 & c_1 & & & & \\
b_1 & a_2 & c_2 & & & \\
 & b_2 & a_3 & \ddots & & \\
 & & \ddots & \ddots & \ddots & \\
 & & & \ddots & a_{n-1} & c_{n-1} \\
 & & & & b_{n-1} & a_n
\end{bmatrix}
\begin{bmatrix}
z_1 \\
z_2 \\
z_3 \\
\vdots \\
z_{n-1} \\
z_n
\end{bmatrix}
=
\begin{bmatrix}
b_1 \\
b_2 \\
b_3 \\
\vdots \\
b_{n-1} \\
b_n
\end{bmatrix}
$$

Note that this sub-problem is an essentially self-contained sub-problem, so it is a natural place for creating a component of our spline software.

18.4.1 Tridiagonal linear systems

Usually we solve the tridiagonal linear system by carrying out an LU factorization as is done for general linear systems. But when we look at what happens in the LU factorization for a tridiagonal systems, we can greatly reduce the time and memory needed. This is well-known and documented in most numerical analysis texts (see, for example, [4] and [18]). We could (and should) use the LAPACK banded matrix routines here. However, we will proceed as if it were not available to illustrate the issues involved. If we write

$$
\begin{bmatrix}
a_1 & c_1 & & & & \\
b_1 & a_2 & c_2 & & & \\
 & b_2 & a_3 & \ddots & & \\
 & & \ddots & \ddots & \ddots & \\
 & & & \ddots & a_{n-1} & c_{n-1} \\
 & & & & b_{n-1} & a_n
\end{bmatrix} =
$$

$$
\begin{bmatrix}
1 & & & & & \\
\beta_1 & 1 & & & & \\
 & \beta_2 & 1 & & & \\
 & & \ddots & \ddots & & \\
 & & & \ddots & 1 & \\
 & & & & \beta_{n-1} & 1
\end{bmatrix}
\begin{bmatrix}
\alpha_1 & \gamma_1 & & & & \\
 & \alpha_2 & \gamma_2 & & & \\
 & & \alpha_3 & \ddots & & \\
 & & & \ddots & \ddots & \\
 & & & & \alpha_{n-1} & \gamma_{n-1} \\
 & & & & & \alpha_n
\end{bmatrix} = LU,
$$

as the LU factorization of our original tridiagonal matrix, we can compute the quantities α_i, β_i, and γ_i in a simple $O(n)$ algorithm:

$$
\begin{aligned}
&\alpha_1 \leftarrow a_1; \quad \beta_1 \leftarrow b_1/a_1; \quad \gamma_1 \leftarrow c_1 \\
&\text{for } i = 2, 3, \ldots, n-1 \\
&\quad \alpha_i \leftarrow a_i - \beta_{i-1}\gamma_{i-1}; \quad \beta_i \leftarrow b_i/a_i; \quad \gamma_i \leftarrow c_i \\
&\alpha_n \leftarrow a_n - \beta_{n-1}\gamma_{n-1}
\end{aligned}
$$

This algorithm can operate *in situ* (that is, without using any additional memory, by overwriting the input arrays with the output) like this:

$$
\begin{aligned}
&b_1 \leftarrow b_1/a_1 \\
&\text{for } i = 2, 3, \ldots, n-1 \\
&\quad a_i \leftarrow a_i - b_{i-1}c_{i-1}; \quad b_i \leftarrow b_i/a_i \\
&a_n \leftarrow a_n - b_{n-1}c_{n-1}
\end{aligned}
$$

Note that we can store both the tridiagonal matrix and the LU factors (in compressed form) in the same data structure:

```
! representation of n x n tridiagonal matrix A
! A(i,i) = a(i), A(i+1,i) = b(i), A(i,i+1) = c(i)
! array sizes: a(max_n), b(max_n-1), c(max_n-1)
type :: tdg
    integer n, max_n
    real(kind=wp), pointer :: a(:), b(:), c(:)
end type tdg
```

Again, this is part of a module which contains data structures and routines, but no variables. Again, we have used the set_precision module to set the precision of the floating point data. Basic routines to create and allocate, destroy, resize, print, and copy these data structures have been written.

This LU factorization code is implemented in tdg_lu below:

```
subroutine tdg_lu(mat,iflag)
  type(tdg) :: mat
  integer, intent(out) :: iflag
  integer :: i, n

  n = mat%n
  if ( mat%a(1) == 0 ) then
     iflag = -1
     return
  end if
  mat%b(1) = mat%b(1) / mat%a(1)

  do i = 2, n-1
     if ( mat%a(i) == 0 ) then
        iflag = -1
        return
     end if
     mat%a(i) = mat%a(i) - mat%b(i-1)*mat%c(i-1)
     mat%b(i) = mat%b(i) / mat%a(i)
  end do
  mat%a(n) = mat%a(n) - mat%b(n-1)*mat%c(n-1)
end subroutine tdg_lu
!------------------------------------------------
```

How can we test this code? We can re-construct the the *LU* matrix, and check the re-construction error: how close are the re-computed a_i, b_i, and c_i to the original values? Note that to do this we need to copy the original values so they won't be changed by tdg_lu. Our re-construction routine should not be *in situ*: the output should be separate from the input. We need this for debugging, not for speed or minimizing memory usage. It also means that we are avoiding bugs that can arise in the *in situ* version of the algorithm. Here is a routine for re-constructing the LU factorization:

```
logical function tdg_lumult(mat,prod)
   type(tdg) :: mat, prod
   integer i

   tdg_lumult = .true.
   if ( .not. tdg_resize(prod,mat%n) ) then
      tdg_lumult = .false.
      return
   end if


   if ( mat%n <= 0 ) return

   prod%a(1) = mat%a(1)
   if ( mat%n == 1 ) return
   prod%c(1) = mat%c(1)
   do i = 2, mat%n - 1
      prod%b(i-1) = mat%b(i-1)*mat%a(i-1)
      prod%a(i)   = mat%a(i) + mat%b(i-1)*mat%c(i-1)
      prod%c(i)   = mat%c(i)
   end do
   prod%b(mat%n-1) = mat%b(mat%n-1)*mat%a(mat%n-1)
   prod%a(mat%n) = mat%a(mat%n) + &
      mat%b(mat%n-1)*mat%c(mat%n-1)
end function tdg_lumult
```

At this point it is also useful to have a routine that gives an indication of how different two type(tdg) variables are. For example, we could simply compute the maximum difference in the entries, as is done in tdg_norm_diff. This is not a regular matrix norm of the difference, but it is enough for these testing purposes. The testing code then becomes quite simple after we have set up and copied a matrix to factor:

```
if ( .not. tdg_lumult(mat1,temp) ) then
    print *, 'Error performing L.U multiplication'
end if
print *, 'L.U ='
call tdg_print(temp,stdout)
print *, 'Maximum difference between L.U & original =', &
    tdg_norm_diff(temp,mat2)
```

The maximum error should be a modest multiple, say 10 to 20 times, of **u** (the unit roundoff, see Section 2.1.1), provided the original matrix has modest-sized entries and is **diagonally dominant**; that is, each diagonal entry has magnitude greater than the sum of the magnitudes of all other entries in that row:

$$|a_{ii}| > \sum_{j:j\neq i} |a_{ij}|.$$

It turns out that the linear systems that arise in computing splines are diagonally dominant. If the error is much larger than 10 or 20 times **u** for a diagonally dominant matrix and n modest, it is likely a sign of a bug.

Solving the linear system can now be carried out using the standard approach for LU factorization. To solve $LUz = y$, we first solve $Lw = y$ and then $Uz = w$. If we write out the equations to solve for w in terms of y we get the following algorithm:

$w_1 \leftarrow y_1$
for $i = 2, 3, \ldots, n$
  $w_i \leftarrow y_i - \beta_{i-1}w_{i-1}$

This can also be done *in situ* with input and output in y:

for $i = 2, 3, \ldots, n$
  $y_i \leftarrow y_i - \beta_{i-1}y_{i-1}$

Solving for z in terms of w from the equation $Uz = w$ is done backwards, starting from z_n and working our way towards z_1. (For solving $Lw = y$ we started with w_1 and worked our way forwards to w_n.) The algorithm for this is

$z_n \leftarrow w_n/\alpha_n$
for $i = n - 1, n - 2, \ldots, 1$
  $z_i \leftarrow (w_i - \gamma_i z_{i+1})/\alpha_i$

Again, this operation can be made *in situ* with both input and output in y.

$y_n \leftarrow y_n/\alpha_n$
for $i = n - 1, n - 2, \ldots, 1$
  $y_i \leftarrow (y_i - \gamma_i y_{i+1})/\alpha_i$

Combining forward and backward substitution gives a single *in situ* algorithm for solving the factored tridiagonal linear system. This is implemented in
tdg_lusolve.

```fortran
subroutine tdg_lusolve(mat,y,iflag)
   type(tdg), intent(in) :: mat
   real(kind=wp) :: y(:)
   integer, intent(out) :: iflag
   integer i
   logical has_zero

   iflag = 0

   ! Solve U.z = y, overwriting y with z
   do i = 2, mat%n
      y(i) = y(i) - mat%b(i-1)*y(i-1)
   end do

   ! check mat%a for zeros
   has_zero = .false.
   do i = 1, mat%n
      has_zero = has_zero .or. (mat%a(i) == 0)
   end do
   if ( has_zero ) then
      iflag = -1
      return
   end if

   ! Solve L.x = z (stored in y), overwriting y with x
   y(mat%n) = y(mat%n) / mat%a(mat%n)
   do i = mat%n-1, 1, -1
      y(i) = (y(i) - mat%c(i)*y(i+1)) / mat%a(i)
   end do
end subroutine tdg_lusolve
!-------------------------------------------------------
```

The solve routine can be tested in combination with the tridiagonal factorization
routine; set up a linear tridiagonal system $Ax = b$ and, after solving for x, check
the residual $b - Ax$.

So far, we have represented a tridiagonal matrix by three floating point arrays a,
b and c, and a length parameter n (a has n entries while b and c have $n - 1$ entries).

The module created for tridiagonal matrices is self-contained and independently tested. It can be used in other contexts.

18.4.2 Some words about accuracy and reliability

Readers knowledgeable in numerical analysis will realize that the LU factorization routine described above does not use partial pivoting (i.e., row swaps). This means that it can fail for some non-singular tridiagonal matrices such as

$$\begin{bmatrix} 0 & 1 \\ 1 & 0 \end{bmatrix}.$$

Even for tridiagonal matrices which are close to this matrix, there are typically large errors in the computed solution due to roundoff errors.

However, the equations solved to determine the unknowns in the spline representation are tridiagonal linear systems with special features.

Let us recall the formula we use for the spline functions: let $h_i = x_{i+1} - x_i$. Then for $x_i \leq x \leq x_{i+1}$,

$$s(x) = \frac{(x_{i+1} - x)^3 M_i + (x - x_i)^3 M_{i+1}}{6h_i} + \frac{(x_{i+1} - x)y_i + (x - x_i)y_{i+1}}{h_i}$$
$$- \frac{h_i}{6}[(x_{i+1} - x)M_i + (x - x_i)M_{i+1}].$$

From this formula we can see that on $[x_i, x_{i+1}]$, $s(x_i) = y_i$ and $s(x_{i+1}) = y_{i+1}$; since the formulas for $s(x)$ match up at the endpoints x_i and x_{i+1} the spline function s is continuous. Something similar happens with the second derivatives: using the formula on $[x_i, x_{i+1}]$, $s''(x_i) = M_i$ and $s''(x_{i+1}) = M_{i+1}$ and again s'' is continuous. We need the equations to enforce the continuity of the first derivatives. Using the formula for $s(x)$ on $[x_i, x_{i+1}]$ we get

$$s'(x) = \frac{-(x_{i+1} - x)^2 M_i + (x - x_i)^2 M_{i+1}}{2h_i}$$
$$+ \frac{y_{i+1} - y_i}{h_i} - \frac{h_i}{6}(M_{i+1} - M_i).$$

The corresponding formula for the interval $[x_{i-1}, x_i]$ is

$$s'(x) = \frac{-(x_i - x)^2 M_{i-1} + (x - x_{i-1})^2 M_i}{2h_{i-1}}$$
$$+ \frac{y_i - y_{i-1}}{h_{i-1}} - \frac{h_{i-1}}{6}(M_i - M_{i-1}).$$

Equating the values at $x = x_i$ for continuity of the first derivatives gives the equation

$$-\frac{h_i^2}{2h_i}M_i + \frac{y_{i+1} - y_i}{h_i} + \frac{h_i}{6}(M_i - M_{i+1})$$

$$= \frac{h_{i-1}^2}{2h_{i-1}}M_i + \frac{y_i - y_{i-1}}{h_{i-1}} + \frac{h_{i-1}}{6}(M_{i-1} - M_i).$$

Rearranging gives the equation

$$\frac{y_{i+1} - y_i}{h_i} - \frac{y_i - y_{i-1}}{h_{i-1}} = \frac{h_{i-1}}{6}M_{i-1} + \frac{h_{i-1} + h_i}{3}M_i + \frac{h_i}{6}M_{i+1}.$$

Since this must be satisfied at every interior knot point x_i, $i = 1, 2, \ldots, n - 2$, there are two equations that are left to be satisfied. What those two extra equations are depends on the kind of spline (complete, natural, periodic, "not-a-knot"). But these $n - 2$ equations for the interior knot points are *diagonally dominant* (that is, each diagonal entry is larger in magnitude than the sum of the magnitudes of the other entries on that row – or column):

$$\frac{h_{i-1} + h_i}{3} > \frac{h_{i-1}}{6} + \frac{h_i}{6},$$

as $h_j > 0$ for all j. Provided the remaining two equations do not break this property, LU factorization with partial pivoting (that is, row swaps) is not necessary.

What if partial pivoting is necessary? Do we need to revert to the standard LU factorization algorithm with its $O(n^3)$ cost in time and $O(n^2)$ memory needs? No. But we would need one more array for an extra set of super-diagonal entries a_{ij}, where $j = i + 2$, to handle the row swaps. And we would have to make sure that the matrices start out tridiagonal. More information on some of these issues can be found in books on numerical linear algebra such as *Matrix Computations* [46].

18.4.3 Handling scratch memory

When we need to construct the spline from the data given knowing the kind of spline we wish to construct, we need to construct a tridiagonal linear system along the way, which is then solved. But this requires more memory. We can either use "scratch space" arrays (provided they are big enough), allocate the array, or use automatic arrays (stored on the stack).

Scratch space arrays are vulnerable to problems with lengths; if the length is too small, then an error will occur. There is no way without dynamic memory allocation of handling arbitrarily large problems, as the extra memory needed is proportional to n, the number of knot points. While scratch space arrays are essentially the only way of dealing with these memory problems in Fortran 77, in Fortran 90 memory allocation means we can avoid passing scratch space arrays.

Stack allocation is possible in Fortran 90, provided the dimensions of the arrays are computable as expressions of the input arguments. But we wish to use the tridiagonal matrix structures. So rather than use stack allocation we will use the more portable and less problematic approach of allocating the type(tdg) structure as needed, and de-allocating it at the end of the routine. This does have a performance penalty. However, construction of splines should be relatively infrequent, so this penalty should not be too significant. If this is found to be too high a penalty, then the stack allocation of the necessary arrays could be implemented. In this case the tridiag module would need to be replaced with a lower level module that worked directly on triples of arrays. In that case, the tridiag module routines could be re-written to be interfaces to the lower level routines.

18.4.4 Setting up the equations

What remains to be done for the spline construction routines is to set up and solve the linear systems to obtain Mlist.

For most of the spline construction routines, the equations for rows 2 through $n - 1$ are the same; it is usually only the first and last equations that are different for the different kinds of splines. A routine spline_basic was written to carry out these common computations:

```
subroutine spline_basic(s,mat,rhs,iflag)
   type(spline), intent(in) :: s
   type(tdg) :: mat
   integer, intent(out) :: iflag
   real(kind=wp) rhs(:), h(s%length-1)
   integer i, n

   iflag = 0
   n = s%length
   if ( .not. tdg_resize(mat,n) ) then
      iflag = -1
      return
   end if

   ! Set up h array
   do i = 1, n - 1
      h(i) = s%xlist(i+1) - s%xlist(i)
```

```
    if ( h(i) == 0 ) then
        iflag = -1
        return
    end if
 end do
 ! Set up right-hand side (rhs) and matrix entries
 do i = 2, n - 1
     rhs(i) = (s%ylist(i+1)-s%ylist(i))/h(i) &
            - (s%ylist(i)-s%ylist(i-1))/h(i-1)
     mat%b(i-1) = h(i-1)/6.
     mat%a(i)   = (h(i-1)+h(i))/3
     mat%c(i)   = h(i)/6
 end do
end subroutine spline_basic
```

Note that we use stack allocation for the h array for efficiency. This routine simplifies the computations in the spline construction routines. For `spline_clamped` we use:

```
call spline_basic(s,mat,s%Mlist,iflag)
if ( iflag == 0 ) then
  ! Now we must set the first and last rows
  h_1 = s%xlist(2) - s%xlist(1)
  h_n_1 = s%xlist(n) - s%xlist(n-1)
  mat%a(1) = h_1/3
  mat%c(1) = h_1/6
  s%Mlist(1) = (s%ylist(2)-s%ylist(1))/h_1 - dy0
  mat%b(n-1) = h_n_1/6
  mat%a(n)   = h_n_1/3
  s%Mlist(n) = dy1 - (s%ylist(n)-s%ylist(n-1))/h_n_1
end if
```

Similar code is in `spline_natural`. Note that if we had used Cholesky factorization, which requires the matrix to be symmetric, then we would not have been able to use this approach.

As usual, we test these codes. We test them two ways: for our example spline function we know the formula for the spline function, and we know the values of the M_i. So we test both. We compute and print the maximum error in the computed values for the M_i, and we select (pseudo-)random points in the interpolation interval and compute the difference between the formulas for our example given above, and via `spline_eval`. This is perhaps redundant, but it is often worthwhile (and not inconvenient) to do both tests; the tests are not redundant when applied to other example splines where the correct M_i values are not given.

For the example test spline, we obtained in double-precision a maximum error of 2.22×10^{-16} in Mlist, and a maximum error in the spline function values of 2.56×10^{-16}. As the unit roundoff $\mathbf{u}$ for double-precision is $\approx 2.2 \times 10^{-16}$, these are very satisfactory values.

18.5 Periodic splines

A periodic spline is a spline function s with the property that for a fixed $p > 0$ (the period of the spline), $s(t + p) = s(t)$ for all t. The periodic spline interpolant of

$$s(x_i) = y_i, \quad i = 1, 2, \ldots, n$$

has period $p = x_n - x_1$; the extra conditions that a periodic spline must satisfy are that $s(x_n) = s(x_1)$, $s'(x_n) = s'(x_1)$ and $s''(x_n) = s''(x_1)$. The first condition says that $y_n = y_1$. Since $M_i = s''(x_i)$ this last condition simply says that $M_n = M_1$. The middle condition is the more difficult one, but reduces to the equation:

$$\frac{y_2 - y_1}{h_1} - \frac{y_1 - y_{n-1}}{h_{n-1}} = \frac{h_{n-1}}{6} M_{n-1} + \frac{h_{n-1} + h_1}{3} M_1 + \frac{h_1}{6} M_2.$$

You can get this equation by setting $i = n$ in the general equation and using the facts that $M_n = M_1$, $M_{n+1} = M_2$, $y_n = y_1$, $y_{n+1} = y_2$, and $h_n = h_1$ for periodic splines. Similarly, for $i = n - 1$ we get

$$\frac{y_1 - y_{n-1}}{h_{n-1}} - \frac{y_{n-1} - y_{n-2}}{h_{n-2}} = \frac{h_{n-2}}{6} M_{n-2} + \frac{h_{n-2} + h_{n-1}}{3} M_{n-1} + \frac{h_{n-1}}{6} M_1.$$

Periodic splines require slightly different treatment from clamped and natural splines as the linear system used for constructing the spline is no longer tridiagonal, rather it is tridiagonal plus a symmetric pair or entries in the top-right and bottom-left corners of the matrix. This gives a so-called periodic tridiagonal matrix. We will now look at how we can solve periodic tridiagonal matrices efficiently using the standard tridiagonal solver.

For evaluating periodic splines we do not use the simple extrapolation technique for evaluating the spline outside the interval $[x_1, x_n]$. Instead, we use the periodicity of the spline function.

18.5.1 Periodic spline evaluation

To evaluate a periodic spline function, we use the *argument reduction* approach: first replace the input t with $t - kp$, where k is a whole number chosen so that

$t - kp \in [x_1, x_n]$. Then we can use the standard evaluation routine for $t - kp$. How do we compute k? Recall that $p = x_n - x_1$. Now $x_1 \le t - kp \le x_n$, so $0 \le t - x_1 - kp \le x_n - x_1 = p$, or, equivalently, $kp \le t - x_1 \le (k + 1)p$. Dividing by $p > 0$ gives $k \le (t - x_1)/p \le k + 1$. So we can take $k = \text{floor}((t - x_1)/p)$; note that $\text{floor}(z) = \lfloor z \rfloor$, the largest integer $\le z$. Using the Fortran 90 FLOOR function runs the risk of overflowing the integer result. Instead, what we really need is $t - pk = x_1 + [(t - x_1) - p \, \text{floor}((t - x_1)/p)]$; $u - p \, \text{floor}(u/p)$ can be computed by the MODULO function in Fortran 90 (fmod in C/C++).

Clearly we need a new routine for evaluating periodic spline functions: spline_peval. We do not have to repeat all the code for evaluating the cubic function on $[x_i, x_{i+1}]$ or carrying out the binary search. In accordance with the principle of *once and only once!* we will call spline_eval from spline_peval to do most of the work. Here is code to implement this:

```
p = s%xlist(s%length) - s%xlist(1)
t_reduced = s%xlist(1) + modulo(t-s%xlist(1), p)
val = spline_eval(s,t_reduced,iflag)
```

18.5.2 Periodic spline construction

Construction of a periodic spline involves solving a linear system with a periodic tridiagonal matrix, which looks like this:

$$
\begin{bmatrix}
a_1 & c_1 & & & & & b_{n-1} \\
b_1 & a_2 & c_2 & & & & \\
 & b_2 & a_3 & \ddots & & & \\
 & & \ddots & \ddots & \ddots & & \\
 & & & \ddots & a_{n-2} & c_{n-2} & \\
c_{n-1} & & & & b_{n-2} & a_{n-1}
\end{bmatrix}
\begin{bmatrix}
z_1 \\ z_2 \\ z_3 \\ \vdots \\ z_{n-2} \\ z_{n-1}
\end{bmatrix}
=
\begin{bmatrix}
w_1 \\ w_2 \\ w_3 \\ \vdots \\ w_{n-2} \\ w_{n-1}
\end{bmatrix},
$$

if we replace M_n with M_1 in the linear system. The technique we will use is the **Sherman–Morrison–Woodbury formula** [46]. This formula allows us to compute the inverse of a matrix that is "almost tridiagonal" in the sense that removing just a few entries will give a tridiagonal matrix. The formula itself is

$$
(A + uv^{\mathsf{T}})^{-1} = A^{-1} - \frac{A^{-1}uv^{\mathsf{T}}A^{-1}}{1 + v^{\mathsf{T}}A^{-1}u}
$$

provided A is a matrix with an inverse and $1 + v^{\mathsf{T}}A^{-1}u \ne 0$. Since for periodic spline functions the matrix in the linear system is symmetric, $b_{n-1} = c_{n-1}$, and we can set

$$
A = \begin{bmatrix}
a_1 - b_{n-1} & c_1 & & & & & \\
b_1 & a_2 & c_2 & & & & \\
& b_2 & a_3 & \ddots & & & \\
& & \ddots & \ddots & \ddots & & \\
& & & \ddots & a_{n-2} & c_{n-2} & \\
& & & & b_{n-2} & a_{n-1} - c_{n-1}
\end{bmatrix},
$$

$$
u = b_{n-1} \begin{bmatrix} 1 \\ 0 \\ 0 \\ \vdots \\ 0 \\ 1 \end{bmatrix}, \qquad
v = \begin{bmatrix} 1 \\ 0 \\ 0 \\ \vdots \\ 0 \\ 1 \end{bmatrix}.
$$

A quick check will verify that uv^{T} is a matrix with zeros everywhere except at the four corner entries which each have the value b_{n-1}, so the linear system we wish to solve really does have the matrix $A + uv^{\mathrm{T}}$.

The Sherman–Morrison–Woodbury formula will work well if A and $A + uv^{\mathrm{T}}$ are well-conditioned. Since A and $A + uv^{\mathrm{T}}$ are diagonally dominant for the periodic spline case, we would expect this approach to be satisfactory. To implement this approach, we first compute $A^{-1}u$, which can be done one column at a time. We write e_k for the vector with kth component one and all others zero; then $u = b_{n-1}(e_1 + e_{n-1})$ and $v = (e_1 + e_{n-1})$. So $A^{-1}u = b_{n-1}A^{-1}(e_1 + e_{n-1})$; we can compute $w := b_{n-1}A^{-1}(e_1 + e_{n-1})$ by means of the standard tridiagonal linear solver. Then we can compute

$$
1 + v^{\mathrm{T}}A^{-1}u = 1 + b_{n-1}(e_1 + e_{n-1})^{\mathrm{T}}A^{-1}(e_1 + e_{n-1})
$$
$$
= 1 + (e_1 + e_{n-1})^{\mathrm{T}}w = 1 + w_1 + w_{n-1}.
$$

To solve the linear system $(A + uv^{\mathrm{T}})z = r$ for z we set

$$
z = (A + uv^{\mathrm{T}})^{-1}r
$$
$$
= A^{-1}r - \frac{A^{-1}uv^{\mathrm{T}}A^{-1}}{1 + v^{\mathrm{T}}A^{-1}u}r
$$
$$
= \left(I - \frac{w(e_1 + e_{n-1})^{\mathrm{T}}}{1 + v^{\mathrm{T}}w} \right) A^{-1}r.
$$

So we can first solve $Ap = r$ using the standard tridiagonal equation solver, and then compute

$$z = p - \frac{p_1 + p_{n-1}}{1 + w_1 + w_{n-1}} w.$$

A minor problem in all this is that the tridiagonal solvers generated by spline_basic are $n \times n$ matrices, not $(n - 1) \times (n - 1)$ as we would use after dropping M_n as an independent variable. However, this is not a major problem: we can set $a_n = 1$ and the other entries in the nth row and column equal to zero. After computing $M_1, \ldots, M_{n-1}$ we can simply set $M_n = M_1$, regardless of what came out of the linear equation solver.

Since the algorithm used is quite complicated, we found it very useful to go through the calculations "by hand" using MATLAB for a specific example periodic spline. Constructing the example periodic spline was done using pen and paper, and also using MATLAB to plot the result so that errors in the pen-and-paper calculations were revealed. Initial computation not only gives a good set of data to compare with the Fortran 90 implementation, but also helps to find problems with the proposed algorithm itself. Doing computations "by hand" is no guarantee that they are error free!

As always, testing was done incrementally as the code was developed. This involved testing the periodic tridiagonal solver (often by comparing with MATLAB's results), hand-computing a periodic spline function explicitly, computing the corresponding M_is, testing the M_is produced by the construction routine, and finally testing the spline function values against the hand-computed formula.

18.6 Performance testing

Here is some performance testing code:

```
if ( .not. spline_get(s,len) ) then
   print *, 'Cannot allocate spline'
   return
end if
do i = 1, len
   xlist(i) = (1.0d0*i)/len
end do
call random_number(ylist)

if ( .not. spline_set(s,xlist,ylist,len) ) then
   print *, 'Cannot set spline x, y entries'
   return
end if
```

```
do i = 1, n
   call spline_natural(s,iflag)
   if ( iflag /= 0 ) then
       print *, 'Cannot compute natural spline,', &
       iflag =', iflag
       call spline_print(s,stdout)
       return
   end if
   do j = 1, n_evals
       call random_number(t)
       s_at_t = spline_eval(s,t,iflag)
   end do
   call random_number(s%ylist)
end do
```

After compiling the program with the -pg compiler option and running the program, running gprof on the executable file produces output which contains a summary of the amount of time spent inside each routine, and a more extensive output listing the number of calls and amount of time spent in each routine *on behalf of* the different calling routines. In our example, each spline has length len $= 100$ while each spline is evaluated at n_eval$= 100$ randomly chosen points; this is repeated $n = 10^5$ times. Using g95 as the Fortran 90/95 compiler, without optimizing switches set, we get the top two routines where most time is spent:

% time	cumulative seconds	self seconds	calls	self s/call	total s/call	name
54.57	5.97	5.97	10000000	0.00	0.00	splines_MP_spline_eval_
12.80	7.37	1.40	100000	0.00	0.00	splines_MP_spline_basic_

That is, spline_eval (54%) and spline_basic (13%) in the splines module are the most time-consuming routines. A detailed analysis of these timings can be made, using information regarding the number of clock cycles typically required to access data and perform operations. The outcome of this analysis is that about 60% to 70% of the clock cycles needed can be accounted for. This means that the time needed could not be reduced to less than 60% to 70% of the times produced by this code under test conditions; perhaps not even that is achievable. The code, therefore, performs about as well as can be expected.

19

Multigrid algorithms

Multigrid algorithms are iterative methods or preconditioners for large linear systems, especially those arising from partial differential equations. While the reader does not need to be knowledgeable about multigrid algorithms, if further information about these algorithms is needed, see [16] or [75] for overviews of how multigrid algorithms work. But the information we need for developing the software will be given here.

Multigrid methods for linear elliptic second order partial equations can solve linear systems with n unknowns to an accuracy of ϵ in $O(n \log(1/\epsilon))$ or $O(n \log n \log(1/\epsilon))$ time and $O(n)$ or $O(n \log n)$ memory. This makes them among the most efficient methods for solving linear systems.

We will only consider multigrid methods for linear systems; nonlinear systems can be treated using the Full Approximation Scheme (FAS) developed by Brandt and described in [16].

19.1 Discretizing partial differential equations

Partial differential equations are differential equations where the unknown function is a function of more than one variable, and involves derivatives of all the variables. For example, the **Poisson equation** in two variables is the equation (for unknown $u(x, y)$):

$$\frac{\partial^2 u}{\partial x^2} + \frac{\partial^2 u}{\partial y^2} = f(x, y) \quad \text{in a region } R,$$

for some given function $f(x, y)$. This equation is useful in electrostatics (there, $u(x, y)$ is the voltage at (x, y), and $f(x, y)$ is the net charge density in the region), or in steady heat flow (there, $u(x, y)$ represents the temperature, and $f(x, y)$ the rate of heat generation at (x, y)). To solve the equation uniquely we need *conditions* that must hold on the boundary of R. For the Poisson equation, these are typically either Dirichlet boundary conditions

$$u(x, y) = g(x, y) \qquad \text{on the boundary } \partial R,$$

or Neumann boundary conditions

$$\frac{\partial u}{\partial n}(x, y) = j(x, y) \qquad \text{on the boundary } \partial R.$$

The expression $\partial u/\partial n(x, y)$ is the derivative of u along the direction perpendicular to the boundary of R at (x, y), going away from R. For steady heat flow problems, Dirichlet boundary conditions represent a boundary held at a fixed temperature (like an ice bath), while Neumann boundary conditions represent heat flow conditions (like meeting an insulator, i.e. no heat flow).

The discretization of partial differential equations is a large and important subject, but goes far beyond the scope of this book. There are three main approaches: the Finite Difference Method (FDM), the Finite Element Method (FEM), and the Finite Volume Method (FVM). What each of these does is turn a partial differential equation (with boundary conditions) into a large system of algebraic equations. If the partial differential equation is linear, the result is a large system of linear equations. Since the unknown in a partial differential equation is a function, we effectively have to find infinitely many quantities. Rather than try to do the impossible, we aim to compute an approximation to the true solution. To get a better approximation, we would normally expect to compute more quantities. Thus for an accurate solution, we will need to solve a large system of equations.

Rather than show in detail how to use these different methods, we will refer the reader to a number of books which describe and analyze these methods in detail. For the Finite Difference Method, [99] is a good starting point. For the Finite Element Method, [36] is a good starting point; [13] is more advanced in terms of both techniques and theory. There are fewer books devoted to the Finite Volume Method than the others, but an introduction with an emphasis on fluid flows (perhaps the biggest area using Finite Volume Methods) is [70].

For what follows, we will say a little about using Finite Difference Methods, since these are the simplest to describe and are used in the computational examples. The test equation we will work with is the Poisson equation in two dimensions: $\partial^2 u/\partial x^2 + \partial^2 u/\partial y^2 = f(x, y)$ on a square region R with Dirichlet boundary conditions $u(x, y) = g(x, y)$ for a given function g on the boundary of R. We start by selecting a grid spacing $h > 0$ and laying down a grid of points (x_i, y_j) where $x_i = x_0 + i h$, $i = 0, 1, 2, \ldots, m$ and $y_j = y_0 + j h$, $j = 0, 1, 2, \ldots, m$. Now we make appoximations to the partial derivatives $\partial^2 u/\partial x^2$ and $\partial^2 u/\partial y^2$ at (x_i, y_j)

based on the values $u(x_p, y_q)$ at nearby points:

$$\frac{\partial^2 u}{\partial x^2}(x_i, y_j) \approx \frac{u(x_{i+1}, y_j) - 2\,u(x_i, y_j) + u(x_{i-1}, y_j)}{h^2} \quad \text{and}$$

$$\frac{\partial^2 u}{\partial x^2}(x_i, y_j) \approx \frac{u(x_i, y_{j+1}) - 2\,u(x_i, y_j) + u(x_{i-1}, y_{j-1})}{h^2}.$$

The errors in these approximations are $\approx \partial^4 u/\partial x^4 \cdot h^2/12$ and $\approx \partial^4 u/\partial y^4 \cdot h^2/12$, respectively. So the exact solution to the partial differential equation would satisfy

$$\frac{u(x_{i+1}, y_j) + u(x_{i-1}, y_j) + u(x_i, y_{j+1}) + u(x_{i-1}, y_{j-1}) - 4\,u(x_i, y_j)}{h^2} \approx f(x_i, y_j).$$

The idea is to replace this approximation with equality in order to compute an approximation u_{ij} of $u(x_i, y_j)$. (This is an example of treating an approximation as if it were exact; see Section 11.3.2.) We get the system of equations

$$f(x_i, y_j) = \frac{u_{i+1,j} + u_{i-1,j} + u_{i,j+1} + u_{i-1,j-1} - 4u_{i,j}}{h^2} \quad \text{for every } (x_i, y_j) \text{ inside } R,$$

$$g(x_i, y_j) = u_{i,j} \quad \text{for every } (x_i, y_j) \text{ on the boundary of } R.$$

The smaller $h > 0$, the more accurate we expect the approximation $u(x_i, y_j) \approx u_{i,j}$ to be, but the larger the system of linear equations is. If R is a 1×1 square and we take $h = 0.01$, then we will have $99^2 \approx 10^4$ unknowns in our linear system to solve. For three-dimensional problems, the number of unknowns can easily be in the millions, and can reach into billions.

19.2 Outline of multigrid methods

Multigrid methods use a hierarchy of "grids", each of which has its own matrix. These grids go from the finest grid (which is associated with the matrix from the linear system to solve) to the coarsest grid (which is associated with a small matrix). These grids are numbered $0, 1, \ldots, N - 1$. Since the number of grids grows logarithmically in the number of unknowns, N is typically no more than about 20. The matrix associated with grid k is A_k with $A_0 = A$, the matrix in the linear system we wish to solve. For each grid we need a smoothing operator R_k which acts as a preconditioner for A_k. Actually, there are two kinds of smoothing operators: pre-smoothers R_k and post-smoothers S_k. The matrix A_k is a square $n_k \times n_k$ matrix. For multigrid methods we need $n_0 \geq n_1 \geq \cdots \geq n_{N-1}$ with $n_0 = n$, the number of unknowns in the original system. To connect the grids there are interpolation matrices I_{k+1}^k which are $n_k \times n_{k+1}$ and restriction operators I_k^{k+1} which are $n_{k+1} \times n_k$. With these ingredients we can write an abstract version of a multigrid algorithm as:

```
multigrid(k,bₖ)/* Solve Aₖxₖ = bₖ */
{
    if k = N
        solve AₙxₙN = bₙ directly
    else
    {
        xₖ ← 0
        repeat v₁ times: xₖ ← Rₖ(xₖ, bₖ)
        rₖ₊₁ ← Iₖ^{k+1}(bₖ − Aₖxₖ)
        eₖ ← Iₖ₊₁^k multigrid(k+1,rₖ₊₁)
        xₖ ← xₖ + eₖ
        repeat v₂ times: xₖ ← Sₖ(xₖ, bₖ)
    }
    return xₖ
}
```

The operations $x_k \leftarrow R_k(x_k, b_k)$ and $x_k \leftarrow S_k(x_k, b_k)$ can each be an iteration of the Gauss–Seidel method [4, p. 548], the Gauss–Jacobi method [4, p. 545], the SOR method [4, p. 555], reversed versions of these, or some other linear iterative method for the equation $A_k x_k = b_k$ such as iterative refinement with Incomplete LU factorization (ILU). Often these can be represented in terms of matrices $\widehat{R}_k$ and $\widehat{S}_k$ via the formulas

$$R_k(x_k, b_k) = x_k + \widehat{R}_k(b_k - A_k x_k),$$
$$S_k(x_k, b_k) = x_k + \widehat{S}_k(b_k - A_k x_k).$$

To guarantee that the overall multigrid method implements a symmetric preconditioner we need $\widehat{S}_k = \widehat{R}_k^{\mathrm{T}}$, A_k symmetric for all k, and $I_k^{k+1} = (I_{k+1}^k)^{\mathrm{T}}$.

Readers familiar with multigrid methods will identify this as a V-cycle multigrid algorithm [16]. Using the same ingredients, variants of this (such as the W-cycle) can be constructed [16].

19.3 Implementation of framework

This framework can be easily implemented *as an abstract framework*. Our implementation language is C++, and we will use templates. The main template class will be an abstract class, so that all the ingredients (the functions A_k, I_k^{k+1}, I_{k+1}^k, R_k, S_k, and support functions) can be overloaded in derived classes. Note that all of these "ingredients" are represented by functions for computing matrix–vector products, computing $y = A_k x$ for example. The main template parameters are the vector and scalar types. This allows us to use the same code for single, double, and extended precision (or even higher precision when it becomes available), and different ways of representing vectors. We have chosen to use the Matrix Template Library (or MTL) developed by the Open Systems Laboratory at Indiana University for the final implementation. Alternatives include MV++ and SparseLib++ developed at the National Institute for Standards and Technology (NIST) which is another template matrix–vector library; Blitz++, originally developed by Todd Veldhuizen; uBLAS, originally developed by Joerg Walter and Mathias Koch, which is part of the Boost C++ library, and is modeled on MTL; there are many more, including wrappers for LAPACK in C++, stand-alone non-template matrix–vector libraries (such as `newmat`). The production of matrix–vector libraries in C++ and other object-oriented languages is almost a small industry in itself!

The interfaces that are assumed to be available for matrices and vectors follow MTL, but we have aimed to keep as much of the code as possible independent of the specific choice of implementation. We chose MTL in part because it has sparse and dense matrices in a common framework, and can provide high performance.

We will need to assume that a number of operations can be performed on the vector class. Some of these will be supported by the STL `vector` template class (such as `size`, `resize`, subscripting, and `iterators`), and some will not (such as arithmetic operations). An important design decision regarding the arithmetic operations is whether they should be "two argument" functions (which construct and return the result) or "three argument" functions (with an output parameter). Since efficiency is the essential reason for multigrid methods, we opted for using output parameters for the vector arithmetic functions, rather than the more convenient but usually less efficient "two argument" versions.

Along with the use of templates, we are using the technique of ***type binders***. Since classes can be used to define operations, a template implementation of an abstract framework can use a collection of classes to implement the basic operations used in the multigrid algorithm. The technique of type binders uses another aspect of classes in C++: types can be defined within a class, and are then "local" to the class. This is used a great deal in the Standard Template Library, where the standard template vector classes contain the type of each entry and the types of the iterators for accessing the vector entries:

```
typedef vector<double> Vec;
Vec x(10);   Vec::iterator i;
for ( i = x.begin(); i != x.end(); ++i )
   cout << *i << endl;
```

This avoids users of iterators needing to know how the iterators are implemented. It also means that we can define classes whose main purpose is to provide a set of types or classes that are related in specific ways. Here is the the main part of the type binder for the multigrid framework:

```
template< typename T, class VectorType,
          class MatrixType, class PermType >
class TypeBinder
{
 public:
   typedef TypeBinder< T, VectorType, MatrixType, PermType >
     Types;

   typedef T              value_type;   // Scalar Type
   typedef unsigned int int_type;       // Integer Type
   typedef MatrixType    Matrix;        // Matrix (dense)
   typedef VectorType    Vector;        // Vector (dense)
   typedef PermType      Perm;          // Permutation or pivot
   typedef typename Vector::size_type size_type;

   // Grid class contains vectors for internal use
   ...
}; //TypeBinder
```

This contains all the types needed for creating the multigrid class. Note that since T (the value_type) is a template parameter, if we want to use single-precision (float), double-precision (double), or extended precision (long double, where available), we just need to change this and the other template types to use this value_type, and all the computations will propagate this level of precision. It is even possible to use user-defined types that provide high accuracy through software, or the complex<double> type for solving linear systems with complex matrices and/or right-hand sides.

Since our multigrid method will need a place to store residuals, right-hand sides, and approximate solutions for each level, the type binder contains a Grid class which is suitable for this purpose.

```
struct Grid
{
  Vector x, b, r;

  // Constructor of dimension dim
  Grid(size_type dim)
  { Vector x(dim), b(dim), r(dim); }
```

```
  // Empty constructor
  Grid() { }
  // resize -- sets new dimension
  void resize(size_type new_dim)
  {
    x.resize(new_dim);
    b.resize(new_dim);
    r.resize(new_dim);
  }
}; // class Grid
```

This class does not provide supporting vectors for all levels. That will be done in the main multigrid template class.

The main multigrid template class is both a template class and an abstract class. The main "ingredients" for the multigrid method – the operators that define the method – are pure virtual functions. That is, they must be defined in a derived class. The routine that defines the multigrid V-cycle is not virtual. Thus, a derived class needs only to define the ingredients for the multigrid method; the base class takes care of how to combine them. There is a performance penalty for virtual functions: time must be spent looking up the virtual function table. However, unless the problem is very small, this will be negligible compared to the time spent applying the operator.

Here is the outline of the multigrid template class using the type binder:

```
template < typename Types >
class multigrid
{
 protected:
  // typedefs from Types for better readability
  ...
 private:
  // Private data items
  ...
 public:
  // Constructor: builds a multigrid method with n_levels,
  // where level k has dimension _dims[k].
  // multigrid(int_type n_levels, const int_type _dims[],
  //            const int_type _nu[])
  ...

  // Constructor: need to use resize() later
```

```
// multigrid(int_type n_levels)
...


// resize -- Note: dims must have length >=
    coarsest_level + 1
// void resize(const int_type _dims[])
...
// set_nu -- update nu[] array; _nu must have length >= 2
// void set_nu(const int_type _nu[])
...


// Destructor: free up grid and dims
// We want
    "~multigrid()"
...


int_type const get_max_level()               const
{ return coarsest_level; }
int_type const get_dim(int_type level) const
{ assert(level >= 0 && level <= coarsest_level );
  return dims[level]; };
int_type const get_nu(int_type i)          const
{ assert(i == 0 ||  i = 1); return nu[i]; };


// residual -- out <- b-A[level]*x
// Vector &residual(const Vector &x, const Vector &b,
//                     int_type level, Vector &out)
...


// The "ingredients" for multigrid (apply_operator,
    pre_relax,
// post_relax, interpolate, restriction, and solve)
...


// MGSolve -- multigrid solver for solving A[0]*x = rhs
// Uses levels up to "top_level"
// Vector &MGSolve( int_type top_level, Vector &x, const
    Vector& rhs )
...
}; // multigrid
```

The private data part consists of the array of dimensions, the array of Grids, and the number of pre- and post-relaxations to do:

```
Grid       *grid;            // Array of grid structures
int_type *dims;             // Array of dimension of each grid
int_type  coarsest_level;  // Coarsest grid
int_type  nu[2];            // Relaxation parameters
```

The constructors allocate and initialize the private data. Here is the main constructor:

```
multigrid(int_type n_levels, const int_type _dims[],
          const int_type _nu[])
{
  dims = new int_type[n_levels];
  grid = new Grid[n_levels];
  coarsest_level = n_levels - 1;
  for ( int i = 0; i < n_levels; i++ ) {
    dims[i] = _dims[i];
    grid[i].resize( dims[i] );
  }
  nu[0] = _nu[0];     nu[1] = _nu[1];
};
```

There is a resize member that can re-set all the dimensions in the dim array. The interfaces of the "ingredients" are fairly similar to each other, although some are meant to represent direct or iterative solution methods, while the others represent the direct application of a matrix:

```
virtual Vector &pre_relax (Vector &v, const Vector &b,
                           int_type level) = 0;
virtual Vector &post_relax(Vector &v, const Vector &b,
                           int_type level) = 0;
virtual Vector &solve     (Vector &v, const Vector &b,
                           int_type level) = 0;

virtual Vector &interpolate(const Vector &v, int_type level,
                           Vector &out) = 0;
virtual Vector &restriction(const Vector &v, int_type level,
                           Vector &out) = 0;
virtual Vector &apply_operator(const Vector &v,
  int_type level, Vector &out) = 0;
```

The main member function of the multigrid class is `MGSolve`, which implements a V-cycle algorithm. Note that it is written in terms of iteration instead of recursion, similar to eliminating tail-end recursion.

```
Vector &MGSolve( int_type top_level, Vector &x,
                const Vector& rhs )
{
    assert(top_level <= coarsest_level && top_level >= 0);
    Vector interpolant(dims[0]);

    copy(rhs, grid[0].b);
    copy(x,   grid[0].x);

    for ( int_type j = 0;j < top_level; ++j ) {
        assert(grid[j].x.size() == dims[j]);
        pre_relax( grid[j].x, grid[j].b, j );
        residual( grid[j].x, grid[j].b, j, grid[j].r);
        restriction( grid[j].r, j+1, grid[j+1].b );
        // We need to set grid[j+1].x to zero as well...
        for ( int_type i = 0; i < grid[j+1].x.size(); ++i )
            grid[j+1].x[i] = 0;
        assert(grid[j].r.size() == dims[j]);
        assert(grid[j+1].b.size() == dims[j+1]);
    }

    solve( grid[top_level].x, grid[top_level].b, top_level);

    for ( int_type j = top_level; j > 0; --j ) {
        interpolant.resize( dims[j-1] );
        interpolate( grid[j].x, j-1, interpolant );
        add( interpolant , grid[j-1].x );
        post_relax( grid[j-1].x, grid[j-1].b, j-1);
    }
    copy(grid[0].x, x);
    return x;
}
```

Next we will see some guidelines for the "ingredients", and a first test example.

19.4 Common choices for the framework

There are some standard choices that are commonly made:

- $I_k^{k+1} = (I_{k+1}^k)^{\mathrm{T}}$.

  That is, the restriction and interpolation operators are transposes of each other.
- $A_{k+1} = I_k^{k+1} A_k I_{k+1}^k$.

  That is, $A_{k+1}x$ is obtained by interpolating x onto the next finer grid, applying the matrix A_k for the finer grid to the interpolated vector, and then restricting the result to the original grid.

These choices are natural from a mathematical point of view, and ensure (amongst other things), that if A_0 is symmetric, positive definite, $I_k^{k+1} = (I_{k+1}^k)^{\mathrm{T}}$ for all k, and all of the I_k^{k+1} have full rank, then all A_k matrices are symmetric, positive definite. However, with functional representations of all these matrices, it is not possible to implement $I_k^{k+1} = (I_{k+1}^k)^{\mathrm{T}}$ in an efficient way. It is possible to implement $A_{k+1} = I_k^{k+1} A_k I_{k+1}^k$ in a moderately efficient way by using

$$
\begin{aligned}
A_k x_k &= I_{k-1}^k A_{k-1} I_k^{k-1} x_k \\
&= I_{k-1}^k I_{k-2}^{k-1} A_{k-2} I_{k-1}^{k-2} I_k^{k-1} x_k \\
&\;\;\vdots \\
&= I_{k-1}^k I_{k-2}^{k-1} \cdots I_0^1 A_0 I_1^0 \cdots I_{k-1}^{k-2} I_k^{k-1} x_k,
\end{aligned}
$$

which could be implemented by interpolating all the way to the bottom level, applying A_0, and then restricting back to level k. A compact representation of A_k, if possible, would generally be more efficient. Usually this can be done using sparse matrix data structures. While there is no general guarantee that the A_k matrices are all sparse, with suitable interpolation and restriction operators, they usually are. How sparse these matrices are should be monitored in general applications. By keeping the abstract software given above, we keep a great deal of flexibility. If we have a perfectly regular problem for which all the necessary operators can be determined analytically, then we do not have to keep the sparse matrices; only a few parameters would be needed for each level. This would give us algorithms which use a minimal amount of memory and could be used for very large, regular problems.

Another common choice is to set, in addition,

- $S_k = R_k^{\mathrm{T}}$.

With this additional choice, the multigrid operator is symmetric if A_0 is.

For multigrid software that uses explicit sparse matrices, we will start with the abstract multigrid routine, and create the ingredients for the abstract algorithm using sparse matrices. Then the typical choices for the smoother operators (based on the Jacobi, Gauss–Seidel or SOR iterative methods) become very easy to implement.

19.5 A first test

Our first test is to solve the $n \times n$ system

$$
A u := \begin{bmatrix} 2 & -1 & & & & \\ -1 & 2 & -1 & & & \\ & -1 & 2 & \ddots & & \\ & & \ddots & \ddots & -1 & \\ & & & -1 & 2 \end{bmatrix} \begin{bmatrix} u_0 \\ u_1 \\ \vdots \\ u_{n-2} \\ u_{n-1} \end{bmatrix} = \begin{bmatrix} b_0 \\ b_1 \\ \vdots \\ b_{n-2} \\ b_{n-1} \end{bmatrix} =: b,
$$

which comes from the one-dimensional differential equation $d^2 u / dx^2 = f(x)$ with the boundary conditions $u(0) = 0$ and $u(L) = 0$. If we set $x_i = i\,h$ with h (the step-size or grid spacing) equal to L/n, then setting $b_i = h^2 f(x_i)$ will give a solution u, where $u_i \approx u(x_i)$.

19.5.1 Implementing the test problem

Since this is a test problem, and the aim is to keep the structure of the code very simple, we assume that $n = 2^k - 1$ for some positive, whole number k. This allows us to use simple code for all the operators. Since this is a test code, hard-wiring most of the choices is acceptable. The need for a concrete test case outweighs the need for generality at this stage. Later we will build more general test cases.

The restriction operator $y = I_{k+1}^k u$ is given by $y_i = \frac{1}{4} u_{2i} + \frac{1}{2} u_{2i+1} + \frac{1}{4} u_{2i+2}$, while the interpolation operator $z = I_k^{k+1} v$ is actually two times the transpose of the restriction operator: $z_{2i-1} = v_i$ and $z_{2i} = \frac{1}{2}(v_{i-1} + v_i)$. The operators $y = A_k u$ have a scale factor that depends on the level k: $y_i = s_k(2u_i - u_{i-1} - u_{i+1})$, with $u_{-1} = u_n = 0$; some pencil-and-paper calculation will show (and MATLAB will confirm) that $s_{k+1} = s_k/4$. The scaling is particularly important for the relaxation steps. We used Gauss–Seidel for the pre-relaxation and reversed Gauss–Seidel for the post-relaxation.

The solver for the top level was a direct LU-factorize-and-solve, which was implemented using MTL's `lu_factor` and `lu_solve` routines. Since the number of unknowns at the top level should always be fairly small, this should give acceptable performance.

All the "ingredients" were implemented in another template class `oneDPois-son` derived from `multigrid`. This template was then instantiated with a `Types` binder made from a collection of basic C/C++ types and instantiations of MTL's types:

```
// Derived class from multigrid which defines the operators
    needed
typedef double value_type;
typedef MY_MG::TypeBinder<value_type,
                          dense1D<value_type>,
                          matrix<value_type>::type,
                          dense1D<int> > myTypes;
typedef myTypes::int_type int_type;
typedef myTypes::Vector   Vector;
```

The main program takes the number of levels from the command line, creates the right-hand side and solution vectors and the multigrid object. The multigrid algorithm is then applied a number of times to compute a usefully accurate solution to the linear system.

19.5.2 *Testing and validation*

It took a number of steps to build, and test while building, the system. The most important steps were to select a modest value of n (we used $n = 7$ and 15) in order to check that each step was being carried out correctly. The main operator matrices (A_k), the interpolation and restriction matrices (I_k^{k+1} and I_{k+1}^k), and the relaxation operators ($\widehat{R}_k$ and $\widehat{S}_k$) were all computed in MATLAB. This gave a reference with which to compare the results from the framework. Using the Op<Vector> template class for operators (described in the following section) and a function to generate a dense matrix representation of such an operator, the matrices for the framework and this example were generated and compared. By going through the steps of the algorithm one by one we were able to locate and fix the bugs in the code. A number of these were syntax errors that were identified during compilation due to misunderstanding how to use the MTL matrices and iterators. Occasionally, templates required typename operators for the compiler to understand the code; these errors were flagged at compilation. In addition, there were a few more serious errors in logic that were identified by a step-by-step comparison with the results of MATLAB for a simple example.

One of the difficulties for testing multigrid algorithms is that there is no simple description of what they do apart from the original pseudo-code. This is different from direct linear solvers: given A and b they compute x where $Ax - b$ should be zero (or very close to it). Thus it is easy to test if a linear solver is working. So for

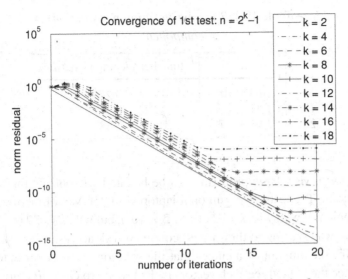

Figure 19.1. Plot of residual norms against iteration number for the first test problem.

multigrid algorithms, it is necessary to test each step to see if it has computed what it should compute. For this task, MATLAB is invaluable.

Ultimately, the whole purpose of the multigrid solver is that it can produce rapidly convergent iterations that approach the true solution. At least it is always possible to compute residuals, and they should go to zero in a rapid way that is independent, or nearly independent, of the size of the problem. To test to see if we have a useful algorithm, we need performance tests – not just correctness tests.

In Figure 19.1 we can see plots of the residual norm $\|Ax - b\|_\infty$ (logarithmic scale) against the iteration number for $n = 2^k - 1$, $k = 2, 4, \ldots, 18$. The number of levels in the multigrid algorithm is k. The exponential convergence of the residual can be seen in the straight, descending part of the plots. These plots flatten out eventually because of roundoff error; for small values of k the level of the residual is clearly not far from unit roundoff for double-precision. For larger values of k it appears to be much larger. However, if we compute $\|Ax - b\|_\infty / \|A\|_\infty \|x\|_\infty$ we find that it is a little smaller than unit roundoff; for $k = 18$ for example, $\|Ax - b\|_\infty / \|A\|_\infty \|x\|_\infty \approx 5.5 \times 10^{-17}$ which is less than $\mathbf{u} \approx 2.2 \times 10^{-16}$. A reason for this is that the condition number of A grows like $n^2 \approx 4^k$; for $k = 18$ we get $n \approx 2.62 \times 10^4$ and $n^2 \approx 6.87 \times 10^{10}$.

The essential point is the straight, descending part of the plots all have a slope that is roughly the same, representing a reduction of the residual with each iteration of a factor of about 0.185. This the most desirable property of multigrid methods: convergence rates that are independent, or very slowing degrading, as the problem size increases. Also, because only functional representations of the operators

Table 19.1. *Time per iteration per solution
component*

k	n	time/iter'n/component (μsec)
14	1.63×10^4	0.275
17	1.31×10^5	0.347
20	1.05×10^6	0.387

have been used, very large problems can be handled without running into memory limitations. The tests were run on a laptop with 256 MB of memory; this test problem could run well with $k = 21$ ($n \approx 2 \times 10^6$), but with $k = 22$ ($n \approx 4 \times 10^6$) the program was starting to thrash with continual disk accesses. With $k = 22$ and $n \approx 4 \times 10^6$, the amount of memory that the solution vector x takes up is about 32 MB. Since there are three such vectors in the level zero Grid structure, this takes up about 96 MB. Adding the memory for all the other levels double this: 192 MB. Adding in the three vectors (solution, right-hand side, and residual) in the main program gives a total memory requirement for $k = 22$ of about 288 MB. While the program could still run using virtual memory (even taking into account the space needed by the operating system), the program was thrashing.

Timings back up the good results on convergence and memory usage: there were no obvious bottlenecks. Using `gprof` we obtained Table 19.1. While there is an increase in the time per iteration per solution component, it is mostly due to caching effects; for $k = 14$ several solution vectors will fit in the L2 cache, but this is no longer true for $k = 17$ or $k = 20$. The difference between $k = 14$ and $k = 20$ is about 112 ns (nanoseconds) per iteration per component, or about 200 clock cycles for the 1.8 GHz computer that gave the timings. This can be easily accounted for by several L2 cache misses per iteration per component.

19.6 The operator interface and its uses

For a more serious application, we used the multigrid framework to handle a more complex task. First, the framework was extended to handle the situation where general sparse matrices can be used to define some or all of the "ingredients" of the multigrid method. This is particularly appropriate for looking at *Algebraic Multigrid (AMG)* methods [97]. The interpolation, restriction, and the main (A_k) operators have to be explicitly represented as sparse matrices. The pre- (and post-) relaxation operators can be defined as Gauss–Seidel (and reverse Gauss–Seidel) operators for the corresponding main (A_k) matrix. Note that implementing the Gauss–Seidel operators requires access to the entries of the A_k matrices.

In between the original framework and the sparse matrices we have an operator interface:

```
// Defines Op class -- transforms vectors to vectors
#ifndef OPERATOR_H
#define OPERATOR_H
template <class Vector> struct Op { // returns y = A*x
  virtual Vector &operator()(const Vector &x, Vector &y)
    = 0;
};
#endif // OPERATOR_H
```

For a sparse matrix we can define the simple application of the matrix to a vector, the Gauss–Seidel method, Successive Over-Relaxation (SOR), the Jacobi method, and so on.

Here is the class for the simple application of a matrix:

```
template<class Vector, class Matrix>
class MatrixOp : public Op<Vector> {
 private:
  const Matrix *A;
 public:
  MatrixOp(const Matrix &_A) : A(&_A)  {  }

  Vector &operator()(const Vector &x, Vector &y)
  { zero(y);  mult(*A,x,y);  return y;  }
};
```

The MTL `mult` operator actually computes $y \leftarrow Ax + y$, so it is necessary to zero y before calling `mult` to get $y \leftarrow Ax$. Here is the code for carrying out one iteration of the Gauss–Seidel method using MTL-style interfaces:

```
template <class Vector, class Matrix>
class GaussSeidelOp : public Op<Vector> {
 private:
  const typename mtl::rows_type<Matrix>::type A;
 public:
  GaussSeidelOp(const Matrix &_A) : A(rows(_A))  {  }

  typedef typename Vector::value_type value_type;
  Vector &operator()(const Vector &b, Vector &x)
  {
```

```
for ( int i = 0; i < A.nrows(); ++i )
  {
      typename Matrix::Row r = A[i];
      typename Matrix::Row::iterator j;
      value_type sum = b[i], diag = 0;
      for ( j = r.begin(); j != r.end();.++j )
        {
            if ( j.column() == i ) diag = *j;
            else  sum -= (*j)*x[j.column()];
        }
      x[i] = sum / diag;
  }
  return x;
}
}; // GaussSeidelOp
```

Note that j is an iterator over the entries of the current row A[i] so that *j is the value of the current entry of the matrix, while j.column() is its column number and j.row() is its row number.

To accommodate these Op<Vector> objects into the multigrid framework, a new template class OpMG was created from multigrid using arrays of Ops:

```
#ifndef OP_MG_H
#define OP_MG_H

// Multigrid using arrays of operators
#include "my-mg.h"
#include "operator.h"

template<typename Types>
class OpMG : public MY_MG::multigrid<Types> {
 public:
  // typedefs from Types
  ...
  typedef Op<Vector> *PtrOp;
 private:
  // These are the arrays of (pointers to) operators that
  // define the multigrid preconditioner.
  // We use pointers to Op's to allow polymorphism
  // via virtual functions
  PtrOp *A, *pre_rel, *post_rel,
        *interp,  *restrikt, top_solve;
```

```
public:
 // main constructor
 ...
 // Destructor
 ...
 // now here we put the essential (virtual) functions
 // defining the multigrid preconditioner
 Vector &pre_relax (Vector &v, const Vector &b,
                    int_type level)
 {  return (*pre_rel[level])(b, v);  }
 Vector &post_relax(Vector &v, const Vector &b,
                    int_type level)
 {  return (*post_rel[level])(b, v);  }
 Vector &solve     (Vector &v, const Vector &b,
                    int_type level)
 {  return (*top_solve)(b, v);  }
 // Note that "out" is on level "level",
 // while "v" is on "level+1"
 Vector &interpolate(const Vector &v, int_type level,
                     Vector &out)
 {  return (*interp[level])(v, out);  }
 // Note that "out" is on level "level",
 // while "v" is on "level-1"
 Vector &restriction(const Vector &v, int_type level,
                     Vector &out)
 {  return (*restrikt[level-1])(v, out);  }
 Vector &apply_operator(const Vector &v, int_type level,
                        Vector &out)
 {  return (*A[level])(v, out);  }
};

#endif // OP_MG_H
```

19.7 Dealing with sparse matrices

In contrast to the situation for dense matrices, there are a great many different ways of representing sparse matrices. Not only this, but there are even more ways of *implementing* sparse matrices and their operations. This means that different sparse matrix systems or packages will be inconsistent, and there are more opportunities for incompatibilities. Since it is possible to develop more efficient code for particular

cases (e.g., tridiagonal, or banded, or periodic tridiagonal matrices), there tends to
be a zoo of routines and data structures for sparse matrices.

This leads to two important observations:

- *The underlying code should not depend on the details of a particular sparse matrix data
  structure.* Efficiency might still depend on the details of the sparse matrix structure, but
  the correctness of the algorithm should not. Whole matrix operations (e.g., matrix–vector
  multiplies) should be preferred to element operations (e.g., accessing a_{ij}) which should
  be preferred to elemental update operations (e.g., inserting a new non-zero entry a_{ij}).
- *Since users need a way of setting up sparse matrices, include or allow a "default" sparse
  matrix data structure.* There are a number of these available publicly, such as MTL and
  SparseLib++. Many more are available. If you do not wish to use a previously developed
  data structure, you could develop one of your own. This is not an easy task, but if you
  insist, you should provide easy-to-use access and operations routines.

In this multigrid example, the iterative methods that we wish to use as smoothers
(e.g., Jacobi, Gauss–Seidel, SOR, etc.) require elemental access. That is, their efficiency relies on efficiently accessing individual elements. Other iterative methods
such as Krylov subspace methods (e.g., conjugate gradients, GMRES, BiCG and
BiCGStab, QMR) require only the ability to compute the matrix–vector products
Ax and possibly $A^{\mathrm{T}}x$ for the sparse matrix A and a general vector x. Other methods
such as sparse LU and sparse incomplete LU factorization require not only efficient
element access, but also the ability to efficiently update entries in the sparse matrix,
and to add new non-zero entries.

Templates allow the choice of essentially any matrix type, as long as they can
satisfy the interface requirements. As noted above, MTL matrix types can do this
for the multigrid system described in this book.

19.7.1 A taxonomy of sparse matrix data structures

For more on sparse matrix data structures, there are the classic references [32, 43].
A short introduction to this topic can also be found in [93].

The simplest sparse matrix data structure is the triplet structure: a sparse matrix
is represented by a set of triplets (i, j, val) with one triplet for each non-zero
entry. Here i is the index of the row of the entry, j the index of the column, and
val the actual value of the entry: $a_{ij} = val$. This is referred to as the *coordinate
representation* of the sparse matrix, see [93, 32]. However, as it stands it is not a
very useful data structure. For a start, accessing a specific entry is not easy: the
entire set must be searched for the correct value of (i, j) before reading off the
value a_{ij}. Most matrix operations access all or part of a specific row or column of
A. This data structure is of no help in doing this.

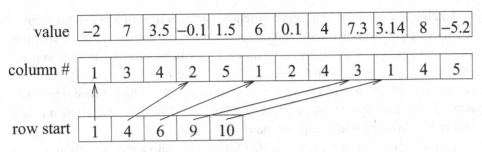

Figure 19.2. Compressed row representation.

The set of triplets can be sorted using, for example, a lexicographical ordering that orders the triplets first by i, and then for the entries in the same row i orders the entries according to j. Then all the entries in the same row will be together, greatly reducing search time and improving memory locality. Alternatively, this could be done by sorting first on the column index j and then (for entries in the same column) on the row index i.

Ordering the entries so as to bring all the entries in a specific row (or column) together is the essence of the *packed* or *compressed row* (or *column*) *representation*. This is illustrated in Figure 19.2. This means that entries in a given row can be accessed very efficiently. However, if we also wanted to access the entries in a given column, this cannot be done very efficiently. Finding an individual entry is reasonably efficient: given (i, j), we can go directly to the list of entries in row i, and scan or search these entries for column index j, and then read off a_{ij}. With binary search, an individual entry can be found in time $O(1 + \log n_i)$ where n_i is the number of non-zeros in row i. However, inserting a new non-zero entry will require updating almost the entire data structure: if we insert a new a_{ij} entry, all the entries following after this new entry have to be shifted up by one space. This is very inefficient. Commonly this is dealt with in sparse matrix factorization routines by splitting the factorization of a matrix into two parts: a **symbolic factorization** and a **numerical factorization**. The first phase is simply to compute an upper bound for the non-zero entries in the factored matrix. The numerical factorization then computes the actual (numerical) values. The symbolic factorization phase can often be done efficiently using specialized algorithms, data structures, and theory. In this way, the problems of inserting new non-zeros individually is avoided.

A partial remedy is to use a separate block of allocated memory for each row. Then when inserting a new non-zero entry into a row, only entries in that row will need to be shifted. The memory block should not be re-allocated every time a new non-zero entry is added. Instead, we should use amortized doubling to double the size of the memory block when extra memory is needed, and track how much of each memory block is actually used. This is the strategy used in Meschach [92].

Another issue is how to access efficiently all the entries in a particular column when using packed row representation (or accessing all entries in a particular row when using packed column representation). This can be done use links from each entry to the next entry in its column. This is done in Meschach [92]. It is also described in [93]. The links needed can be constructed in $O(nnz)$ time where nnz is the number of non-zeros, however, the links need to be updated when a new non-zero is inserted into the sparse matrix structure.

Two other options can be considered for sparse matrix representation. One is to use *hash tables*. This is suitable where a sparse matrix is accessed in an essentially random fashion, and also allows "random" updates with $O(1)$ cost. However, traversing rows or columns is difficult, and memory locality is lost. Nevertheless, it is a useful option for certain operations.

Another option is to treat each row and each column as a *linked list*. That is, each entry will belong to two linked lists, one for its row and one for its column. This makes insertion of a new entry fast (once you know where to put it). Accessing entries in a row and a column can be done reasonably efficiently, but because of all the pointers and memory allocations involved, there is substantial loss of memory locality.

19.8 A second test

A second test for the multigrid framework comes from the two-dimensional partial differential equation

$$\frac{\partial^2 u}{\partial x^2} + \frac{\partial^2 u}{\partial y^2} = f(x, y)$$

over a region Ω with the condition that $u = 0$ on the boundary of Ω. For this test we take Ω to be the union of three squares forming an "L", as shown in Figure 19.3. This is discretized using the standard 5-point stencil for the $\partial^2/\partial x^2 + \partial^2/\partial y^2$ operator: if $u(x_i, y_j) \approx u_{ij}$ with $x_i = x_0 + i\,h$ and $y_j = y_0 + j\,h$, where h is the common grid spacing, then

$$\frac{\partial^2 u}{\partial x^2}(x_i, y_j) + \frac{\partial^2 u}{\partial y^2}(x_i, y_j) \approx \frac{u_{i+1,j} + u_{i-1,j} - 4u_{i,j} + u_{i,j-1} + u_{i,j+1}}{h^2}.$$

Setting $b_{i,j} = -h^2 f(x_i, y_j)$ we get a linear system

$$-u_{i+1,j} - u_{i-1,j} + 4u_{i,j} - u_{i,j-1} - u_{i,j+1} = b_{i,j}.$$

A difficulty here is that we have to map the (i, j) pairs for a two-dimensional domain into a single index k for a vector, and because we have a more complicated region,

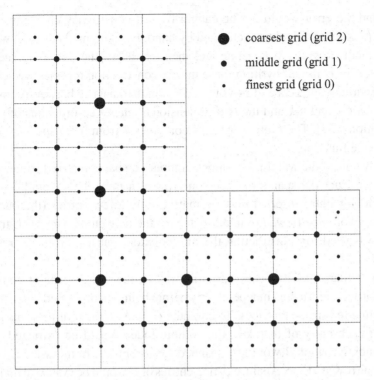

Figure 19.3. "L"-shaped region for second multigrid example. Note that points in coarser grid are included in finer grids.

this can be a substantial problem. Rather than try to hard-wire the choices, we implemented the algorithm to use general sparse matrices which can be modified as needed.

We used the OpMG template class to define the multigrid operator using the Op-derived classes (MatrixOp, GaussSeidelOp, LUSolveOp, etc.) to define the component operators.

We could have started using the Op classes to define operators and built a version of OpMG without needing the original multigrid class. Then why have a multigrid class? The two classes have different roles: OpMG is appropriate when the operators in the multigrid algorithm are implemented using independent data structures, while multigrid is appropriate when the different operators are defined in terms of a common data structure.

Several routines required careful debugging. This was particularly true for the routine to construct the matrix A_0 that defined the linear system to be solved, and the routine to construct the restriction operators. Since all the other matrices were defined in terms of these, if these matrices were wrong, everything else would be wrong and the error would not be caught by self-consistency checking. A small test case was set up which was checked by hand. For automated testing, we would write a small program to generate and then test all of the entries to see if they are correct. To help with writing these matrix construction routines we set up two support routines, my_idx and rev_my_idx, which translated between components of the solution vector k and the two-dimensional integer co-ordinates of the point in the region (i, j). The routine my_idx computes k from (i, j) and rev_my_idx is its inverse function.

Since we used the MTL row-major compressed sparse matrix format, we took care to construct the sparse matrices one row at a time. This would ensure that with each new entry inserted into the matrix, only a few entries (the ones in the same row) would be moved to make space for the new entry. The MTL transpose routine was used for constructing the interpolation matrices from the restriction matrices.

A sparse matrix multiplication routine was written for row-major compressed sparse matrices, and tested independently before being incorporated into the routine constructing the sparse matrices. To compute $C = A\,B$, the routine scans the rows of A; for each entry of that row, the column index would be extracted, and the corresponding row of B would be scanned for its entries. In this way, C could be built up one row at a time. Again, existing entries of C would be moved to make space for new entries, but only entries in the row under construction. To facilitate this, a sparse vector was constructed for each row before adding the values in the sparse vector to C.

The resulting routine (after debugging) gave excellent convergence results. These are shown in Figure 19.4. The convergence rates are remarkably consistent across the size of the problem: residuals are typically between 0.186 and 0.217 of the previous residual.

However, there is a big performance problem. From times reported by gprof, most of the time was spent in assigning values to sparse matrix entries A(i,j) = val.[1] The second largest was an internal insertion operation. Table 19.2 shows the timing results for the "A(i,j) = val" operation.

As can be seen from Table 19.2, the dimension increases by roughly a factor of four as we go down the table, as do the number of calls. This means that the number of sparse matrix updates is only linear in the dimension of the problem. This is good news. However, the time per call is increasing by a factor that is also close to four as we go down the table. Furthermore, for the largest problem in the table, the "A(i,j) = val" operation and the internal insertion operation

---

[1] More precisely, the function call with the most time (not counting the functions it called) was mtl::elt_ref<...>::operator=(double).

Table 19.2. *Timing results for sparse matrix entry assignment*

dimension	total time (sec)	# calls	time/call (μsec)
2 945	0.19	30 745	6.18
12 033	3.03	128 939	23.49
48 641	50.87	528 061	96.33
195 585	872.57	2 137 295	408.00

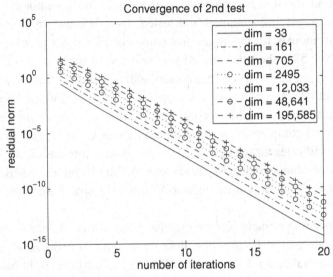

Figure 19.4. Plot of residual norms against iteration number for the second test problem.

together account for about 98.7% of the total time. Given that we have been careful to add entries by rows, why is this happening? The cost of shifting entries may have been avoided, but the cost of allocating new memory has not. The writers of MTL could have used an amortized doubling scheme which would only require $O(\log n)$ calls to new and only copying $O(n)$ sparse matrix entries. However, it seems that this was an optimization that was not implemented, perhaps because of the memory overhead. Modifying the library to incorporate amortized doubling would involve considerable effort, and any new version of the library would require a new "fix". Instead, we decided to use hash tables for constructing the sparse matrix; once the hash tables have all the sparse matrix entries entered and updated, it can be converted into an MTL sparse matrix. Since MTL can use external arrays to define a compressed sparse matrix, we can avoid going through "A(i,j) = val" in converting the hash table into a sparse matrix.

To ease the implementation of a hash table for sparse matrices we used the hash_map template class. While hash_map is not part of the Standard Template Library [96, pp. 497–504], it is available with GNU C++ as an extension. Note that hash_map is also available in the SGI implementation of the STL [91]. A hash_matrix template class was derived from hash_map for the purpose of assembling matrices – hash_matrix is not a general matrix class; instead it has a convert member which converts the hash matrix into an MTL matrix.

Four routines needed to be replaced with ones that use the hash_matrix class: the sparse matrix multiply, the transpose routine, the routine constructing the main matrix A_0, and the routine constructing the restriction operator for each level. With these changes implemented and tested, the performance of the algorithm improved enormously for the larger problems. For the largest problem considered (dimension 195 585) the time needed was reduced from 26 minutes, 22 seconds (without hash_matrix) to 17.75 seconds (with hash_matrix), a reduction by a factor of about 90. The convergence rates per iteration were just the same as before.

We did not try to run this second test on the next larger problem (dimension 784 385) to completion: we noticed that it was doing a great many disk accesses which indicates thrashing, and the memory requirements (as reported by MS Window's Task Manager) would come close to 200 MB on a 256 MB laptop. The solution vector would only need about 6 MB, but the sparse matrices would need much more.

The memory requirements can be estimated as follows: A_0 needs about 45 MB; the interpolation and restriction operators need about 21 MB each; the level zero Grid structure takes up 3×6 MB = 18 MB; the solution, right-hand side and residual vectors of the main program need 6 MB each totalling 18 MB. Together these account fo 123 MB. The A_1 probably accounts for another 20 MB. Temporary structures, such as hash tables and temporary matrix products, would account for the remaining 50 to 60 MB.

The redesign using hash tables illustrates some points about designing for efficiency: it is often best to start with a good design without worrying about low-level efficiency issues. Then profile the result to see what needs improving. A simpler design is usually easier to debug and check. It can then be used as a reference for debugging an improved version. And good designs are easy to change, so it is usually not hard to make them more efficient.

Appendix A

Review of vectors and matrices

Since linear equations are basic to much scientific computation, and linear equations are represented by vectors and matrices, we outline a basic review of vectors and matrices. For more information about vectors and matrices, see linear algebra texts such as [2, 100].

Vectors are usually represented by columns of numbers like this:

$$x = \begin{bmatrix} x_1 \\ x_2 \\ x_3 \\ \vdots \\ x_n \end{bmatrix} \in \mathbb{R}^n$$

for an n-dimensional vector.

A word about notation There are a number of different notations used to represent vectors. These include using bold face letters ($\mathbf{x}$), letters with arrows above them ($\vec{x}$), tildes underneath ($\underset{\sim}{x}$), or no extra notation at all (x). In spite of attempts to unify the notation for vectors, no agreement was reached. In this book, no extra notation is used to indicate vectors.

There are two basic operations on vectors: multiplying by a scalar (that is, a real number), and adding. Suppose α is a real number and x and y are two n-dimensional vectors. Then

$$\alpha x = \begin{bmatrix} \alpha x_1 \\ \alpha x_2 \\ \vdots \\ \alpha x_n \end{bmatrix}, \qquad x + y = \begin{bmatrix} x_1 + y_1 \\ x_2 + y_2 \\ \vdots \\ x_n + y_n \end{bmatrix}.$$

An $m \times n$ matrix is a matrix with m rows and n columns and has the form:

$$A = \begin{bmatrix} a_{11} & a_{12} & \cdots & a_{1n} \\ a_{21} & a_{22} & \cdots & a_{2n} \\ \vdots & \vdots & \ddots & \vdots \\ a_{m1} & a_{m2} & \cdots & a_{mn} \end{bmatrix} \qquad (m \times n).$$

Usually matrices are represented by capital letters. Note that an n-dimensional column vector can be thought of as an $n \times 1$ matrix. The transpose of a matrix is the result of reflecting the entries across the main diagonal – the entries where the row number is the same as the column number:

$$A^{\mathrm{T}} = \begin{bmatrix} a_{11} & a_{21} & \cdots & a_{m1} \\ a_{12} & a_{22} & \cdots & a_{m2} \\ \vdots & \vdots & \ddots & \vdots \\ a_{1n} & a_{2n} & \cdots & a_{mn} \end{bmatrix} \qquad (n \times m).$$

If x is a column vector $(n \times 1)$, then x^{T} is a row vector $(1 \times n)$.

Like vectors, matrices can be multiplied by scalars, and added (provided they have the same number of rows and columns). But matrices can also be multiplied by vectors and by matrices, provided the sizes are consistent. If A is $m \times p$ and B is $p \times n$, then $C := AB$ is the $m \times n$ matrix with entries given by the formula

$$c_{ij} = \sum_{k=1}^{p} a_{ik} b_{kj}.$$

The most common use of matrices and vectors is to represent systems of linear equations. The equations

$$
\begin{aligned}
b_1 &= a_{11}x_1 + a_{12}x_2 + \cdots + a_{1n}x_n \\
b_2 &= a_{21}x_1 + a_{22}x_2 + \cdots + a_{2n}x_n \\
&\vdots \qquad \vdots \qquad\qquad \vdots \\
b_m &= a_{m1}x_1 + a_{m2}x_2 + \cdots + a_{mn}x_n
\end{aligned}
$$

can be represented as a single matrix–vector equation

$$b = Ax,$$

where b is an m-dimensional vector, A an $m \times n$ matrix and x an n-dimensional vector. We don't expect to have one solution of a system of equations unless $m = n$ – that is, the matrix A is *square*. If $n > m$ there are more unknowns than equations (called an *underdetermined* system), and if $n < m$ then there are more equations than unknowns (called an *overdetermined* system). In underdetermined systems there are usually solutions, but there may be infinitely many of them. In overdetermined systems, unless we are lucky, there will not be any solutions at all.

Even if the matrix is square, there might not be solutions. Try this system, for example:

$$
\begin{aligned}
1 &= x_1 + x_2, \\
1 &= 2x_1 + 2x_2.
\end{aligned}
$$

If we subtracted twice the first equation from the second, we would get $-1 = 0$, which is impossible. So there are no solutions to this system of equations.

A.1 Identities and inverses

To understand how matrices are used to solve linear systems, we need to introduce a special matrix: the $n \times n$ *identity matrix*. This is the matrix that has ones on the main diagonal and zeros elsewhere:

$$I = \begin{bmatrix} 1 & 0 & \cdots & 0 \\ 0 & 1 & \cdots & 0 \\ \vdots & \vdots & \ddots & \vdots \\ 0 & 0 & \cdots & 1 \end{bmatrix}.$$

The reason why it is special is that for any $m \times n$ matrix A, $AI = A$, and if B is $n \times p$ then $IB = B$. There is also the zero matrix where every entry is zero, usually denoted O: $A + O = A$, $AO = O$, and $OB = O$ for compatible matrices A and B.

In the algebra of $n \times n$ square matrices, some matrices A are *invertible*: that is, they have an inverse A^{-1} with respect to matrix multiplication: $A A^{-1} = I = A^{-1} A$. For square matrices, if $AX = I$ then we also have $XA = I$, so $X = A^{-1}$ is the inverse of A. The identity matrix is clearly its own inverse: $I^{-1} = I$ since $I I = I$.

Knowing that an inverse exists is very helpful (at least theoretically) for determining if a linear system can be solved uniquely: if $Ax = b$ then if we multiply from the left by the inverse of A we get

$$A^{-1} Ax = A^{-1}b, \quad \text{that is,}$$
$$Ix = A^{-1}b, \quad \text{so}$$
$$x = A^{-1}b$$

is the unique solution of the linear system.

For example, if

$$A = \begin{bmatrix} 2 & -3 \\ -1 & 1 \end{bmatrix}$$

then

$$A^{-1} = \begin{bmatrix} -1 & -3 \\ -1 & -2 \end{bmatrix}.$$

Note that if A and B are square matrices and $AB = I$, then $B = A^{-1}$ and also $BA = I$.

A.2 Norms and errors

In numerical computation we do not expect to get exact answers. So we need a way of measuring how big an error is, and a way of measuring the size of a number, or a vector, or a matrix. For numbers we can use the absolute value:

$$|x| = \begin{cases} +x, & \text{if } x \geq 0, \\ -x, & \text{if } x < 0. \end{cases}$$

For vectors we need something more. Usually we measure the size of a vector with a *norm*, which is usually denoted by double vertical bars something like this: $\| \cdot \|$. Different authors in different situations might use a slightly different notation, but it means the same thing.

What is a norm? It is a real-valued function of vectors $x \mapsto \|x\|$ with the following properties:

1. $\|x\| \geq 0$ for any vector x, and $\|x\| = 0$ only if $x = 0$ (the zero vector);
2. if α is any real number and x is a vector, then $\|\alpha x\| = |\alpha| \|x\|$;

3. $\|x + y\| \leq \|x\| + \|y\|$ for any vectors x and y. (This is called the ***triangle inequality***.)

There are a number of standard norms that are commonly used, but other norms are also used if they are appropriate or convenient. In a program or routine you should say what norm you are using, or how it is defined. The most common norms used are the following.

1. The Euclidean norm: $\|x\|_2 = \sqrt{\sum_{i=1}^{n} |x_i|^2}$. This is the usual way of measuring the size of a vector in three-dimensional space. This formula can be derived using Pythogoras' theorem for right-angle triangles.
2. The maximum norm: $\|x\|_\infty = \max_{i=1,...,n} |x_i|$. This is suitable if you want to see the maximum error.
3. The 1-norm: $\|x\|_1 = \sum_{i=1}^{n} |x_i|$. This norm has some close connections to the maximum norm, and is appropriate if each x_i is adding to some important quantity.

All norms on n-dimensional vectors are *equivalent* in the sense that each can be bounded by the others. Suppose $\| \cdot \|_a$ and $\| \cdot \|_b$ are norms on n-dimensional vectors. Then there are numbers C_1, $C_2 > 0$ where

$$C_1 \|x\|_a \leq \|x\|_b \leq C_2 \|x\|_a \qquad \text{for all } x.$$

These numbers C_1 and C_2 can depend on n:

$$\|x\|_\infty \leq \|x\|_1 \leq n \|x\|_\infty,$$
$$\|x\|_\infty \leq \|x\|_2 \leq \sqrt{n}\|x\|_\infty.$$

There are also norms for matrices. These norms satisfy the same conditions, plus an additional one for matrix multiplication:

$$\|A B\| \leq \|A\| \|B\|.$$

The usual way of defining matrix norms is in terms of vector norms. These are called *induced* matrix norms. The general formula for these is

$$\|A\| := \max_{x:x \neq 0} \frac{\|Ax\|}{\|x\|}.$$

Note that the norms on the right are all vector norms. Calculating the induced norm on a matrix in general is not easy but fortunately there are some formulas for the most common cases:

1. $\|A\|_\infty = \max_i \sum_j |a_{ij}|$;
2. $\|A\|_1 = \max_j \sum_i |a_{ij}|$;
3. $\|A\|_2 = \sqrt{\lambda_{\max}(A^T A)}$, where $\lambda_{\max}(B)$ is the maximum eigenvalue[1] of B.

Some matrix norms are not induced by any vector norm. One such norm is the Frobenius norm:

$$\|A\|_F = \sqrt{\sum_{i,j} |a_{ij}|^2};$$

that is, it is the square root of the sum of the squares of all entries of the matrix.

---

[1] Eigenvalues are described in texts on linear algebra and most texts on numerical analysis. See, for example, [4, 18, 46].

A.3 Errors in solving linear systems

If we try to solve a linear system

$$Ax = b$$

for x, but we have inaccurate data, what we actually solve is

$$(A + E)(x + d) = b + e,$$

where e is the error in b, E is the error in A, and d is the error in the (computed) solution. There is a formula that bounds the error d in the solution:

$$\frac{\|d\|}{\|x\|} \le \frac{\kappa(A)}{1 - \kappa(A)(\|E\|/\|A\|)} \left(\frac{\|E\|}{\|A\|} + \frac{\|e\|}{\|b\|} \right),$$

where $\kappa(A)(\|E\|/\|A\|) < 1$. The number $\kappa(A) := \|A\| \|A^{-1}\|$ is the **condition number** of A. Of course, when we take norms of matrices, we need to use the matrix norm generated by the vector norm that we choose to use. For example, if A is the 2×2 matrix $\begin{bmatrix} 2 & -3 \\ -1 & 1 \end{bmatrix}$, then if we use the $\|\cdot\|_\infty$ vector norm, the condition number is

$$\kappa_\infty(A) = \left\| \begin{bmatrix} 2 & -3 \\ -1 & 1 \end{bmatrix} \right\|_\infty \left\| \begin{bmatrix} -1 & -3 \\ -1 & -2 \end{bmatrix} \right\|_\infty$$

$$= 5 \times 4 = 20.$$

This condition number can never get smaller than one, so we would rather that the condition number "is not too big". How large does $\kappa(A)$ need to become to cause difficulties? Since we can never expect better accuracy in our data than $\|E\|/\|A\|$, $\|e\|/\|b\| \approx \mathbf{u}$, the unit roundoff, if $\kappa(A) \gtrsim 1/\mathbf{u}$ we do not expect any accuracy at all in our computed results. In double-precision this means that $\kappa(A) \approx 10^{15}$ or higher will probably make the results of a numerical algorithm in double-precision meaningless unless there is some special structure to the matrix. Even for lower values of $\kappa(A)$ there can be a significant loss of accuracy; if $\kappa(A) \approx 10^n$ then you lose approximately n significant digits in the final solution.

Appendix B

Trademarks

MATLAB is a trademark of The MathWorks, Inc.

Pentium is a trademark of Intel.

GNU (which stands for GNU's Not Unix), and gcc are trademarks of the Free Software Foundation.

68000 is a trademark of Motorola.

RS/6000 and PowerPC are trademarks of IBM.

Java is a trademark of Sun Microsystems.

Unix is a trademark of AT&T.

Microsoft Word and RTF (Rich Text Format) are trademarks of Microsoft.

PostScript and PDF (Portable Document Format) are trademarks of Adobe.

Connection Machine, CM-2, CM-5, *Lisp and C* are trademarks of Thinking Machines, Inc.

References

[1] ANSI/ISO/IEC. *Fortran 2003 Standard: ISO/IEC 1539-1:2004*, 2004. A draft standard from 2002 is available for free download from `http://webstore.ansi.org/ansidocstore/default.asp`; search for 1539-1.

[2] Howard Anton. *Elementary Linear Algebra*. John Wiley & Sons, 9th edition, 2005.

[3] Douglas Arnold. Some disasters attributable to bad numerical computing. URL: `http://www.ima.umn.edu/~arnold/disasters/disasters.html`, August 1998.

[4] Kendall E. Atkinson. *An Introduction to Numerical Analysis*. John Wiley & Sons Inc., second edition, 1989.

[5] Z. Bai, C. Bischof, S. Blackford, J. Demmel, J. Dongarra, J. Du Croz, A. Greenbaum, S. Hammarling, A. McKenney, and D. Sorensen. *LAPACK Users' Guide*. SIAM 3rd edition, 1999.

[6] Zhaojun Bai, James Demmel, Jack Dongarra, Axel Ruhe, and Henk van der Vorst, editors. *Templates for the Solution of Algebraic Eigenvalue Problems: A Practical Guide*. Number 11 in Software, Environments, and Tools. SIAM 2000.

[7] Richard Barrett, Michael W. Berry, Tony F. Chan, James Demmel, June Donato, Jack Dongarra, Victor Eijkhout, Roldan Pozo, Charles Romine, and Henk van der Vorst, editors. *Templates for the Solution of Linear Systems: Building Blocks for Iterative Methods*. SIAM 1993.

[8] BLAS technical forum. URL: `www.netlib.org/blas/blast-forum/`, 1999.

[9] Hans Boehm. Bounding space usage of conservative garbage collectors. In *Proceeeedings of the 29th ACM SIGPLAN-SIGACT Symposium on Principles of Programming Languages*, pages 93–100, New York, January 2002. Association for Computing Machinery.

[10] R. F. Boisvert, J. Hicklin, B. Miller, C. Moler, R. Pozo, K. Remington, and P. Webb. Jama: A Java matrix package, 1998. Library available through `http://math.nist.gov/javanumerics/jama/`.

[11] Ronald F. Boisvert, Jack J. Dongarra, Roldan Pozo, Karin A. Remington, and G. W. Stewart. Developing numerical libraries in Java. *Concurrency: Practice and Experience*, 10:1117–1129, 1998.

[12] Ronald F. Boisvert, Sally E. Howe, and David K. Kahaner. GAMS: A framework for the management of scientific software. *ACM Transactions on Mathematical Software*, 11(4):313–355, December 1985.

[13] Susanne C. Brenner and L. Ridgway Scott. *The Mathematical Theory of Finite Element Methods*, volume 15 of *Texts in Applied Mathematics*. Springer-Verlag, second edition, 2002.

[14] R. P. Brent. Algorithms for matrix multiplication. Technical Report TR-CS-70-157, Stanford University, March 1970.

[15] R. P. Brent. *Algorithms for Minimization without Derivatives*. Automatic Computation. Prentice–Hall, 1973.

[16] William L. Briggs, Van Emden Henson, and Steve F. McCormick. *A Multigrid Tutorial*. SIAM, second edition, 2000.

[17] Frederick Brooks. *The Mythical Man Month*. Addison-Wesley, 1982.

[18] R. L. Burden and J. D. Faires. *Numerical Analysis*. Wadsworth Group, 7th edition, 2001.

[19] Conor Cahill. *Dbmalloc documentation*, 1990–1992. Available via
`http://dickey.his.com/dbmalloc/dbmalloc.html`.

[20] J. Carrier, L. Greengard, and V. Rokhlin. A fast adaptive multipole algorithm for particle simulations. *SIAM J. Sci. Statist. Comput.*, 9(4):669–686, 1988.

[21] Chromatic. *Extreme Programming: Pocket Guide*. O'Reilly & Associates, 2003.

[22] James W. Cooley and John W. Tukey. An algorithm for the machine calculation of complex Fourier series. *Math. Comp.*, 19:297–301, 1965.

[23] T. H. Cormen, C. E. Leiserson, R. L. Rivest, and C. Stein. *Introduction to Algorithms*. MIT Press, 2nd edition, 2001.

[24] BitMover Corp. Bitkeeper. Available via `http://www.bitkeeper.com/`.

[25] Intel Corp. *IA–32 Intel Architecture Optimization Reference Manual*. Number 248966-011. Intel Corp., 1999–2004. Available via
`http://developer.intel.com`.

[26] C. J. Date. *An Introduction to Database Systems*. Pearson/Addison Wesley, 8th edition, 2004.

[27] Mark de Berg, Marc van Kreveld, Mark Overmars, and Otfried Schwarzkopf. *Computational Geometry: Algorithms and applications*. Springer-Verlag, 1997.

[28] Erik Demaine. Cache-oblivious algorithms and data structures. In *EEF Summer School on Massive Data Sets, Aarhus, Denmark*, Lecture Notes in Computer Science. Springer, June–July 2002. To appear.

[29] J. Dongarra, J. DuCroz, I. S. Duff, and S. Hammarling. A set of level-3 basic linear algebra subprograms. *ACM Trans. Math. Software*, 16:1–28, 1990.

[30] J. Dongarra, J. DuCroz, S. Hammarling, and R. J. Hanson. An extended set of Fortran basic linear algebra subprograms. *ACM Trans. Math. Software*, 14:1–32, 1988.

[31] Dale Dougherty and Arnold Robbins. *sed & awk*. O'Reilly Media, Inc., 2nd edition, 1997.

[32] I. S. Duff, A. M. Erisman, and J. K. Reid. *Direct Methods for Sparse Matrices*. Monographs on Numerical Analysis. Oxford University Press, second edition, 1989.

[33] I. S. Duff, M. A. Heroux, and R. Pozo. An overview of the sparse basic linear algebra subprograms: The new standard of the blas technical forum. *ACM Transactions on Mathematical Software*, 28(2):239–267, 2002. Current code available via `http://math.nist.gov/spblas/`.

[34] Alan Edelman, Eric Kostlan, and Michael Shub. How many eigenvalues of a random matrix are real? *J. Amer. Math. Soc.*, 7(1):247–267, 1994.

[35] E. Elmroth, F. Gustavson, I. Jonsson, and B. Kågström. Recursive blocked algorithms and hybrid data structures for dense matrix library software. *SIAM Rev.*, 46(1):3–45, March 2004.

[36] K. Eriksson, D. Estep, P. Hansbo, and C. Johnson. *Computational Differential Equations*. Cambridge University Press, 1996.

[37] James D. Foley, Andries van Dam, Steven K. Feiner, John F. Hughes, and Richard L. Phillips. *Introduction to Computer Graphics*. Addison-Wesley, 1st edition, 1993.

[38] Association for Computing Machinery. Collected algorithms of the ACM. URL: http://www.acm.org/pubs/calgo/, 1960–2005. The algorithms in thic collection are mostly from the journal *Transactions on Mathematical Software*.

[39] Matteo Frigo, Charles E. Leiserson, Harald Prokop, and Sridhar Ramachandran. Cache-oblivious algorithms. In *Proceedings of the 40th Annual Symposium on Foundations of Computer Science*, pages 285–297, New York, October 1999. ACM.

[40] E. Gamma, R. Helm, R. Johnson, and J. Vlissides. *Design Patterns: Elements of Reusable Object-Oriented Software*. Addison-Wesley Professional Computing Series. Addison-Wesley, 1994.

[41] United States General Accounting Office (GAO). GAO report: Patriot missile defence – software problem led to system failure at Dharhan, Saudi Arabia. Available via http://www.fas.org/spp/starwars/gao/im92026.htm, 1992. GAO/IMTEC report # 92-26.

[42] M. R. Garey and D. S. Johnson. *Computers and Intractability: A Guide to the Theory of NP-completeness*. Freeman, 1979.

[43] A. George and J. Liu. *Computer Solution of Large, Sparse, Positive-Definite Systems*. Prentice–Hall, 1981.

[44] A. Goldberg. *SmallTalk-80: the Language*. Addison-Wesley, 1989.

[45] David Goldberg. What every computer scientist should know about floating-point arithmetic. *ACM Computing Surveys*, 32(1):5–48, 1991.

[46] G. Golub and C. Van Loan. *Matrix Computations*. Johns Hopkins Press, 2nd edition, 1989.

[47] Leslie Greengard and Vladimir Rokhlin. A new version of the fast multipole method for the Laplace equation in three dimensions. In *Acta Numerica, 1997*, pages 229–269. Cambridge University Press, 1997.

[48] E. Hairer, S. P. Nörsett, and G. Wanner. *Solving Ordinary Differential Equations I*. Ser. in Comp. Math. #8. Springer–Verlag, 2nd edition, 1993.

[49] E. Hairer and G. Wanner. *Solving Ordinary Differential Equations II: Stiff and Differential–Algebraic Problems*. Ser. in Comp. Math. #14. Springer–Verlag, 1991.

[50] D. Harel and Y. Feldman. *Algorithmics: The Spirit of Computing*. Addison-Wesley, 3rd edition, 2004.

[51] Donald Hearn and M. Pauline Baker. *Computer Graphics, C Version*. Prentice-Hall, 2nd edition, 1994.

[52] N. J. Higham. *Accuracy and Stability of Numerical Algorithms*. SIAM, 1996.

[53] Glenn Hinton, Dave Sager, Mike Upton, Darrell Boggs, Doug Carmean, Alan Kyker, and Patrice Roussel. The microarchitecture of the Pentium 4 processor. *Intel Technology Journal*, (Q1):1–12, 2001. Available at URL http://developer.intel.com/technology/itj/q12001.htm.

[54] Ivar Holand. Sleipner A GBS Loss. Report 17. Main Report. SINTEF: Civil and Environmental Engineering report STF22–A97861, 1997.

[55] R. A. Horne and C. A. Johnson. *Matrix Analysis*. Cambridge University Press, 1985.

[56] J. C. Hubbell. You are under attack! The strange incident of October 5. *Reader's Digest*, 78(468):37–41, April 1961.

[57] Thomas Huckle. Collection of software bugs. URL: http://www5.in.tum.de/~huckle/bugse.html, March 2004.

[58] Andrew Hunt and David Thomas. *The Pragmatic Programmer*. Addison-Wesley, 1st edition, 2000.

[59] IEEE. *IEEE Standard 754–1985 Standard for Binary Floating Point Arithmetic*, New York edition, 1985.

[60] Intel Corp., Denver, CO. *IA-32 Intel Architecture Software Developer's Manual, Volume 1: Basic Architecture*, 2004.

[61] Intel Corp., Denver, CO. *IA-32 Intel Architecture Software Developer's Manual, Volume 3: System Programming Guide*, 2004.

[62] W. Kahan and Joseph D. Darcy. How Java's floating-point hurts everyone everywhere. Technical report, Department of Mathematics and Department of Electrical Engineering and Computer Science, University of California, Berkeley, Berkeley, CA, USA, June 1998.

[63] Willliam Kahan. How futile are mindless assessments of roundoff in floating-point computation? Technical report, Department of Computer Science, University of California, Berkeley, June 2005. Available via `http://www.cs.berkeley.edu/~wkahan/Mindless.pdf`.

[64] Willliam Kahan and Charles Severance. IEEE 754: An interview with William Kahan. *IEEE Computer*, 33(3):114–115, March 1998.

[65] B. Kernighan and P. J. Plauger. *The Elements of Programming Style*. McGraw-Hill Publ., 2nd edition, 1978.

[66] J. Kleinberg and E. Tardos. *Algorithm Design*. Pearson/Addison-Wesley, 2005.

[67] G. Krasner, editor. *SmallTalk-80: Bits of History, Words of Advice*. Addison-Wesley series in computer science. Addison-Wesley, 1983.

[68] Michael J. Laszlo. *Computational Geometry and Computer Graphics in C++*. Prentice Hall, Inc., 1996.

[69] C. L. Lawson, R. J. Hanson, D. R. Kincaid, and F. T. Krogh. Basic linear algebra subprograms for Fortran usage. *ACM Trans. Math. Software*, 5:308–325, 1979.

[70] Randall J. LeVeque. *Finite Volume Methods for Hyperbolic Problems*. Cambridge University Press, 2002.

[71] J. L. Lions. Ariane 5: Flight 501 failure, report by the inquiry board. Originally appeared at `http://www.esrin.esa.it/htdocs/tidc/Press/Press96/ariane5rep.html`. Available via `http://www.ima.umn.edu/~arnold/disasters/ariane5rep.html`, July 1996.

[72] David Loshin. *Efficient Memory Programming*. McGraw-Hill, 1999.

[73] Mark Lutz and David Ascher. *Learning Python*. O'Reilly Media, Inc., 2nd edition, 2003.

[74] M. Mason. *Pragmatic Version Control: using Subversion*. Pragmatic Bookshelf, 2005.

[75] S. F. McCormick, editor. *Multigrid Methods*. Frontiers in Applied Math. SIAM, 1987.

[76] R. W. Mecklenburg. *Managing Projects with GNU Make*. O'Reilly Media, Inc., 3rd edition, 2005.

[77] Bertrand Meyer. *Eiffel: The Language*. Prentice-Hall, 1991. Second revised printing, 1992. Third edition in preparation. Tutorials on Eiffel available online at `http://docs.eiffel.com`.

[78] Webb Miller. Computational complexity and numerical stability. *SIAM J. Comput.*, 4:97–107, 1975.

[79] Webb Miller. *The Engineering of Numerical Software*. Prentice-Hall, Inc., 1984.

[80] Jean François Monin. *Understanding Formal Methods*. Springer, 2003.

[81] Gordon E. Moore. Cramming more components onto integrated circuits. *Electronics*, 38(8):114–117, 1965.

[82] J. Nocedal and S. J. Wright. *Numerical Optimization*. Springer, 1999.

[83] Jesper Holm Olsen and Sœren Christian Skov. Cache-oblivious algorithms in practice. Master's thesis, Department of Computer Science, University of Copenhagen, December 2002.

[84] Michael L. Overton. *Numerical Computing with IEEE Floating Point Arithmetic*. SIAM, 2001.

[85] Bruce Perens. *Electric Fence documentation*. Available via http://perens.com/FreeSoftware/.

[86] Shari L. Pfleeger. *Software Engineering: Theory and Practice*. Prentice Hall, 2nd edition, 2001.

[87] W. H. Press, S. A. Teukolsky, W. T. Vetterling, and B. P. Flannery. *Numerical Recipies in C: the Art of Scientific Computing*. Cambridge University Press, second edition, 1992.

[88] Harald Prokop. Cache-oblivious algorithms. Master's thesis, Massachusetts Institute of Technology, Cambridge, MA, June 1999.

[89] John Reid. The new features of Fortran 2003. Technical Report JTC1/SC22/WG5 N1579, ISO/IEC, JKR Associates, Oxon, UK, 2003. Available via URL http://www.kcl.ac.uk/kis/support/cit/fortran/john_reid_new_2003.pdf.

[90] Ellen Siever, Stephen Spainhour, and Nathan Patwardhan. *Perl in a Nutshell*. O'Reilly Media, Inc., 2nd edition, 2002.

[91] Silicon Graphics Inc. (SGI). Standard template library programmer's guide. Available via http://www.sgi.com/tech/stl/, 1993–2006.

[92] D. E. Stewart and Z. Leyk. *Meschach: Matrix Computations in C*. Australian National University, Canberra, 1994. Proceedings of the CMA, #32.

[93] G. W. Stewart. Building an old-fashioned sparse solver. Technical Report TR-203-95 or TR-4527, University of Maryland, College Park, Institute for Advanced Computer Studies, Department of Computer Science, August 2003.

[94] David Stoutamire and Stephen Omohundro. *Sather 1.1*, August 1996. Available via http://www.icsi.berkeley.edu/~sather/.

[95] Volker Strassen. Gaussian elimination is not optimal. *Numer. Math.*, 13:354–356, 1969.

[96] Bjarne Stroustrup. *The C++ Programming Language*. Pearson/Addison-Wesley, 3rd edition, 1997.

[97] K. Stüben. A review of algebraic multigrid. *J. Comput. Appl. Math.*, 128(1–2):281–309, 2001.

[98] Sun Microsystems. *The Java Tutorial*, 2004. Available via http://java.sun.com/docs/books/tutorial/.

[99] J. W. Thomas. *Numerical Partial Differential Equations: Finite Difference Methods*, volume 22 of *Texts in Applied Mathematics*. Springer-Verlag, 1995.

[100] Lloyd N. Trefethen and David Bau III. *Numerical Linear Algebra*. SIAM, 1997.

[101] U. Trottenberg, C. W. Oosterlee, and A. Schüller. *Multigrid*. Academic Press Inc., San Diego, CA, 2001. With contributions by A. Brandt, P. Oswald and K. Stüben.

[102] Todd L. Veldhuizen and M. E. Jernigan. Will C++ be faster than Fortran? In *Proceedings of the 1st International Scientific Computing in Object-Oriented Parallel Environments (ISCOPE'97), Marina del Rey, CA*, Springer-Verlag, 1997.

[103] J. Vespemann. *Essential CVS*. O'Reilly Media, Inc., 2003.

[104] Gray Watson. *Dmalloc Documentation*. Available via http://dmalloc.com/.

[105] R. Clint Whaley, Antoine Petitet, and Jack J. Dongarra. Automated empirical optimization of software and the ATLAS project. Technical Report 147, LAPACK Working notes, September 2000. Available via netlib.

[106] J. H. Wilkinson. *The Algebraic Eigenvalue Problem*. Oxford University Press, 1965.

[107] Edward Yourdon. *Rise and Resurrection of the American Programmer*. Yourdon Press Computing Series. Prentice-Hall, 1996.

Index

Printed in the United States
By Bookmasters